The Blessings of My Storms

By

Andrew Wilkinson

When I left Auburn University in 1993, my good friend Drew was the handsome, charismatic, multimillionaire president of our fraternity and chairman of the Interfraternity Council. He and his brother, Glenn, were in line to inherit the business empire his father, the former Governor of Kentucky, and his mother had built from the ground up. Before I would see Drew again, he became a destitute addict and ex-con with no immediate family left alive.

Andrew's stirring memoir, <u>The Blessings of My Storms</u>, is a gritty plunge into the journey of a boy who had absolutely everything and lost it all. It is the story of a broken man restored by God and transformed into the grateful, abundantly blessed family man he is today.

Josh Hopkins
Actor and Director

~

He was born to a life of extreme privilege, wealthy parents, family aircrafts, large farms, fancy cars, a table on Millionaire's Row at the Kentucky Derby, private schools, a bedroom at the Governor's Mansion, and all of the many other trappings of wealth and influence.

Then it was gone.

More than the money and prestige, ultimately, he would lose his father, mother, and his older brother, Glenn.

Where did he turn? After prison, a life of self-destruction, and playing the victim as he ran from everything using alcohol and drugs, Andrew turned to God.

This is his story. From an arrogant, selfish young man, to humility and the recognition of his blessings while looking to God. It is one you will not forget.

Ralph Hacker
Broadcast Executive
Sports Commentator

It is a great blessing that I can share about my dear friend Andrew Wilkinson. From the first time I met him, his humble and gentle spirit grabbed my heart. I am thrilled and excited about his memoir, <u>The Blessings of My Storms.</u> I am confident all who read it will be blessed, encouraged, and inspired to recognize often overlooked and taken for granted blessings in their own lives. I believe this is the beginning of great things to come for my friend and brother in Christ, Andrew.

Raeanne Hance
God Behind Bars, Inc.
Executive Director of Florida
Global Director of Community/Corrections

~

Some books make us laugh, some bring us to tears, some may even put us to sleep. As I read Andrew's <u>The Blessings of My Storms,</u> I often found myself laughing only to follow up two pages later with heartfelt tears. It is a raw true story that brims with genuineness and speaks to the human heart.

Leo Schofield
Inmate, Hardee Correctional Institution, Bowling Green, Florida

To my father, Wallace, my mother, Martha, and my brother, Glenn…my family that was.

To my wife, Nadine, and our daughter, Melina….my family that is.

How I wish words could express my love for all of you.

The Lord has looked down from heaven upon the sons of men

To see if there are any who understand,

Who seek after God.

Psalm 14:2

Foreword

A couple of years ago, tragedy befell a childhood schoolmate of mine. His wife, with whom he had built a family and a life, died of breast cancer. My friend was left with his own deep grief and a traumatized heart, along with three children under 12 years old needing answers and their mother.

It was the kind of a situation that changed absolutely everything in the lives of the people it affected. Although I have never lost a spouse and cannot speak of the heartsick pain associated with it, I have experienced similar times in life. Times when life has kicked us so hard we can't move and we don't know what to say or do; times that stagger us and break down our truths right in front of our eyes. Times when things are destroyed and a barren wasteland is laid out before us.

I read in the newspaper about his wife's memorial. I couldn't think of anything save how he and his children were suffering. How life can be harder than anything we ever imagined.

I wrote him a letter. In it I shared one of the most important blessings I have ever received from God. After I accepted Jesus Christ into my heart, I understood a profound truth. In this life there are mighty and dark storms. Storms that bring destruction. However, in the darkest of clouds, loudest cracks of lightning, and deafening booms of thunder, God has not forsaken us and blessings come forth. Blessings of love, faith, mercy, strength, compassion, relationships, circumstances, understanding, and heavens more. When we are in pain, God gives.

I never heard from my old schoolmate. I have prayed for him and his children. Perhaps he read my letter and concluded that the years took a toll on me, that Andrew had lost his mind. I hope not. I hope that if he has not yet, he still will one day see and understand the blessings of his storms. They are definitely there. They are there for all of us.

Chapter 1

The left wing of the Bombardier Challenger dipped around 20 degrees, allowing for a magnificent view of the Mediterranean Sea and the sun glowing off its waters from the left side of the aircraft. From about 7,500 feet, each of the four passengers aboard could see the magnificence of Monte Carlo and what makes it so beautiful — the Prince's Palace, the port of Monte Carlo, the Hotel de Paris, and, of course, the Monte Carlo Casino. I was 26 years old.

My father asked the pilots to circle the spectacular principality one more time. As I sat on the sofa, my customary place when I flew on my family's jet, my mind began to wander. What in the world had I done to deserve this? A life like I had? Like this? I needed to appreciate things more. I needed to take stock of so many parts of my life. Only a few short years later, I would be asking myself this same question. Not in a jet 7,500 feet over Monte Carlo, but under a vastly different set of circumstances.

Fast forward three years to 2001. The sun was beginning to set in the late afternoon of a February day in central Kentucky. I was driving west on the Bluegrass Parkway, a 70-mile stretch of interstate running directly through the heart of Kentucky. I needed no map or GPS to reach my destination. Wilkinson Farms was approximately another 20 miles away. Normally I drove my Jeep Sahara Wrangler when I escaped to the farm, and today was no different — neither the mode of transportation nor the fact I was escaping.

The farm was a place to go and be removed from everything else. It had been in my family since I could remember, and over the years had increased in size by purchases and lease agreements my father had made. The farm had seen it all — the antics, hunts, accidents, good, and bad times that a bunch of weekend cowboys and soldiers could throw at it. The weekend cowboys and soldiers were me, my older brother Glenn, and all of our family and friends that descended on the farm for countless getaways and weekends.

But today I was alone. It seemed today I needed the drive as much as the farm itself. I knew the drive like the back of my hand. It was comfortable and familiar — the water towers, the horse farms, the rolling hills through the farms and pastures. It was home.

While I was off in a type of daydream somewhere listening to the K93 FM country radio station, my cell phone rang. I looked down to see who was calling and the display read simply "Dad."

Bringing the phone to my cheek, I greeted him, "Hi, Dad."

My father didn't seem to hear me. "Where are you?"

"I'm headed down to the farm for the night," I answered.

"Where is your brother?"

"I have no idea, Dad. I haven't talked to him since this morning."

"I need you to come out to the house," he commanded.

After a momentary silence he went on, "I've got some trouble."

Never in my life had I heard my father say anything like that or remotely close to it.

"Sure, Dad, sure. I'm coming right now."

As I drove to the next exit to change direction and head to my childhood home, Greenbrier, I looked at the setting sun one more time. I knew something was terribly wrong.

There had been emergencies before. This was something different.

"I've got some trouble." These four words spoken by my father, Wallace G. Wilkinson, the 57th governor of the Commonwealth of Kentucky and successful businessman, would mark the beginning of a journey for me. A personal journey into the deepest recesses of human and spiritual darkness. A personal journey toward all out self-destruction that would ultimately only cease when God Himself trapped me, leaving nowhere else to run or hide.

Pain would come and it would come in abundance; pain which I suffered and that which I administered. This was the beginning of very bad times. Times so harsh and desperate the fact I survived is proof the hand of God was over me, protecting me. I would be caught in a terrible, destructive storm of life — hurricanes, tornadoes, and earthquakes all wrapped into one.

But in the storm too were blessings. There would be invaluable lessons about God, life, and love swirling around in the dark funnel clouds, in the violent waves crashing on my shores, and the huge chasms in my very foundation as many faults gave way.

I would learn who Andrew Wilkinson was — not the wealthy man's son and not the governor's son. I would come face to face with myself stripped completely down. I can never say I would recommend anything about my life to others, but it is my life and I embrace it fully. Where I have been and what has happened are why today is what it is. And more importantly, I suppose, why I am the man I have become.

A little more than an hour after my dad's call, he, my mother Martha, my brother Glenn, and myself were gathered at home in a room we called the sun room. It sat below and behind the kitchen separating the house from the backyard. Through an underground tunnel, it also connected the main house to the indoor swimming pool.

My dad loved this room, and this is where he read the morning newspaper all of my life. It had windows on all sides, and he and my mother enjoyed watching the squirrels and birds in the large trees that were all over our backyard. This room bore witness to many decisions, characters, and meetings throughout the years.

Years earlier, in 1984, it was here my dad had discussed his abduction for ransom at the hands of Stan. A former business partner, Stan, had come onto hard times. He was broke, called a hotel room home, and lived off alcohol and pills. My mother and I had been in France while my father and Glenn stayed behind at home. My father had known Stan for a long time. Our family knew his family, and I remembered him from when I was a little boy.

My father felt compassion for him. Compassion was a character trait of his that I saw displayed many times.

Stan had come to him several times and asked for money, and Dad had always acquiesced. It was April when Stan came to his office a final time to ask for more money. This time the answer was "No."

As Dad would recount it to us, "I told him I was no longer willing to help someone who was not willing to help themself." Stan pulled a gun and put it to the side of my father's head, and instructed him to cooperate or he would kill him. Stan demanded $500,000 in cash, a condominium in a place of his choosing, and an automobile. He was under the influence much of the time he held Dad hostage, which applied more terror to an already terrifying situation.

At one point, Stan described how he could kill my brother Glenn and put him in the trunk of my dad's car. As they sat in a diner in Frankfort, Kentucky, my father had thought about sticking a fork in Stan's neck while he ate. Dad ultimately decided against it, because he believed Stan still might have time to get off a couple of shots. The two stayed the night in our condominium atop a hotel Dad had developed several years earlier — the Capital Plaza Hotel.

The following day, one of Dad's airplanes, a turbo commander flown by a Wilkinson pilot, carried them to Glasgow, Kentucky. It was there at the small municipal airport they met the president of a bank. Dad had arranged for him to bring the $500,000. Stan was given the cash and he let Dad go.

Later I would ask my father if Stan did not realize he would call the authorities when he let him go. Dad told me he believed Stan had gone crazy between the alcohol, pills, and desperation, and was no longer capable of rational decision-making. Freed, Dad alerted the FBI and they apprehended Stan in Lexington later the same day. He was found to be in possession of two handguns, several pairs of handcuffs, and the money.

About two months later, released on bond, as he awaited his trial for federal extortion charges, Stan died alone in a hotel room where he had been living for months. I remember riding the subway in Paris and my mother, seemingly out of nowhere, breaking down and sobbing. After everything was over in the States, those involved in the situation had contacted my mother and explained what happened. At this point there was no more danger, so the decision was made not to tell me until we returned home in two days.

Later, business and political enemies would start a rumor concerning it all. That Wilkinson had concocted the whole "scheme" for exposure only a couple of years prior to the launch of his gubernatorial campaign. As a result of the kidnapping, we had armed security at our home from that time on. They took care of our family very well. One in particular, although primarily there for protection, became much more to us. Dave Herald protected me as a boy. I am certain today I could still trust him with my life.

Everyone who ever knew my dad knew he had always given utmost attention to how he looked and he presented himself.

Glenn told me, "Andrew, I am telling you, if you could have seen Dad right as it was over like I did you would understand. I have never seen him look so rough. His clothes were wrinkled, soiled, and a mess. He was not shaven. It was just awful."

In the days after his kidnapper's death, my father wondered out loud if he should attend the funeral. I guess he wanted to remember the Stan from years earlier that he and Mom had known and trusted. I don't know. What I do know is that my mother would not allow it. There were only a few instances that Mom outright forbade something. She knew the severity of what had transpired between her husband and his captor. She knew he could have killed him. Dad did not attend that funeral.

That had happened 17 years before, and once again we were in the sunroom. Unbeknownst to us, this day was the final time that my family, the four of us, would come together the way we always had been. Following that day, every time we gathered would be consumed in uncertainty regarding matters of financial law and health.

My father stood as the three of us sat. My mother stood and took his hand. She guided him to sit beside her on the sofa. There are really no words to explain or capture a moment like this. The weight of it all was absolutely colossal, and we all felt it. When a man must disclose he is about to file for the single largest personal bankruptcy in the history of a state, it is a hell of a thing.

Chapter 2

Dad proceeded to explain to us that friends and longtime business associates, many of whom I had known since I was a child, were forcing him into bankruptcy with personal debt of over $415 million dollars.

Through a series of decisions over the course of the past several years, my father, Wallace G. Wilkinson, self-made businessman and 57th governor of the Commonwealth of Kentucky, was unable to pay what he owed. The entrepreneur, the warrior, the fighter, the underdog, the winner I was raised by was insolvent.

How could this be? Was it possible? Wallace Wilkinson was broke. I often think what it must have been like for him, a very proud man, to explain to his family that all was lost. That he was defeated. That the Wilkinson family of Kentucky was going down.

A lifetime's worth of work by him and my mother would be no more. Everything that was ours would be gone in a matter of time. All would be seized or dismantled. I looked at him through heavy tears. I loved him very much and respected him. It was precisely at this moment and several others during his own bankruptcy that my respect for him would grow.

As Glenn and I walked to our automobiles that cold February night, Mom stayed in the house. Dad was with us, and even at such a truly horrible moment as this he stayed true to form. His sense of humor, which I always loved, would show itself.

He made a statement I have never forgotten, "If you're going to play in the arena, boys, you have to be prepared, take what happens in the arena. Well, boys, they won't ever be able to say I did anything small," he said with that sly smile I can still see so well.

He was not trying to be funny. He was trying to comfort us.

Dad continued, "We will be all right. Listen, we have to stick together. They will try to split us up. The four of us have got to stick together."

He was right and we did. Dad was absent much of the time as Glenn and I were boys and he knew it. He made up for it in his own way by always letting us know we were welcome with him no matter where he went. I accompanied him several times all over the United States to meetings, where there were big time players on both sides of the table…and me.

My brother and I travelled the world with Dad. He gave us access to a vast amount of resources. I met countless CEOs, businessmen, and community leaders, many governors, and two presidents. Glenn and I were not in his way. He loved having us around.

So many wealthy people cheat on their spouses and don't have time for their children. It wasn't like that for me and Glenn. I wish that we had been more responsible for Dad and Mom. They deserved it.

It took three days from when Dad told us what was going on to when it made headlines. Having to deal with the reality of what had happened and waiting to deal with the tidal wave when the news broke was torture in itself. Those days were fuzzy. Almost like a dream.

Then the morning arrived, "Creditors: Wilkinson owes $420 million." This is how it read on the front page. All hell broke loose. For days the phones were ringing constantly at the offices, my parents' house, Glenn's house, and my house. Television reporters, journalists, people from the business world, people from the political world.

My dad had his team of attorneys, my mom had hers, and Glenn and I had to get our own representation. To say it was chaotic is an understatement.

At some point I went to my bank and withdrew several thousand dollars. I didn't know if I had to make sure I had some cash or what. I can remember every eye in that place being focused on me. Everybody knew who I was and what I was doing.

The next year and a half was marked by actions, delays, decisions, and indescribable uncertainty except for one matter. The men who forced my dad over the edge were coming after everything. Absolutely everything — businesses, properties, interests, farms, livestock, houses, aircraft, boats, automobiles — all of it. This was a time when the darkest attributes of mankind came into full view. Sometimes it was insanity.

Some of the men even contacted me to arrange secret meetings. I actually met with one I had known and trusted for many years. He ducked in and out of several cars before he jumped into my car wearing a baseball cap and sunglasses. We drove to my house and met for a couple of hours. When he finally realized I didn't have a number for an account in Switzerland or the Caymans, he left.

People abandoned us left and right. People we had known for long periods of time. All types of accusations were made. Lies filled the air. People turned against us fast. A distrust of people was born in this time that I continue to struggle with today.

Although I had spent great deals of money before, I was generally in good shape with my finances. Just a few weeks after everything broke I decided to resign my post as vice president of Wallace Bookstores, Inc. I was on my way to work one morning, but instead I drove to Greenbrier, my parents' house. Once there I called Dad at his office. He told me not to go anywhere; he was on his way home. In 10 minutes he got there.

We sat together and I told him I didn't need money from income. I could get out. We stood together. He put his hands on my shoulders and looked me in the eye like only a father could. Dad said one word, "Go." I believe it relieved him that I did not have to endure watching everything crumble around us.

Chapter 3

When a man is shoved into bankruptcy with $420 million in debt, many are hurt. Not only Wallace Wilkinson. Not only his creditors. But a large portion of folks who had worked for my family for years. Some had been with Dad since the very beginning. Indeed, some we actually thought of as part of our family.

Some people deserted us at the first trumpet of disaster. Some stayed true to the very end.

Byron Wagner worked at our home for over 20 years. Greenbrier sat on 12 acres with an indoor swimming pool and a tennis court. It was a full time job to keep it up. He also took care of all sorts of personal needs. My father trusted him as much as anybody he knew, and I know he shared some things with Byron in private conversations he never would disclose to others. He was family, along with his wife, Joan.

Angela Hicks worked for us for 20 years. She began as assistant to the controller for Wilkinson Enterprises and later was named a staff accountant. Her devotion and loyalty, however, naturally landed her a job as Mom and Dad's administrative assistant. Ange (as Glenn and I called her) was also the one put in charge of "the boys'" finances.

One of her job requirements was to deal with Glenn and me when we needed money. I am still close with Ange today, and we often joke how we both would call her constantly with an "emergency" with our apartments or something at school. For example, the refrigerator wasn't cooling properly, the disposal wouldn't work and the landlord wouldn't help, or our cars were broken down. The list of problems that required only money to resolve was never-ending. She worked with us within bounds, but we sure did pester the living daylights out of her for years.

There were others — my father's driver, personal secretary, pilots, the farm manager, officers of all the companies and groups, and mid-level managers. The ripple effect was just enormous. Apart from the sadness of seeing my dad, who so many people respected, lose everything, all of those affected had bills and mortgages to pay. All of them had to start again. The sadness was thick and deep.

We all still had a leader in Dad though. Even during his own financial demise, he was graceful. Day after day he would go to the office to meet and talk with attorneys all day long. On occasion he would inspire the attorneys with ideas and maneuvers.

This is a rather brutal thought I share, but in this world we see people end their lives quite often after experiencing this type of calamity. Wallace Wilkinson was not of that ilk. He worked his own bankruptcy just like everything else he had ever worked in life. He was methodical and meticulous. He could still have a profound effect on important matters.

I still have a letter from one of the lead attorneys describing the admiration he had gained for Dad, not for his accomplishments, but for his conduct and demeanor during the end. I too share this emotion. As drivers came to take his cars away, I watched Dad walk out to shake hands and introduce himself to them. I saw the surprise on their face at his show of character.

I hope one day my daughter, Melina, will recall a moment when she was in awe of my character like I was his. Never to believe I was perfect or anything foolish like that, but to look on in a time of great adversity, devastation, and, yes, embarrassment, and see a real man.

Chapter 4

Dad had grown up very poor, and he hated it. It was Casey County, Kentucky, and most folks were pretty poor. His family was no exception. Although he loved his family, he wanted out of there. There was no opportunity. So many wanted out and so few made it. Dad made it. He used his hatred for being poor to fuel his ambition throughout his life.

This book is not about Dad's bankruptcy. But as someone who knew him, as someone who was there, and as a son, to tell my story it is necessary to touch on his. Over the years I have heard and read terrible things about him. Dad was a worker and his raw ambition was that of a tragic hero.

Between his extremely shrewd political and business acumen and his work ethic, he was formidable at whatever it was he undertook. He was decent, honest, and fair in his personal and professional life. When he played hardball, as I was witness to more than once, it was serious business. But this is how he came up. No one ever gave him anything. He fought for everything he ever had.

Dad once gave a next door neighbor a Cadillac limousine, which was in the fleet of a limousine company he owned, because the neighbor gave up a couple of feet on the property line dividing our homes.

Another instance, I saw him force the insurance company that covered hundreds of his employees to accept a pre-existing condition (terminal cancer) of the spouse of someone he had employed for years. He was ready to move the entire, huge account for the one lady who was very sick. Ironically as it would prove to be, Dad did not ever want to do anything to give someone a reason to say he was not fair.

The pursuit of massive wealth caused what ultimately came on my father. It was greed. We had more than enough money to live how and where we wanted to, but it was not sufficient. The taste of that kind of money proved too much for him. His reason and logic were affected, and he put himself in places he normally never would have gone. Dad was overconfident and believed he could make it work for everybody.

Many of the men who forced him into bankruptcy had earned millions of dollars in their dealings with him. His intentions were spectacular success for everyone. Some people remember him as a bad guy, but he was not. I know who he was and there are many others who know, too.

Mom, on the other hand, did not deal with poverty growing up. Sure, it was Casey County, and no one was that well off. But her father owned the only Chevrolet dealership in town, and her mother ran a country store where my mother, her older sister Katherine, and younger brother Gary, helped. There was a bit of an internal joke in my family that Mom would equate her childhood to Dad's as far as hardship and doing without goes. I don't know if I ever believed that, but she had rock solid values.

My parents had been introduced as young children and continued a close friendship through their teenage years. After graduation, they became more than friends as they headed to Lexington to attend the University of Kentucky. My father fell in love with her for reasons other than just the heart, though his heart was there. He saw in Martha Carol Stafford someone he needed. He wanted out and he was going to need a partner. Someone who worked as tirelessly as he did and someone he could trust. A person who was absolutely committed to family and would help him build something. Mom fit the bill on all of that and much more.

On September 16, 1960, they were married. They truly were a remarkable team and downright impressive when the two of them went at something together. Both Dad and Mom had a way of connecting to everyday people and they enjoyed it. However, my mother's ill-fated campaign for governor in 1991 to continue a Wilkinson administration was not of her and him. It was of him and everybody knew it.

As First Lady, Mom shone so bright and brought so much to the post. It was natural for her and she did it all — the countless hours crisscrossing Kentucky's 120 counties, the fundraisers, the BBQ rallies, the county and state fairs, her adult literacy program, and her real support of youngsters. As much as she lived up to the First Lady image, she did not as a candidate for governor. I recall reading letters she had written to me during the first months of her campaign.

They all pretty much started the same way, "Dearest Andrew, It is so late. We have just now come home to the mansion from another…"

The "mansion" being the Governor's Mansion. I was always melancholy as I read the letters. It was crystal clear that she was unhappy. The day she dropped out of the race was, ironically, one of the best days of the ill-fated campaign. I also heard from several people there that her withdrawal speech was beautiful and graceful — her finest hour.

Dad later shared with Glenn and I that he would regret getting Mom involved in that for the rest of his life. Through all of the deals, the possessions, and the millions, the best asset he ever had was the one asset he would never lose — Martha.

Chapter 5

I never needed God for anything. According to the world, my life was full of all the things that make it complete. I was the son of a wealthy and successful man, the son of a governor. I grew up with access, privilege, and a whole lot of material possessions.

Dad and Mom instilled in us the difference between right and wrong, and loved Glenn and me very much. However, both of them always had to be somewhere. So, Glenn and I figured out that we could get away with a lot pretty early. We were wild, and my father did have to deal with us a few times.

Only days after Dad had been sworn in, I was caught driving a friend's car doing 90 in a 35 on a stretch of road below a cliff underneath the Governor's Mansion. Dad was setting up his new administration with a huge amount of matters to see to, and I am brought to the mansion along with my friend by Frankfort city police. This friend of mine was a guy named Pierce DeVan. Pierce was my best friend for a lot of years and we did it all; we had a whole lot of adventures, leading to a modest amount of headaches for our parents.

Pierce crunched up the front end of my dad's Mercedes SL 600. Of course, I was riding shotgun. It didn't necessarily matter that it was the fault of the other driver. Pierce and I still share a laugh sometimes, remembering the response when Dad found out, "Pierce! Is there anything of mine you haven't wrecked?"

Pierce was also the driver as we returned to the Governor's Mansion after a weekend night out. I was seriously drunk. My quarters were on the third floor of the mansion and the family quarters were on the second. Many times Pierce and

I stepped on that elevator, praying it would run uninterrupted to the third floor. It was equipped with those old school sliding cage doors found on many residential and hotel lifts. One could hear them as they were opened and closed.

Mom sat up that one particular night and was waiting on the second floor. When we got on she heard us, and when the number two button lit up the elevator stopped. Our hearts sank as the door opened and there was Mom. That was not a good night, and Pierce and I don't recall it with humor.

On another occasion, I was driving my new Ford Thunderbird Super Coupe with Glenn in the passenger seat on Interstate 75, which connected Lexington and Frankfort. We were clocked doing well over 120 miles an hour. A Kentucky State Trooper came after us, and we ran from him on side roads, almost losing control several times.

We had a radio in my car and heard it all play out on the airwaves. The pursuing trooper did not know who we were. And we got away from him, getting into Lexington and hiding out in a Howard Johnson's parking lot for about three hours. We constantly discussed what kind of trouble this would be if we were apprehended and what Dad would do. I don't know if we were more afraid of the state police or Dad if he found out.

As we arrived at our personal home, Greenbrier, the on-duty governor's detail trooper came out to greet us. He had heard all the ruckus on the radio, and said he knew it was us as soon as he heard it was a grey Thunderbird Super Coupe they were in pursuit of.

As far back as I can recall, Dad was one of the most active entrepreneurs in the state. It was normal for him to be gone frequently and my mother to look after Glenn and me. His business interests were extensive and it was normal for a helicopter to be landing in the backyard or to watch his airplane race down the runway as his ambition led him off once more.

There were some public disappointments, but they did not define the day. Time after time, Dad seemed to come out on top, despite constantly being the underdog and underrated. He made an art out of coming out of nowhere and seizing the prize. His recipe for success?

He would tell me countless times, "Outwork the other guy and do your homework. Always be prepared. The man that shows up prepared is the one who will win."

Growing up and seeing him operate was something else. College textbooks, banking, developing, coal, farming, or retail. It didn't really matter. Vision is critical and he had it. Yet another one of his nuggets of wisdom he offered throughout the years, "Andrew, people will tell you no or you cannot do something all of your life."

I still have a three-ring binder an employee from the pre-political days made for him. It is full of newspaper clippings and articles about Dad and his pursuits. On the cover is the title, "Wallace the Warrior." He was a warrior. Flawed, but a warrior.

He was loyal to employees that were loyal to him, and there were several who were part of the family. He had always financially assisted members from both sides of my family, and it was not a problem for him to do so. Dad had always presented himself as tireless, organized, and with a dream. Those who recognized this about him were the ones who had helped him somewhere along the way. He helped back when it was his turn.

Chapter 6

I had my first drink of alcohol when my parents were at one of their fundraisers. I was 14 years old and I got hammered to the point of vomiting and passing out. I had filled a 12-ounce Coca-Cola can with Maker's Mark bourbon and drank it all.

In high school, I would move on to marijuana. Marijuana IS a gateway drug. Everyone who denies it is just that — in denial. All the people I knew who used drugs fell in line to this structure. First alcohol, then weed, then on to next level (mushrooms, cocaine, ecstasy, etc.)

I experimented once with cocaine in high school with some older people. I attended Auburn University, and during my freshman year I lived next door to some guys who did quite a bit of it. In time, so would I.

I did everything at Auburn except graduate.

I was elected president of my fraternity, Lambda Chi Alpha, and was later appointed chairman of the Interfraternity Council Court. Known as the IFC, it was the governing body of member fraternities on campus. This was, perhaps, the biggest irony in the history of humanity. I was known all over the Auburn campus as a huge partier. How I was selected for that position I will never understand.

Auburn is where my ability to be a real asshole came out. I betrayed friends, and I did not treat the opposite sex well. I was out of control there, and after six years my father had enough of wasting money. He sent the plane, with Glenn on board, down to Alabama to get me. I had no idea they were coming until I heard the knock on my door and my brother's voice. I was at least sober that night, which made a pretty bad situation a little better than it could have been.

Once back in Kentucky, I immediately started working for Wallace's College Book Company. During this time, a maturation of sorts took place. I began to take things more seriously and I experienced living, working, getting involved, getting out, and breathing. I had not done that at Auburn for quite some time. I had long overstayed my welcome there. I was so stale. Most of the students I started with in 1990 were long gone.

Auburn is a college town out in the middle of the pastures. There is nothing there other than the university. At that point it was kind of embarrassing to walk into any one of the bars and to strike up a conversation with a sophomore, freshman, or another dude like me. "So, Drew, when are you finally gonna get out of here, man?" was the question I was hearing everywhere I went.

I had dug such a deep hole I didn't know where to even begin to get my crap together. Everywhere I turned I was lagging behind and I had told a lot of lies by that point. As years progressed, I proved to be adept at getting myself into that type of situation.

I began in the University of Kentucky bookstore at the main campus in Lexington, which Wallace's leased. After about a year I moved on to the executive offices located across town. There, Dad applied significant pressure on me to go into the retail side of things. Wallace's had 100 stores it either leased or owned outright. In 1996, the total sales for the retail division were around $150 million.

During Dad's political years, Wallace's had basically stood still while the two largest competitors, Follett of Nebraska and Barnes and Noble College Division, forged ahead picking up lease after lease on college campuses all over the country.

My father 100 percent dedicated himself to being governor. He and my mother loved the people of Kentucky. Their desire to help them was authentic, and they were good and successful at it. The education reform act (known as KERA), stacks of competently negotiated successes in economic development, mile after mile of newly paved roads, fresh laid water lines all over the state, and much more connected the folks of the Commonwealth to the rest of the state and country.

He was one of them. So was Mom. He wanted to give something, as governor, to the people of Kentucky he had to fight so hard for — a chance for something better. In this regard, the Wilkinson Administration was a success. Even his enemies had to admit it.

Ironically, his businesses and interests suffered deeply due to his time in office. In the world of politics, unfortunately, we hear often of those, who once they obtained office, abused the office to augment their financial position. For Wallace Wilkinson it was the exact opposite.

In the beginning of the campaign, no one gave him a chance to win. How could he? He was running against two former governors, a sitting lieutenant governor, and a candidate who had already vied for the state's highest office once. A little-known outside of the business circles entrepreneur wasn't taken seriously. He bankrolled his own campaign until he won the Democratic primary.

Of course, after he stunned everyone with the primary victory, donations and support flooded in. All told it was seven years of political distraction that Dad's business interests endured. It was here the seeds of his personal and financial demise were planted. I believe in the depth of my heart if Dad had not gone to Frankfort, he would never have found himself in the position he was in to take on the colossal debt.

He came home, and we were getting seriously outpaced by the other guys. Wallace's had to grow, grow, grow. And fast. From 1996 to 1999, over 35 on-campus bookstore leases were awarded to Wallace's throughout the country. I was present at the meetings where we put together lease proposals. They were very aggressive with tens of millions of dollars committed for renovations. Barnes and Noble and Follett's were rolling out upscale, modern bookstores with all the ticks.

Very few people realize this about the Wallace Wilkinson story. But the men he dealt and socialized with were extremely wealthy and influential. Somewhere in this span of time the powerful flavor and taste of real, big time money crept in. Relationships and decisions became more and more purely about money and getting more of it. Simultaneously the dot com explosion was dominating the business and financial trends nationally. Wallace's created an internet presence to accompany its wholesale division and brick and mortar stores. Dad raised huge sums of money from investors all over the country.

Chapter 7

Admittedly, I had lived a pretty lavish lifestyle, especially for a 20-something. I had a beautiful home in old Lexington just outside of downtown, a Mercedes-Benz E55 AMG, a Jeep Sahara Wrangler, a Harley-Davidson Fat Boy, a watch collection, and two walk-in closets full of custom tailored clothing and shoes. But I was not extreme, especially for the amount of money I had access to.

After my resignation, I listed my house on the market and it sold quickly. The funds to make that purchase were secured from my father and I immediately paid that back in full. I let the motorcycle go as well as the Jeep. I turned everything I could into cash and headed to Florida.

It was a day or two before I would leave Kentucky for good. A very good friend of mine, Justin Fister, came to see me at home. I have known Justin and his brother, Morgan, for years. They are salt of the earth Kentucky people. One of the local news vans was circling my house. Justin was very upset and at a loss for words.

I had a Smith & Wesson .357 Magnum stainless steel revolver that had been given to Dad by a state trooper. It was their standard issue weapon before they started to carry automatics. It had the Kentucky State Police stamp on it. He accepted it with watery eyes and expressed his concern for me.

"I will be fine, Justin. Don't worry about me. Everything will be okay, buddy," I assured him. We waved to each other as he drove away.

By this time, I had seen and experienced the true heartache of so many who knew us. Those who were close to the Wilkinson family. It would be more than 10 years until I spoke to Justin again. Today, our friendship is alive and well.

In the months after the bankruptcy, I lived in our family home in Naples, Florida. It was large with an open floor plan. Just outside of my double bedroom doors on the second floor there was a balcony overlooking a large portion of the living space. I can't count the times I rested on that balcony with my morning cup of coffee and tried to get a handle on everything that was going on. There was a whip-poor-will that sang to me every morning.

The house was so big and empty and quiet. I can still sense the loneliness and emptiness of those long, long days. Really the only things that separated one from another was a phone call to or from Kentucky with attorneys, a briefing on motions filed and decisions rendered on those motions, or a conversation with Dad, Mom, or Glenn.

On a particular weekend, I drove north on I-75 115 miles to Sarasota. I spent the day driving about and taking in the neighborhoods. A house that attracted me was in an old north Sarasota neighborhood. I decided I liked Sarasota and paid cash for that house. There was no way we could stay in Kentucky, and Naples wasn't an option either. Everybody knew us there too. When all of this was over, we were going to start again in the artsy beach town.

I paid $200,000 for the property and immediately put another $100,000 into it for tiling, woodwork, new roof, landscaping, lighting, a well, irrigation system, security system, etc. You name it. Florida is a debtor-friendly state. Creditors cannot take your home in a bankruptcy filing as opposed to other states.

Therefore, you see many "house rich, money poor" situations. I had still around $450,000 in stocks and cash I brought to Florida with me. Altogether, it was around $750,000 in money and property. This was going to make starting over possible, and under normal circumstances it would have been more than enough.

You see, what was happening in Kentucky, though bad enough, was not necessarily the end of me. I still had a home and assets. I was not in bankruptcy. I was young and healthy. I think back on this time and wish I had somehow come to my senses. To realize what I still had.

Like so many times I would illustrate in my life, it was my character, my nature, to take things to the extreme. Warning shots were never enough for me. Major warning shots. The only way I learned is when I absolutely had no choice.

Dad, Mom, and Glenn were primarily in Kentucky and battling every day. Glenn, bless his heart, had always been more spendthrift and could not get out. He needed the income and had to stay on the job. He had been president of Wallace's College Book Company for several years. This is the flagship company that was successful from the very beginning. Dad started it in 1962 while he was attending the University of Kentucky. Business was so good so fast, he decided to leave school and commit himself fully to the venture.

At the time, high school students in Kentucky had to purchase their own textbooks. Although the textbooks were used again the following semester there was no marketplace for them. Dad bought the books back and offered them for sale at a "used" price to incoming students the following year. In 1965, the first Wallace's College Bookstore was opened at the University of Kentucky. Again, Wallace's purchased used textbooks back from students at the end of a semester. These were the students who didn't necessarily care about the selling price. Basically, they were happy that finals were over and they were getting a little pocket or beer money. Wallace's held on to the textbooks that were to be utilized again by the university the following semester. The textbooks that were not to be used in the upcoming semester, Wallace's found a home for them at another campus or school. The information about classes offered, enrollment, and course books to be used was accessible. So much of the educated guessing about product offerings was eliminated. I heard my father exclaim many times it was hands down the best business to be in ever. Wallace's was the one success that led to so many others. It supplied capital and a lot of it. At the time of the bankruptcy, Wallace's wholesale division and retail division had combined sales of over $250 million annually.

The information about classes offered, enrollment, and course book to be used was accessible. So much of the educated guessing about product offerings was eliminated. I heard my father exclaim many times it was hands down the best business to be in ever. Wallace's was the one success that led to so many other successes. It supplied capital and a lot of it. At the time of the bankruptcy, Wallace's wholesale division and retail division had combined sales of over $250 million annually.

Glenn was the president. No doubt, neither Glenn nor I earned our positions. We were the owner's kids and it was clear to all. But Glenn attended the University of Mississippi and returned home to work with a degree. More than I did. And Glenn possessed a way of analyzing and breaking things down to find the weak or "attack" spot. It was a talent in his blood, and he was extraordinary at it.

If you had a dispute with another party, Glenn was the guy to call. He could take a stack of documents and sum it up in a couple of sentences, pointing out flaws and weaknesses of the opposing party all along the way.

Chapter 8

The first Mercedes-Benz E55 AMG I had was the first one in the state of Kentucky. Mercedes had begun production in 1998 and had only shipped several hundred to North America. The Mercedes-Benz dealership in Lexington had sold many cars to the Wilkinsons. I was able to get them to hold for me the first one they received. I was very proud of that car, and it was a heck of a machine.

I had travelled out of town for work and dropped it off at the airport valet. I returned to the Lexington airport and called the office to check in. I always called a lady named Kimberly Barnes; she was a main stay at Wallace's and everyone (including Dad) simply called her, "Sunshine." Her demeanor and presence always seemed to light everything up. "Hey Sunshine, what's going on? I'm home. At the airport. Getting ready to get my car."

She didn't say anything for a second. Then she asked me if I was sitting down. "The Mercedes is down," is how she put it.

I still laugh when I think of it. The lease company that performed valet parking at the airport had already called. A young employee just couldn't help himself and gave into temptation. He took the keys and drove the automobile off of airport property.

The airport in Lexington is surrounded by horse farms with stone and wood fences everywhere. The young driver had accelerated through a curve and the power of the back end overpowered him. He slammed sidelong into an old stone fence bordering one of the horse farms. It basically stripped three quarters of the right side of the car off. I maintained to my insurance carrier that the car was rare and normal depreciation methods did not apply. They contended that the normal methods for calculating values in a claim did apply. So, the fight was on. My brother, Glenn, proved to be much more assistance in the conflict than my attorney.

For months on end, Glenn had to go to work and participate in the step-by-step process of the company being shut down. Not only was he involved by virtue of his blood, but also he was reporting to work daily and experiencing the ever-tightening circle until game over, doors closed. The creditors' committee, attorneys from countless parties and interests, bankers, were all present only for one reason — to pick everything apart and decide what goes where.

The book company itself had several hundred employees. Glenn's presence was only required to a certain point and then he would be cut out. How terrible for Glenn, who was not at fault or to blame. This was such an awful experience for him.

Glenn was Wallace G. Wilkinson, Jr. He emulated our father and always had. Growing up, Glenn never wanted to be a firefighter, policeman, or an astronaut like most of the other kids. Glenn wanted to be just like Wallace G. Wilkinson. If this time was torture for the rest of us, it was water boarding for my brother. Like me, he had no relationship with God. No foundation to rely on outside of himself.

Understandably, Glenn began to falter in this time. He had been married only two years earlier. Her name was Cindy. She was a beautiful girl, and my family approved of her. But she was caught up in everything that was happening to the Wilkinsons. It was not about her, and she found herself isolated and alone much of the time. When she was with Glenn, she could not manage or comfort him. She gave a real effort. But the ongoing situation with us consumed everything else. Their marriage ended as she packed her

SUV and drove north to her family in Ohio. I never did hold it against Cindy. I would have done the same thing.

Dad had dealt with non-Hodgkin's Lymphoma for 10 years when the bankruptcy hit. Twice it had gone into remission with aggressive radiation treatments at the University of Kentucky hospital. The doctors and staff there were always very competent. Dad liked them very much, as did Mom. Everyone who knew this and was close to us watched his health intently, fearing the worst.

The cancer did return. The astronomical level of stress had taken Dad's immune system down to nothing. He had nothing to offer, in terms of defense, and the cancer returned quickly and with force.

By May 2002, 16 months after it all had begun, Dad and Mom were spending more of their time at the house in Florida. Mom had been in Kentucky to testify at her deposition. I too had been deposed and was still in Kentucky staying at Greenbrier. She returned to Florida late in the evening. Dad came to the door to greet her. He was in his bathrobe. There were no lights on. Mom later told me how terrible this was for her. It was clear to see what was happening.

Dad was ghost pale and sweating profusely, so weak that walking was more of a sliding of his feet in the house shoes. But he had heard the car outside and walked through the house to her. He was barely audible as he spoke. Mom, alarmed and still in her professional attire from the prior requirements of the day, helped steady him. "Mother, you are so pretty," he whispered.

As a son, I think about that moment still. Of these two people. Just the two of them. All of the life shared. All of the everything they had shared. Experiences and successes too numerous to count. Personal and private. Everything coming to pieces around them. Crumbling down. Here they were, in the dark. In the foyer of that big house embracing each other. That picture has remained in my mind for all of these years.

Mom was calm, but very shaken. Immediately she contacted me and Byron Wagner. Byron was the caretaker for the Wilkinson family. We all loved him. Years before, Wilkinson Enterprises had acquired the old, historic Phoenix Hotel in downtown Lexington. It had sat abandoned for a number of years and was slated for demolition. A number of different projects were being considered for the space. On a tour of the structure, Dad came across Byron, alone and still tending to the once-luxury hotel. The new owner of the building asked him if he had employment going forward.

Byron answered, "I guess that depends on you, Mr. Wilkinson."

My father gave him the address of the offices at Wilkinson Enterprises and told him to go there saying they had met. So Byron and his family came into our lives.

For now, airports and flying were completely out of the question. Dad requested that we get him back to Kentucky to see his doctors. If he flew, there was the real possibility of an inflight emergency forcing the pilots to land. He would be taken to the nearest hospital. It seemed the only solution was to drive him from Naples to Lexington — almost exactly 1,000 miles straight up I-75.

With Dad and Mom at the house in Florida were two black Labradors, Pupper and Baby, our beloved family pets. They would need to make the journey as well. It was decided that Byron would drive an SUV from our home to Naples. He left immediately. I was going to stay in Lexington on standby and man the telephones. In approximately 15 hours Byron would reach Naples. Then immediately he would pack the dogs in his car and follow as Mom drove with Dad in her SUV. This is how they would drive to Kentucky. That night Mom made Dad as comfortable as she could and stayed with him constantly.

Early the next morning, I got a telephone call. It was Mom. Byron was there and they were heading north. I remember how strong her voice seemed to me. I spoke with Byron briefly. I wanted to know how it was with Dad. I had known Byron since I was a young boy and knew he would give it to me straight up. "He looks bad, Andrew. He just looks bad," is what I heard on the other end of the line.

"Thanks Bee-roan."

I didn't have any more questions.

With Mom leading, they drove about eight hours that day. Occasionally stopping for gas, Dairy Queen soft serve ice cream, and a basket of fresh peaches as they crossed over into Georgia. They stopped at one of those $65 a night interstate exit hotels and called me. Dad was lethargic, but conscious, and the dogs had been so well behaved.

The next morning they were again on the road early and after four hours or so had crossed the Tennessee - Kentucky border. This is when Mom really began to push it. She was averaging between 90 and 95 miles per hour. Byron, with the dogs and following, told me of the difficulty keeping up with her.

My mother knew as a former First Lady if she was pulled over she could explain the situation to any Kentucky law enforcement official and they would have honorably assisted. Less than 30 miles out, Mom called me on her cell. They would be in Lexington within 30 minutes. Be ready and outside. I waited 20 minutes and dialed 911 and asked that an ambulance be sent to our house. I could not know it then, but in the end I would dial that number for all three of them — Dad, Mom, and my brother Glenn.

Their mini-caravan pulled into the large half circle front driveway as I watched, waiting on the front porch. Both automobiles came to a stop and both my mother and Byron jumped out, hustling to the passenger door of the SUV. Byron opened the door as Mom reached in to assist.

In life, we all have certain moments. I believe no matter how long or intense we have endured something, there is on some unconscious, hidden level a tiny morsel of hope left that all will be all right. That somehow everything can work out. Then comes the moment when reality wins out and destroys that hidden, little ray of hope.

As Mom helped Dad pull his right leg out from the floor space, he placed his right hand on her shoulder and looked up at me from underneath his black Oakley cap. The gold Rolex Presidential that a group of coal operators had given him rattled on his brittle wrist. His tired, weary eyes greeted me with a faint smile as tears filled mine. The calf muscles of both his legs were gone and hanging flesh had replaced them. It had been several weeks since I had seen him. The cancer had done its part.

We managed to bring him in the house and made it to his favorite chair in the family room. I sat by him as Mom and Byron tended to the dogs and waited for the ambulance. I remember the exchange, "Hey Spruder, how are you, pal?"

"I'm fine, Dad, how are you?" is all I could manage.

"I don't know, Spruder. I don't know."

Spruder was a variation of many nicknames I had from childhood in my family. Spruder is what Dad used. Even today, when I dream of him he still calls me Spruder.

The ambulance arrived and the paramedics entered the house. All of us thanked them as they performed the necessary tests and prepared him to be transported to the hospital. He was taken to Saint Joseph Hospital two miles southwest of downtown Lexington. Mom and I followed closely as the lights and sirens blared. I can't remember us speaking. The doctors wanted to stabilize him and then proceed with the customary investigative tests. After hours of waiting, a doctor emerged and explained to Mom and I what we already knew. It was the cancer.

I was astonished when, the next day, Dad was released and we brought him home. I believe now the situation was so critical and advanced the physicians simply let us take him home until the next whatever happened. Byron had the numerous prescriptions filled at the pharmacy, and Mom and I did the best we could to help Dad settle in and have some comfort. An oxygen tank was used to help with his breathing.

Dad was only home for one and a half days as he began to suffer serious chest pains. This time, Mom and I drove him to the hospital. At the emergency entrance, Mom ran inside and came out with a wheelchair. Both of us had to pick him up so he could get in the chair. I drove to the parking garage. As Mom pushed her husband of 41 years into the emergency room entrance, he asked her to stop for a moment.

"Mom," he said. "This is the beginning of the end."

He was right. He did not leave the hospital again.

This time arterial blockages were found and he was scheduled for bypass surgery. Almost simultaneously another lymphatic mass, a tumor the size of a lemon, was found in his chest. It took medical precedence over the blockages and was surgically removed. After this, chemotherapy began.

Over the course of the next few days we all held vigil by his bedside. My mother, Glenn, the rest of our family, close friends, and employees came in and out laughing, crying, visiting, and saying goodbye. Dad was in and out of consciousness as we bathed and shaved him, combed his hair, brushed his teeth, and clipped his nails.

The situation deteriorated and a ventilator was brought in to assist in breathing. Nine days later, as Mom and I came to check on him early in the morning, Mom noticed him immediately as we walked in. It was over. Mom didn't utter a word. She went to him.

I watched her through water-drenched eyes as she gently pushed his hair away and placed her hand on his cheek. Together we removed the tape on his face holding the mouthpiece of the ventilator as our hands trembled. The swelling was so severe his skin had pulled apart on his right cheek. Dad had suffered a major stroke. Mom and I were there. We saw him. His chest moved up and down only from the effort of the machine.

This was the end he had prophesied. Wallace Wilkinson was gone. It was July 4, 2002. That night, according to his wishes, the ventilator was removed and it was only a few short minutes before the faintest of his involuntary, tiny little breaths ceased. He was 60 years old.

Chapter 9

It goes without saying that upon my father's death an already horrible situation became downright horrendous for us emotionally. Arrangements were made, and a memorial service was held for him at a church in downtown Lexington. Many people from business, politics, and all walks of life attended. Family, friends, strangers, and even rivals attended. For the awful circumstances surrounding it, it was as beautiful as it could be.

As I looked at him in his casket, that I was his son is the only reason I recognized him. He appeared to be 100 years old. As I stared down at him, a part of me went dark inside. A last meaningful moment transpired as the funeral procession made its way out of town several miles to the cemetery.

At a large construction project the workers, knowing it was Wallace Wilkinson's procession, paused from their work and came to the edge of the site with their hats in their hands. They watched for minutes as the long caravan drove by. Of the remembrances, stories, and all that was said that day, I know that would have been what my father was most proud of.

At his memorial someone approached me and said, "Andrew, Wallace was a worker. That's how he did everything."

So, those men, those workers, were saluting another worker on his last ride. By that time everything had been blown up so much. On all levels everything was so fantastic and exaggerated — claims of corruption, embezzlement, lies, and evasion. Those people with their hats in their hands were paying respect to the core of the man. Mom, Glenn, and I saw that a lot that day and were grateful for it.

I saw Wallace Wilkinson just like everyone else did. He was impressive and he was a force. The end was bad and people were hurt because of decisions he made. Public opinion will always remain mixed on who he was and what he stood for. I have to accept that.

As his only surviving heir, I say he was more than rock solid in many ways that count. There was something about him even his enemies wished they had. Yes, he went down. He went down in a firestorm. But there was much more to him and his life than what the end portrayed. Many people benefited from their business with him, many forgotten Kentuckians benefited from his service, and I benefited from being his son. This is where I leave it.

The creditors' committee, made up of the largest Wilkinson creditors and former friends, decided enough was enough. The governor was gone. They reached a settlement with Mom, Glenn, and I. We kept the house in Naples and a few very personal belongings.

One week later, Mom and I walked out of the front door at Greenbrier, the only personal home I had ever known. We left everything in the house. It was not ours anymore. We turned around and stood a moment. Looking up, down, sideways, silently reliving over 25 years of life. Then we walked away.

Glenn had largely isolated himself during this time, only participating in things as he had to. He had found a home in Ocala, Florida. Ocala is Florida's horse country, and he believed he could find a measure of peace there. Glenn had owned and showed quarter horses in Kentucky, so we all understood his move. Mom headed to Naples and I was returning to my house in Sarasota. Dad was gone and now we were all out of Kentucky.

As painful as this was for Glenn and I, it was devastating for Mom. She was a genuine Kentucky girl, and a former

First Lady who had always been connected to the state and its people. Now she was leaving what had been her life with the man she loved. How could Florida be a welcome destination? It couldn't, and part of my mother's what I call life spirit, was destroyed then. In time, it would take more direct hits from her two boys.

Chapter 10

As mementos from my travels, I used to collect matchbooks. In 2002, matchbooks were not as readily available as they had been as a result of more and more restrictions being placed on smoking. So I started taking laundry bags from the hotels I had visited. I had stuffed my bag from the Hotel Bel-Air with every valuable of my family's I could get my hands on that was not my mother's. Platinum, gold, precious stones, and silver in every form — rings, watches, lighters, cuff links, bracelets, necklaces, pins, pens, and coins. There was every bit of $100,000 in that laundry bag.

I drove south down I-75 with it in the floorboard of my car. I stopped in Atlanta, Georgia that night, in an area called Buckhead. I drove to Martin Luther King Drive and bought an 8-ball of cocaine. I suspect if that drug dealer knew what I had only feet away from him, the chances of my survival would have dropped dramatically during that transaction. This was a mild form of the countless brushes with danger and death that were to come.

I checked into a local, seedy hotel and stashed the bag under the bed. I did more cocaine before I walked to a neighborhood bar to drink for most of the night. After a couple hours of sleep, I continued on to Sarasota with my loot and my drugs.

Concerned for all three of us, family and friends were reaching out to Mom, Glenn, and I. I lied and let everyone believe I was being strong. By this time I had decided that the "alias" of someone to feel sorry for suited me. I was out of Kentucky. It was no longer my home.

I had a girlfriend at the time and she was also a Kentuckian from Lexington. We had been dating for seven or eight months at the time of the collapse. She came to Sarasota with me. Her name was Robyn and she cared about me very much. Although she couldn't understand it all, she tried the best she knew how. Many times she was there when nobody else was. A friend. A listener.

She had recently graduated from the University of Kentucky, and quickly landed a good job with a local theatre company in Sarasota. So began the storm for her. I had a house and some money. Other than that I had no clue what I was going to do.

Scared and confused, I began to take on the role of a victim more and more. I was drinking in excess and I learned where to find the drugs to keep me far away from reality. Their grip was tightening on me and drinking or using or both was an everyday thing.

Sure enough, it was not long until I was in the ghetto one night looking for cocaine, and I was arrested the first time. I picked up two local girls and told them I would give them money to take me where I could score. As they were climbing into my car, a police officer drove by. Two black girls getting in the car with a white guy late in the night in an area known for drugs?

The cop quickly did a U-turn, came up behind me, and hit the lights and sirens. Although it looked exactly like what it was, the officer couldn't prove anything because no transaction had taken place yet. But I did have a loaded Walther PPK 9mm pistol under my seat. I was placed under arrest for carrying it illegally under my seat and taken to the Sarasota County jail. I called Robyn, and she came to bail me out. I obtained an attorney, and the charges were later dropped on a technicality. No one from my family or in Kentucky learned of the arrest.

I guess for most this would be a type of wake up call. It was nothing of the sort for me. I continued with my activities unabated and was frequenting the same area for my supplies within days. I created relationships with a few dealers. In fact, it came to the point when I drove to a pick up they would come running from all directions as I stopped, hoping to be the one I gave my money to.

Before long, it was the other way around. The dealers were coming to me. I would call them and place the cash in my mailbox or somewhere similar, and they would drive by, make the switch, and call me as they were driving off. I was becoming known in the Sarasota ghetto just as I had been at Auburn. All along, Robyn was holding on for dear life. She was not perfect, but was stratospheres away from where I was. I was a monster growing uglier and nastier and gaining force.

So began a four-year period that saw my life go from a wild, irresponsible, spoiled young man to a full-blown addict. There was some type of cocktail consisting of alcohol, pills, and cocaine flowing through my veins constantly. There were days of not using, but they were becoming less and less common. Normally only when I couldn't find something and had to wait. I began the systematic shutting out of those who cared about me the most, especially the ones closest to me like my childhood friend Pierce and my cousin Myra.

In my early life both Glenn and I were extremely close to all of our cousins. But Myra and I had always been like siblings. We were the two youngest and spent a lot of time together. I think I was the brother she would have liked to have and she the sister I would have liked to have.

Chapter 11

Concerned for all three of us, family and friends were reaching out to Mom, Glenn, and I. I lied and let everyone believe I was being strong. I was out of Kentucky. It was no longer my home. I had a house and some money. Other than that I had no clue what I was going to do.

I exploited Robyn's compassion and feelings for me to get what I needed from her. I needed her to feel sorry for me and see how nobody could possibly understand what I was going through. Stay on my side and be quiet. Let me do what I needed to do in my misery. I manipulated her over and over with these lies. I put her in a bad place in her own life. The stress, the hurting, the chaos, and the danger. And it didn't subside. With every day, week, and month that passed I kept ratcheting it up on her.

It was late summer 2002. Mom was in Naples preparing to list the house on the market. Glenn was in Ocala alone and struggling, and I was in Sarasota dropping the hammer on a life of all out, full force addiction. I had thought to become a certified real estate agent, so I enrolled in a one-week course.

The night before the course finished I stayed up snorting powder and swallowing pills. I actually drove to the course the next morning completely messed up. I pulled into the parking lot just to turn around and drive away again. Addicts love run down little strip motels and Sarasota had at this time plenty of them. I checked in one and continued my binge all alone for four or five hours until I had nothing else to ingest.

For two years this type of behavior ruled my life. In the beginning people did not know the depths of it. As the weeks and months passed the telltale signs started to show.

I was not returning phone calls or emails. My appearance became haggard and tired. I blocked out every single person in my life.

Even my childhood best friend, Pierce, and my first cousin Myra, didn't reach me. Glenn and I had always been close to all the cousins we had on both sides of the family, but Myra and I had a special connection. We were more like brother and sister.

Another cousin, Michelle, was the "mother hen" of all of us. She was very mature looking for her age and people routinely believed Myra and I were her children. Absent the parents, we did see Michelle as the mother. So, we had our own little micro-family in the family and often times did our own thing when we were all on vacation with each other. The three of us have some wonderful memories together.

In November 2001, Myra and her husband, Steven, visited me at my new place in Sarasota. I had purchased tickets to the grand opening of the Ritz-Carlton Hotel and I invited them down to attend with Robyn and me. My erratic behavior and using put a damper on what should have been a wonderful time together. I love Myra very much and today we are again very close. After she and Steven left for Kentucky, I would not see Myra again for 11 years.

Somewhere during this time I also tried crack for the first time. I believe it was a time I could not find any powder so I took a bag of crack home with me instead. Crack is brutal and intense. The high is powerful, but short-lived. It leaves the user immediately craving more.

Another danger with crack is how readily available it is on the street. Within a week or two of trying crack it became a staple on my "grocery list" every time I bought drugs. Whatever else I bought, I also bought crack. Usually I was smoking it before I even returned home.

Eventually the house in Naples sold, and Mom was able to buy a house in Sarasota. The same old beach neighborhood I was in. I drove to Naples to help her move. This was the first time she noticed something was wrong.

As we packed boxes together, I was ducking in and out every few minutes. I was running to an apartment over the garage and smoking and snorting cocaine at the same time. I heard the door below open and it was Mom checking to see where I was. I heard her coming up the stairs and I shoved the pipe into my pocket while the coal was still red. It burned a hole into my skin that is still there today. I was sweating profusely and the smoke from the crack filled the air. I was so high I could barely talk. Mom looked at me and actually stepped back to get a better look. She knew.

Mom didn't have a deep understanding of drugs, but I will never forget the look on her face...in her eyes. She turned and walked back down the stairs. I was left standing there with powder on the counter and a burn the size of a nickel on my thigh. I believe the disappointment, the realization was so deep that Mom didn't know how to respond. I think she was in shock, heartbroken, and already overwhelmed by everything else in our lives.

I was somehow able to pull it together and help with the rest of the packing in silence. The moving van arrived the next morning on schedule, was loaded, and then pulled off heading north. This is the way Mom left Naples and went to her new house and life in Sarasota.

I look back on this time and it is a miracle I am alive, and a miracle I didn't take the life of another. All of my neighbors knew exactly what was going on with me. Soon after I moved in, I had befriended a French couple who owned a bakery in town. Now they would no longer speak to me or allow their children to come over to my house. I had gone from being out of control to dangerous.

One night I was returning from Tampa to Sarasota driving Glenn's Chevrolet Suburban. Somewhere along I-275 South I nodded off and veered far left and ran the truck down the side of concrete dividers separating the highway. As I woke up in panic, I corrected so hard that I entered into a full spin back across the four lanes to the other shoulder of the road. Eventually I came to a stop facing the wrong way with grass and dust filling the air on the right side of the highway.

I sat in shock with my hands clenched on the steering wheel for what had to be a few minutes. My headlights were still on as car after car kept driving straight by me. With the left side of the Suburban severely damaged I managed to come around and slowly get back on the road and finish the drive to Sarasota.

Chapter 12

I discovered Delano in South Beach, Miami on one of my drug-fueled road trips. Anybody who knows Miami knows what Delano is. It was a fabulous property. I was flying to Barcelona, Spain the following morning and needed a room for the night. I have no idea why I was flying to Spain other than it sounded good at the time. I rented a convertible Ford Mustang for the night and the airport drive in the morning.

That evening I drove to a random area of town that appeared a likely place to buy. A seasoned addict can spot an area, or even an individual, and ascertain within a moment if drugs are available. I had graduated to this level. To this day, back in everyday, normal life with other healthy people, I silently recognize these types of things all the time.

Along the way somewhere I needed to pass through a toll stop on one of the Miami area highways. As I approached I hit a guardrail with the yellow and black decals on the end of it that protected the tollbooth employees from life-threatening people like me. The airbag deployed and the front end was crunched halfway up toward the windshield. This time the car was not drivable. This time the police did arrive on the scene. How I got away with this I will never know; I explained to the police officer that another car had come over on me and I had to swerve to avoid impact. Another driver stopped and corroborated my story! As high as I was, I remember standing there on the open road with a crashed car only feet away and a police officer nodding up and down as he wrote down my story.

No field sobriety test was administered. I wasn't even asked if I had been drinking. The car was impounded, and that same police officer drove me back to Delano. I thanked him and continued on with my night that at one point had me doing a line of cocaine with a complete stranger in one of the poolside bungalows. After maybe a couple hours of sleep, I began stirring to prepare for my transatlantic flight. My passport and my stash were nowhere to be found.

After I collected my thoughts and tried to think straight, I thought of the crashed Mustang. Where was it now? I called downstairs to the hotel staff and they helped me locate the impound yard where it was and called a taxi for me. Once downstairs, I saw the cab and was getting in when a doorman opened the door for me and said, "There's the man! Good morning."

When a doorman at Delano in South Beach recognizes you and refers to you as "the man," that is saying something. It is an accomplishment of sorts. Albeit, a pathetic one.

Once at the impound yard, I convinced the employee I needed access because I believed my passport was there. He showed me where the car was and gave me the keys. I walked there alone and opened the door looking everywhere inside.

By this time I had missed the flight to Spain, but it didn't matter. I was happy. Beneath the seat and all over the back floorboard I found my passport and my cocaine and OxyContins from the night before. The car had not even been searched!

I bought a BMW R-1150R motorcycle and took another road trip, explaining to everyone that would listen I needed to get away, to get some air, and clear my head. I rode over to the East Coast, picked up I-95 North, and took it straight up to Daytona, through Savannah, and on into Charleston, South Carolina.

I rode in severe rain and was forced to stop under a few overpasses. I rode that motorcycle as high on cocaine as I could get. I can remember laying my chest down on the gas tank as the rain pelted my bare cheeks like needles.

The visibility was so bad other motorists were driving with their hazards on. The danger felt good to me.

I had an mp3 player loaded with old Rod Stewart, Seal, Coldplay, Alanis Morissette, the Rolling Stones, and the like. When I hear Train's "Calling All Angels" I am soaking wet and on the back of that bike again. "I won't give up if you don't give up…"

The same as in Atlanta, I sought out the road or street named after Martin Luther King in both Savannah and Charleston to buy drugs. It should be noted that drugs can be found on many streets across the United States today, but I can't help but believe that the great civil rights leader would be distressed and saddened by this.

In hindsight, it seems clear that I was running from something. But I certainly didn't have to be physically moving. I was running just the same inside. The nights ended when I ran out of chemicals and the mornings began as I drove to pick more up.

One afternoon in a parking lot meeting with my dealer, I was not happy about the price I paid for the quantity I received. It escalated into a shouting match between both of us. The next thing I know I was grabbing a Maglite flashlight out of my car to rush him or defend myself — which one I don't know.

As I turned from the car with my weapon in hand, he pulled an automatic pistol out of his waistband and stuck it in my chest. The barrel of the gun was in my ribs. Nearby people noticed the commotion and started to approach. My dealer jumped in his car and sped off. I too hopped in my car and got out of there…with my fix. Everything was okay. It was just a misunderstanding, I told myself. I still can see

Robyn's wide eyes as I rather nonchalantly shared with her my adventure.

One night as I snorted and smoked cocaine all night long my heart began jumping and skipping beats. It was so serious I went to the bathroom and looked myself over in the mirror. I was pale and sweat poured down my face. My mouth was open as I gasped for air. I felt my heart beat and then pause momentarily before it laboriously pounded again. I was groaning like an animal in its death throes. My lips were caked white and as I beheld myself in the mirror, I had a solitary thought — I had done too much.

My heart couldn't take it. I had done too much and my heart was going to explode. In a matter of hours I would be found on the floor of that bathroom dead, and my mother would see how I died. She would see what my final moments were like. As a father now, to think that my daughter, Melina, could ever experience that terrifies me. So sadly the power of addiction is profoundly more powerful than any moment of horror. I kept going.

In yet another motel room binge I had taken so many uppers and downers that my body and mind couldn't decide which way to go. Paranoia came on, and I became crazed. I left the room as is, with drugs and paraphernalia everywhere, and drove the short distance to my mother's house.

Once there I beat on the door screaming for her to let me in. As she opened it I ran inside crying and totally incoherent. She tried her best to calm me down by hugging me and wrapping me in her arms. I threw her off of me. As she watched I had a complete and total mental and nervous drug-fueled meltdown. I collapsed to the floor screaming and writhing in anguish.

Meltdown is used commonly in clichés of all kinds and vastly overused, but a true meltdown is a terrifying scene.

Especially the sort provoked by illicit drugs. My dear mother could only watch. What happened next is how I know she knew The Lord.

With complete terror in her eyes, she dropped to her knees and cried out to Jesus Christ to help me. I still see the pain, fear, and water in her eyes as she watched me and prayed. She knew of nothing she could do but turn to God. As mothers do, she took care for me that night, nursing me back to whatever normal for me was. Even though the motel I left had a copy of my driver's license, I never heard from them.

Chapter 13

The Florida Mental Health Act of 1971, commonly known as "The Baker Act," allows for the involuntary institutionalization of individuals to be examined over a 72-hour period. The process is meant to establish if a person is a danger to society or themselves. Only a day or two after my mental episode, Mom appealed to a judge to have me "Baker acted."

A marked police unit came to my house in the morning and detained me. I was taken to a mental health facility and forced to stay for three days while they studied me to ascertain if I was an addict, a danger, or nuts.

After the obligatory three-day stay, outpatient therapy was recommended to me…recommended! I could really act when I needed to. It wasn't all acting, however. I found a history book at the facility and brushed up on my Romanian history and the 1989 revolt that saw Nicolae Ceausescu and his wife, Elena, overthrown and executed.

I returned to my house and immediately checked my trusty "spots" — hiding places everywhere for my drugs. To my disappointment my mother had been through everything and removed whatever she had found. But she did not find the Stetson. I checked the inside band of the new cowboy hat I kept in the original box in my closet. Bingo! She didn't find everything after all.

At some point, no matter how many dealers a person has, the day comes when nothing can be found. Everybody is "dry." When thishappened I would systematically go through my house…sweater drawers, vitamin bottles, refrigerator, toolbox, even outside in the courtyard. Sure enough I would come across something I had hidden while completely high.

That instance was always such a moment of complete happiness. Being sober and desperate, then finding something to end all of that misery. Pure bliss. That in and of itself was a drug.

I was 25 pounds underweight and pale. All the while thinking I was slim and looking fit. It was Thanksgiving 2003. My mother's sister, my Aunt Kathy, her husband, my Uncle Gene, their daughters, my cousins Michelle and Carol, and Carol's family came to Sarasota. They came to be with Mom, Glenn, and I over the holiday in what they knew was a tough time after the bankruptcy and Dad's death.

They had been affected as well, and must have been horrified by what they learned was going on. Staying at my mother's place, they did not see me. Uncle Gene and Aunt Kathy came from Lexington. Michelle came from Nashville. Carol and her family travelled from Houston.

Carol and I, too, had a close relationship. We had, with her close friend, Christie, spent an entire summer working together at Lake Barkley State Resort Park in Kentucky and left there with some hilarious stories. The cottage we stayed in was out in the woods. Every night, we heard all kinds of noises in those trees. One night I couldn't take it anymore and ran and jumped in the bed with them armed with a steak knife to protect us. A steak knife!

They came from hundreds of miles away and all over only to leave without having laid their eyes on me. It was one of the recurring instances when over time I had done so many drugs I was broken down. By not eating, not sleeping, and overall exhaustion. I stayed on the floor in my living room smoking cigarettes and sleeping the entire weekend.

When my mother showed up with a Thanksgiving dinner plate for me I asked her to tell everyone I said "Hello," and I was sorry I couldn't make it because I was sick. I had a contagious eye infection. She only nodded her head in deep sadness and said she would as she left me with my plate of sustenance.

Glenn, battling his own demons, did at least show up for the meal. Also severely underweight, he was nodding in and out over his turkey while the rest of our family watched. That weekend, Thanksgiving weekend, they learned the extent of what was happening in Florida with Martha and the boys.

It is a tragic, sad truth that I could continue on with tale after tale of me like this in such loss and addiction. I have painted this canvas sufficiently. During many events or circumstances taking place while I was high there is a moment or action that "woke me up." Something that knocked me into coherence. Slamming into something, being slammed into something, and so forth. The black Suburban when I hit the concrete divider, the yellow Mustang as I slammed into the yellow containers, the guy sticking his pistol in my chest, etc.

But regarding the events of March 3, 2004, I have no recollection. I have very faint, fuzzy visions, but nothing more. What comes next is taken directly from an incident report of the Sumter County (Florida) Sheriff's Department.

I was on the interstate again heading to St. Augustine, Florida, this time in a brand new Jeep Rubicon Wrangler. Sometime around noon I decided to stop and I exited to pull into the parking lot of a Shell gas station in Tarry Town, Florida. Tarry Town is not a town, but rather a rural two-gasoline station crossroad in Sumter County.

I was there for around 40 minutes with the engine running while I sat motionless in the automobile. The manager of the store became concerned about a suspicious vehicle and phoned the police. As the Sumter County Deputy Sheriff approached from the left rear side of the Jeep I was slouched over with my head leaning on the steering wheel. There was "…a yellow substance running from his (my) nose and he (I) was sweating profusely." I had a mini M&M candy tube full of crack on my lap as well as several exposed pieces. In a search of the vehicle they found a black cloth bag filled with "an assortment of pills." Also in the Jeep were two automatic pistols: a Para-Ordnance .45 caliber and a Smith & Wesson .22 caliber both not chambered, but the magazines were full.

The charges were one felony count of possession of cocaine with intent to distribute and three felony counts of possession of controlled substances (Valium, Xanax, and hydrocodone). It should be noted I was fully compliant at all times. I guess I still had that going for me.

The Jeep and pistols were seized. I was taken to the Sumter County Detention Center and booked. The jail was extremely overcrowded. In 2004 many rural, small-town jails were flooded with inmates held on some type of charge relating to the recent explosion of crystal meth. In some places just as many people were being held for "cooking" it as were for using it.

I lay on the floor of a cell on a mat for two days without eating one meal. My body and brain were completely spent from months of heavy drug abuse. I was exhausted to the core of my being. The officers and other inmates made sure I was breathing, but didn't panic because they knew what they were looking at. They saw it often.

At last, a fellow inmate woke me up with a tray of food in front of me on the floor. "Brother, you got to eat some food, man." He was right and I did. I had lain so long on my right side with only a thin mat between me and the floor I had what I call "floor sores." Not from the bed, but from the floor. I was that emaciated.

I waited another six days before I had the courage to call my mother. Nine days I was in jail before she heard from me. I had not called for a day or two before I was arrested. All of this time, all my mother knew is that I had a massive drug problem and I was on a motorcycle.

Good God. Oh, the pain that a child can inflict. This would not be the last of it. I am, to this day, heavily remorseful over how much my loving, loyal mother suffered at the hands of "her Andrew."

When I did call and announce I was still alive and in jail her response was, "I know." She said she had expected I was dead or in jail, and that to receive the collect call meant the obvious. If I was dead, she said, she would have been notified after they identified me.

She posted my bond, and drove three hours north to pick me up and return me to Sarasota. Over the next year and a half she made that drive three more times as I repeatedly violated probation and house arrest conditions. On the original charge I received two years supervised probation and no jail time. I had two DUIs years earlier, but they did not count against me. This was the "first offense." Little did they know. Also, as a condition of my probation, I had to complete 30 days of inpatient rehabilitation.

I went to a rehabilitation center in St. Petersburg. My mother and the rest of my family were understanding and supportive. They still had hope for me and believed in me. I met some great people there — Jep, Allison, and Cameron. It is here where I developed the philosophy that only because someone has numerous diplomas and certificates on their wall doesn't necessarily mean jack.

Accomplished learning in any given field is always a good thing. I am not saying only a person who has experienced addiction can help an addict. What I am saying is that empathy with the addict is a huge tool. The skill of connecting to someone who doesn't want to be connected with is paramount in the addiction rehabilitation field.

Most addicts are also very intelligent. A huge frustration for me, and I think as well for other addicts, is that when you are strung out on drugs you have zero credibility. Addicts are told all the time their minds are broken. But I still had so many things I needed to say, needed to communicate. So many real thoughts that were given hardly any credence by those with the task of helping me.

I came to the conclusion real quick that my counselor did not know how to begin relationship building with me, and I still feel that way today. At one point, as I became increasingly frustrated with her, she punished me by telling me I could not speak for one full week. I was told at a support and rehabilitative facility that I could not open my mouth for a full week outside of meetings to communicate with anyone! I was to be silent.

I lost hope this counselor could help me. I had no trust in her ability to connect herself to me. When trust is not established or is torn down, then it is game over. I had sat in pain and silence for so, so many times as I loaded my brain with chemicals to escape, to push feelings so far down and deep that they disintegrated. But they didn't and I needed help to pull them out one by one and learn to deal with them in reality.

Instead, here I was at a treatment center being forced to continue suppressing them and shut up. I would say that had to be a very bad joke. But it wasn't, and it affected me deeply in a negative way. I look back at that version of myself sitting there in that office, that chair, and listening to what he was being told. I want to cry for him.

Chapter 14

I completed my 30 days inpatient treatment and used the afternoon of the day I was released. I moved into a small beach house on Treasure Island. It was just minutes up the strip from the treatment facility I attended. Immediately, I dropped contact with anything or anybody from rehab and was constantly using. It was in this time I first pierced my skin with a needle and shot heroin into my veins.

In less than three months, the landlord evicted me because I wasn't paying rent. I was dodging my parole officer. It all came to an unbelievable head one morning. The day before, I had rented a moving truck to begin moving out. A couple of neighbors I had gotten to know a little bit were helping me. I was also giving them items I was tired of moving. We worked well into the night and made good progress.

That night I bought some cocaine and did it all night long in a hotel room about a half mile from the house. I fell asleep sometime as the sun was coming up. The next thing I know it was 11:00 a.m. and I had told the people helping me we would meet at 7:00 a.m. to finish. I had to be out that day by a court order. So, I arrive at the house and see this…a Sheriff's Deputy, my parole officer, the landlord, and neighbors from the area loading my belongings into the moving truck. I could still taste the residual cocaine in my nose, and my head felt like a frozen pineapple. Exactly like Julian's in "Less Than Zero." Holy cow, was that pressure. I can feel it now.

I approached and the police officer notified me immediately I could not step foot on the property. The landlord, that morning in my absence, had secured a court order allowing for the immediate removal of me and my belongings and it restricted me from setting foot on the property. I stood off the property and listened to the police officer. Then I had to deal with my parole officer.

I thought absolutely I was going to jail. I convinced him I was okay and just dealing with a lot of stress trying to get my act together. He let me schedule an appointment to see him in the next couple of days to discuss where I was moving and to give a urine sample.

I knew how to beat the urine tests by then. If I knew when it was then I never had a problem. The problems were always when they surprised me and they surprised me a lot.

Next up was the landlord. I could see clearly in his eyes he had zero use for me and wanted the whole situation to be over. As he walked away he said, "Whatever you're dealing with, I hope you get it under control." He knew exactly what I was doing. All the while other people I knew very little emptied the house and loaded the moving truck. I thanked everyone for their understanding and assistance and drove off in the truck.

At Auburn once, I copied the master version of a final and shared it with others in the class. When many answers appeared identical on different students' tests, the professor became suspicious. He called the students in and everyone involved promptly offered me up. Cheating like that at a major state university is a huge deal. Certainly cause for expulsion. The professor called me into his office. I was busted and there was no denying it.

The long and short of it is not only did I not get expelled, but also I was able to reschedule and take another final. I was president of Lambda Chi Alpha at the time. I marched into that fraternity house with my reschedule note from the professor and dared anybody to EVER top that. If that moving day didn't top it, then it certainly rivaled it.

Addicts are master thespians, manipulators, and cons. Even I surprised myself at my ability to escape unscathed at times. In time, though, everything caves in and catches up in grand fashion.

I was broke by this time. All of the fluid cash I had before was gone and I had even borrowed against my house. The real estate market was raging in Florida. I asked my Mom if she wanted to buy my house. She saw the opportunity and took it. I sold it to her for only what I had in it.

I had dumped money into the property, and it was a nice little deal for her. She listed it, and in about two months made $135,000 when she sold it. She would do the same thing with another property that same year, but with more principal and more profit. She really did well in 2004 on those two deals.

There was no joy or celebration, however. The reality of mine and Glenn's problems loomed over everything. All the wounds from Kentucky were gaping and raw. We were all still trying to deal with the fact that what had happened had happened, and Dad was dead. There was no healing. Glenn and I made sure of it.

My mother had lost her husband and partner of a lifetime. She had lost everything they built together. Now she had two sons that were indiscriminately scorching everything in front of and behind them. It didn't matter at all to us. We were burning everything down.

I was bouncing nomadically around. Staying at my mother's when I could. Staying with Robyn when I could. I had to report every week to my probation officer. I was attending recovery meetings. Staying clean for short spurts at a time. Finding work, then losing it, and then looking again. This is pretty much the cycle that prevailed for about a year and a half.

I waited tables. I washed hair in a salon. I parked cars. I did whatever people in my situation do. Ultimately the day always came when I would use again. There is much more to the meaning of sober than being chemical or alcohol free. Sober is a state of mind. Sober is a mentality. And I was not sober at all.

Addiction is a horrible thing. Addiction kills the addict. But it also kills families, relationships, and life. An addict and their addiction is an extremely intimate thing. I do not believe in blanket solutions and approaches. There are some common denominators involved, but the road of an addict is extremely personal and unique. The results are the same, but the journey is not.

I believe the single largest common denominator of all addicts is extreme selfishness. We focus on our pain, our suffering. How no one understands us. How we have or had it so much worse than everyone else. The focus is on us, us, us. To hell with everyone else. But we still have things to say. We need so desperately to learn to listen and interact productively. It takes serious skill to help an addict. Much more than only a heart for it.

I have the highest respect for anyone genuinely trying to help addicts and the curses of addiction, no matter their approach. It is an honorable endeavor. Fighting addiction is saving lives. Some approaches may work for some, but not for others. That is why I say it is an intimate relationship between the addict and the addiction.

The percentage of addicts that relapse after treatment is huge. Figures vary, but it is safe to say that 60% to 80% of alcoholics or addicts relapse. No one can claim they have it all figured out. A treatment program has to be tailored to the individual, with the intent of going in very deep into their spirit, psyche, and experiences with hardcore understanding and compassion. A change of perspective has got to be introduced and implemented early to the addict.

In my opinion, there is but one tool for this change of perspective — God. Addiction is spiritual darkness. Addiction is a spiritual disease. I have an extremely addictive personality. God made me this way and it is my cross to bear, among others. We all have a cross to bear. The glorious truth is that the power to overcome is readily available to all of us through Jesus Christ.

There are those who believe once an addict always an addict. No matter what happens in the future a person, once an addict, is always one. There are those that believe addiction can be left behind and what a person was in the past is no more. I am of the latter. Jesus Christ tells us this, as well.

I have been to meeting after meeting where a person was two, three years clean and still self-identified, rather miserably, as an addict. Drug and alcohol free not just a few weeks, months, or even a little over a year, but a long time. Life had progressed, family had lovingly reclaimed them, friends compassionately forgiven them, and they were still mired in the darkness, shame, and guilt.

I have wanted to stand up many times to interrupt and shout out loud, "Stewart the addict, keep going! Don't stop here. You're stuck. You have life and wings…fly!…fly! Go forth and live!! Don't call yourself an addict or you will think like one. Bust out of that shell, my friend. Bust it down and come on!!"

Of course, I never did that or I would have been thrown out. And I respect that. But I sure have wanted to. Many people choose to and support the notion of always self-identifying as an addict in recovery. If this is what works for them, then great. This is why I hold fast to the idea that addiction is profoundly intimate and personal and must be tailored to the individual.

However, in the end a spiritual life must begin for success. I am but one opinion in this much debated and discussed subject. I am not an authority on anyone else's life. I know the love of God and my own experiences.

I believe that people can get hung up in that stage too long and it hurts them. Again, any efforts to fight addiction have my respect, and it is certainly not an us against them thing. But I have seen so many people drag themselves in and out of meetings day after day, even hour by hour, with a willing heart. But they are stuck. The wheels are spinning, and they are in a rut. They have got to push on and up and into life.

There is no place for an addict in true life. Now, I have an awesome responsibility to never, ever forget the addict that I was and the death and destruction he carried with him.

As I already mentioned, I had a string of jobs that came and went as I was on probation. Wait a second. I am the one that came and went. The jobs stayed put. I waited tables at an upscale restaurant adjacent to the Sarasota Opera House. The owner's wife and her family dined there one night, and I made her pay the tab. She didn't appreciate it. I was fired.

I entered a salon and spa randomly one day that was also downtown. It was a nice operation and the owner, I believe, saw something in me. He hired me on the spot. I washed and conditioned hair for customers, primarily women, prepping them for whatever service they had scheduled an appointment for. Washing and conditioning hair is a little bit personal on some level, I guess. I collected numerous unsolicited telephone numbers after I towel dried the hair of women I had just washed and conditioned. None of which I ever dialed.

There was once an extremely busy day, and everyone was behind a bit with their clients. The owner instructed me to give a hot oil treatment to a woman who was there to see him. I had absolutely no idea what I was doing, and she knew it. She sat there quietly fuming as I fumbled around with her hair and a plastic hair cap. At one point she turned and looked up at me with a kind of disbelief in her eyes. Like, "Is this really happening right here, right now?!?" Normally, I always had or have something to say. At that moment all I could do was offer a shrug and a smile. It wasn't enough, and she left before her session was complete.

I also found work at an old school beach resort motel on Lido Key. I worked the desk at night taking reservations. Another employee had dropped the deposit envelope into the safe slot as his shift finished. It did not fall completely through the slot, and as I came on for my shift I noticed it. I worked my entire shift watching that envelope edge sticking up from the box. All it needed was a small tap and it would have fallen flush through.

I closed that night and made my rounds as usual. I shut the system down and dimmed the lights. I grabbed that envelope and walked out the door with it in my pocket. I had just stolen over $400. All of which was spent on drugs within 24 hours. The next day the manager knew I had taken the money, even though I denied it. She fired me, rightfully so.

The guilt from that was heavy in my heart for a long time. A couple of years later, when I could, I contacted her with a letter and admitted my guilt and shame. As I could, I made restoration with installments until I had paid back in full what I had taken.

I was talking or communicating with no one from my life except Robyn. She was trying. Everyone else could not get in. My mother did not want me at her house because the police were always looking for me and they knew her address. I was ashamed. I never wanted Myra to see what I had become. What life had done to me as opposed to the innocent childhood times, stories, and memories we shared.

Finally, my old friend, Pierce, hired a private detective to find me and give a report of what I was doing. When I found out I promptly contacted him and spoke to him horribly full of deception and anger. What a way for an old, true friend to be treated. How his heart must have felt as he listened to my voice. Nobody is safe from the heartbreaking wake the engine of an addict throws out.

Chapter 15

All in all, I violated my probation three times. Every time with a dirty urine sample. Each time I had to attend a "VOP" (violation of probation) hearing at court. The first time I violated, I was reinstated with some outpatient treatment requirements. The second time I was taken off of probation and placed under house arrest for one year. I had to submit a weekly schedule of my comings and goings, and if I deviated from my schedule I was busted. At that time the judge informed me if he saw me again there was going to be prison time involved.

At last, the day came when I had submitted yet another dirty urine sample and the court had a warrant for my arrest. I was at the apartment I was sharing with Robyn one afternoon and suddenly there it was…the loud, shocking knocks of police serving a warrant. I went to the door, knowing what was happening, and opened it.

"Sheriff's Department! We have a warrant for Andrew Wilkinson! Are you Andrew Wilkinson?"

"Yes, I am," I responded.

There was no excessive force involved, but a scene like that is not a walk in the park. I respect law enforcement for the job they do every day. They never know what they will face. I could have been high on 10 chemicals and ready for a life-threatening fight. It is a home invasion, they don't know what to expect, and they can't take chances. They have families at home and people that need them.

They grabbed me and spun me around pretty tough to subdue and cuff me. At some point I said something about how tough they must have thought they were, needing three of them to deal with me or something like that. That escalated the situation, and there was some physical wrestling for a few moments. Robyn was home and heard all of this. She became shocked and afraid, and ran up the stairs to the second floor. An officer pursued her. It was just an awful scene.

I was led to the patrol car in only what I had been wearing at the time. A pair of underwear and shorts. No shirt, no shoes, no jacket. It was so out in the open what was going on, and a lot of neighbors were watching as the police pushed my head down into the patrol car. I cussed the officer hardcore that drove the car. I was aggressive and personal. I called him everything. I think I even made up a couple of words. He kept his cool like a professional.

In a matter of minutes it was all over. Robyn, after having experienced that, was left in the apartment alone. Yet again, this is what addicts do. We blow everything up so sensationally, and then we are nowhere to be found when the dust settles on the pain we dish out.

I was booked into the Sarasota County jail, just as I had been the previous two times. When I caught my original charges in the Jeep I was in Sumter County. Every time I violated probation, I was taken to the Sarasota jail where I waited to be transferred to Sumter County and see the judge there. People serve their probation not where they were arrested, but where they live. Probation is transferred to the county of residence.

When I made the call to my mother explaining I was detained again, her voice was flat and emotionless. She was numb at that point. While I was being arrested pretty much every six months, Glenn was on his end doing the same things I was. He just wasn't being caught.

People suppose that being locked up is being locked up, but that is not altogether true. There are differences between county lock-up and prison. County can be much worse. In county, everybody just got brought in. Whatever happened just happened and nerves and emotions are raw, let me tell you. People are hurt, sobering up, in shame, and coming to terms with what kind of trouble they are in.

Things can go down real quick. It is very tense. The tension on Christmas Day, with everybody separated from their family and loved ones, is so thick. Thick and heavy. Extreme caution should be exercised in all activities. Plus, there is no going outside or recreation. It is like a tinderbox. All there needs to be is a spark, and yours truly was adept at throwing off a spark or two.

I had been there a couple of weeks, and my cellmate and I did not get along so well. He had decided I was a cop undercover on the inside or a "rat." A rat is somebody working with law enforcement to improve their own situation. There is real hatred and danger for anyone suspected of being a rat — in confinement or on the streets. I had to deal with this suspicion more than once. I guess it was how I looked, talked, or held myself. Whatever the case, it was not good. There are three things you do not want to be or suspected of being among criminals — a cop, a rat, or a child molester. So, my cellmate had a serious beef with me.

At the time, the floor of the jail I was on consisted of four pods holding inmates with a control center in the middle of all the pods. From the control center, the officers could see through the thick Plexiglas viewing windows that ran the length of the pod walls. Each pod could house around 30 to 40 prisoners. There were the cells, the common area where chow and congregating took place, and the shower. Although sanitized every day, the shower was disgusting and filthy. Every single time I used it to clean my body I could smell the strong odor of semen.

I was "called out" of the pod one day for a routine reason by the guards. As I returned, I noticed a string of items had been strewn from my cell out into the middle of the common area. A sleeping pad, blankets, toiletries, and a paper bag with cards, letters, and pencils. As I continued to my cell I could sense every eye of every man in that pod following me. Getting closer to the cell I saw it was the top bunk's items that had been disturbed. I was the top bunk.

I turned to see my cellmate in the center of the pod sitting nonchalantly at one of the metal tables watching me. All the other inmates were making space standing on the outer edges of the area. I had never been a fighter. Glenn and I had had a few good ones throughout the years, and I had gotten into a couple of fights at Auburn. But I had generally always looked for the party, not the fight.

That day I didn't look for anything. It looked for and found me. This wasn't some trendy, politically correct Tweet or culturally enlightened Facebook post about manhood or womanhood in today's modern world. One doesn't stop to say, "Excuse me one moment, if I may, my good cellmate. Have you, perhaps, considered the changing thoughts, ideas, and society's expression of what a man is in our evolving and highly sophisticated global community?" Sometimes we have to play ball by the rules of the field we are standing on.

This was a jailhouse challenge to my manhood. A direct statement from this guy telling me he thought I was a part of the female anatomy. I had no choice. I had to confront this guy. He wanted to fight and there was no way around it. If I didn't fight him the consequences for me would have been far worse than any beating he might have given me. That is how it works on the "inside." It is hard in there. A lot like the natural world.

The fear inside of me increased with every step I took toward him. As I was about halfway to him, he jumped up and stood in his spot waiting for me. He was taller than I was by a couple of inches and, I would say, 15 or 20 pounds heavier. Long, stringy, brown hair came down both sides of his face onto his shoulders. His Fu Manchu mustache was longer than his jawline on both sides.

As I was standing directly in front of him, I could smell the "buck" on his breath. Buck (sometimes called hooch or other names) is jailhouse alcohol fermented from basically anything the distillers can get their hands on — mainly fruit, oranges, apples, and even banana peels.

We were standing face-to-face, opposite each other like a sanctioned bout. Not only the inmates in our pod, but the inmates in every pod were yelling and screaming by now. Everyone wanted to see what I was going to do.

I asked him, "Are you the one who did this to my belongings?"

He responded, "Yeah, what are you gonna do abou…"

My right fist interrupted him. I hit him as hard as I possibly could on his mouth. At that moment, the fear was gone. I was a child of wrath and it was pouring out of me. The blood spurted out of his lip as I stood him up and pushed him back with punch after punch. Right, left, right, right, left. I attacked him and he never came to his senses. He never even got his hands up. I hurt him, and it felt good. I have often thought how he was just a lost sinner like I was, and if God would ever give me the chance to ask his forgiveness.

After the unexpected assault he fell to one knee, stunned, as I hovered over him like a man deranged. Trying something, at least, he slashed at my face with his open hand. One of his fingernails dug into my left eye and tore a divot out of my sclera (the white of the eye). I howled in pain it hurt so bad. I was bent over with both hands on my eye when the guards got to us.

My cellmate was on the ground with his face completely splattered with blood. Blood was everywhere. Even in the shower area on the wall a few feet away. They didn't ask a lot of questions, and my opponent was quickly led away. To the doctor or confinement, I didn't know.

One of the guards checked on me and said outright, "Are you okay? Don't worry; we're not going to do anything with you. You're not in trouble. We know what happened."

To put it in the vernacular, homeboy messed with the wrong cracker that day.

Blood from other people is taboo in jail. I understand why. Jail is full of drug addicts, prostitutes, and people generally not known to lead low-risk lives. Hepatitis C and HIV are real concerns day by day.

Someone had pushed a cleaning cart over by me and people were saying out loud to me things like, "You spilled it, now you got to clean it up."

That's right, I thought. I didn't expect anyone to help me clean up blood from my fight. I stood there for a moment taking my own hand from my eye to see blood, and then surveying the blood situation all around me. There was a bottle of disinfectant and a sponge on the cart, so I picked them up and started on the shower wall because I didn't see a mop.

As I rested one hand on the wall and brought the other hand with the sponge up to clean, I saw the blood on both my fists. I could barely see, but I kept my mouth shut and started cleaning.

After a short moment, I noticed a black kid and a white guy had grabbed a mop and towel and were helping me. I stopped, a bit surprised, and looked to them with my eye beginning to swell shut and gave a small nod of appreciation. Both of them responded in kind. I never spoke a word to either one of them about it, but I took it as a show of respect. At that moment it meant a great deal to me.

I was taken just outside of the pod and a staff member with a cart gave me two pain relievers and quickly taped a patch on my eye. I was told someone would take a more extensive look at the eye in the morning.

As I looked around to the other pods guys were either giving me fist pumps and replaying what had happened by air fighting or standing motionless staring at me. I guess they were the ones rooting against me.

When I returned to my cell, I discovered all of my belongings had been returned. It was my former cellmate's things that were now gone. I entered my cell. Slowly and quietly I climbed on my bunk. The pain in my left eye was so intense, and water and pus were streaming out of it. As I took a deep sigh, water began to stream down from my right, uninjured eye as well. I was so tired. And this wasn't even the beginning yet.

I slept. That is, until I heard, "Wilkinson! Andrew Wilkinson! Come on! Roll your bunk up! Get your stuff! Let's go! Let's go!"

I opened my eyes in as much disbelief and disgust as the poor woman with the botched hair oil treatment. I knew what this was. I was being transferred to Sumter County from Sarasota County. I had done this twice before. For a person to drive it straight is about a two-hour drive.

Transporting prisoners is different. Stops are made all over the state of Florida to pick up and drop off other transportees. The two previous times had both lasted several hours longer than the normal drive time. Now, I had an eye swollen shut, still raw in pain from the fight, and draining. Plus, I knew by now they take you in what they detained you in. I only had a pair of shorts on when they picked me up at the apartment. I was given an old, broken down pair of the plastic orange jail slippers. Nothing else, except chains.

This ride, the third time for me, would be much different than the previous two. This ride would change my life forever. The other two had taken approximately seven or eight hours from start to finish. This ride would last more than 20 hours. It was in the middle of night when we left Sarasota and 20 some hours later in Sumter County it was almost one o'clock in the morning when the deputies checked me in.

We entered the transport van from the rear. There were two metal benches running the length of the cargo section — one on the left and one on the right. Each bench could hold four or five passengers. I was the first to enter, and slid all the way up toward the front just behind the driver. Metal grating separated the two benches left and right as well as the prisoners from the forward area. I was hand and ankle cuffed. The handcuffs were secured to a chain around my waist, and the ankle cuffs were secured to the belt by another short length of chain.

An inmate for transport was picked up in Key West, and after 10 or 11 hours we were headed back north again. It was February, and I can still remember how cold I was. One of the guys had thrown up and the vomit was streaming everywhere on the metal flooring. The stench was awful.

The side of the van I was on was fully occupied. The pressure from everyone on my left side had pressed my bare skinned right shoulder against the metal grating for so long the skin was breaking. I had travelled the Seven Mile Bridge by car many times to the Keys and out to return to the mainland of Florida. The driver yelled back at us saying we were crossing the bridge.

By now, the patch on my eye had come off. A yellowish-orange pus of water and infectious fluid now filled my eye. I could see through the grating and windshield and noticed the glow of moonlight on the water of the Atlantic Ocean. Pure white out of the right, and yellow-orange out of the left.

So, here I was. This is what it had come to. Andrew Wilkinson chained up in a cage like an animal. One eye messed up. Only a pair of shorts to clothe me. Everything gone and Dad was dead. I had broken the heart and trust of my mother many times over, and she wasn't the only one. I had nothing left. I had nowhere else to run. No matter the pain, no matter the confusion, no matter the addiction, shame, and humiliation I had never given up. Until then.

As I looked out at the spreading fan of the moon's reflection on the water I let go. I gave up. I would have welcomed and yes, wished for, that truck to take a sudden swerve and plunge into the black water windshield first drowning every one of us trapped inside. I didn't give a damn. At long last I was defeated, and I was alone. Utterly and coldly alone.

Turning my eyes to the yellow-orange moon, I offered the first sincere prayer of my life. It was an utterly broken spirit and desperately contrite heart that I held in sacrifice. My sacrifice was accepted.

There was no "if, then" exchange with God about His very existence. No, "God I'll never do that again if You'll do this now" plea. It was an instantaneous and complete acknowledgement and confession of my inability to fix what had become my life.

I didn't know what it truly meant to be a Christian. To be born again. At that moment I was not alone anymore. Right then I knew I was dealing with Jesus Christ, and He was dealing with me.

No trumpets sounded and no angels lit the sky singing a heavenly chorus as they did for the Wise Men. There was, however, absolute appropriateness and truth. I was exactly where I was supposed to be. All the hours, days, months, and years of my life pointed precisely to this moment. This was my time to embrace my loving, forgiving God. So I did.

My spirit was told I had used my God-given talents and gifts for my own destruction. It was told there was a way out of the beast-like condition I was in. His name is Jesus Christ, and He is my living Savior. But I had to submit. There could be nothing left of the former things. Jesus would take me forward, but I could not dwell on yesterday. Release was a command, and I obeyed. Security and peace flowed through and into my heart. I felt a confidence so strong, I lifted off of the grating cutting my skin and held my chin in the air just as a victor would.

On my way to be sentenced to state prison, saturated in a defeated life of addiction and misery, I felt the unmistakable touch of my Savior. I beheld the power in the name of Jesus Christ. It was not possible for me to create this experience on my own. To imagine it. I shed tears of thankfulness and joy. I had seen and felt my Good Light. I was delivered and I knew it.

Chapter 16

Being booked in for a third time in a year and a half, I actually knew inmates and guards by name at the Sumter County jail. Soon after I was processed I was hearing things like, "Wilkinson, oh no, man, what are you doing, man? Thought you were gonna get it right this time. Didn't the judge tell you next time and…?"

Then they would make the sign of a knife across their throat with their finger. The judge had said if he saw me again on this same case it would definitely mean prison time. The maximum time I faced was 20 years — five years per charge. I had no prior record, so it was highly unlikely I would get anything near that. But I had made a mockery of the system and it was conceivable that the judge, especially if he was in a bad mood or had a fight with his wife the night before, could give me two to four years.

Fresh from the most important thing that had ever happened to me, I was not in fear. I wasn't concerned with that. What I was concerned with was getting a Bible and learning.

I was taken to a normal doctor's office where my eye was examined. I actually sat in the waiting room in my prisoner's garb and handcuffs. The deputy sat next to me. I got some looks from the other waiting patients, I can tell you. The diagnosis was there was nothing to be done with my eye except take care of it while it healed. I was given some heavier duty pain relievers, which the jail nurse would administer to me, antibiotics, and more patches.

I found a jailhouse Bible and started reading. The first time I opened its pages, I came to the Gospel of Luke 19:10, "For the Son of Man has come to seek and to save those who are lost."

When I read that, the words came off of the page and seared my spirit. In my spirit, I immediately knew that the Word of God is the Truth. In a few days, my mother had sent me another Bible and I spent every moment I could with my face in it. I had always said I was a Christian. I was baptized as a child. Did I truly know who Jesus Christ was? No. Could I explain to someone the plan of salvation for all sinners through God's grace and mercy? No. Did I know how all of the Old Testament prophets pointed directly and exactly to Christ Himself? What?!?!?

Being incarcerated is when the Holy Spirit taught me how to recognize blessings. I had been immensely blessed all of my life, and the blessings continued to spill from God all over me. The difference is I wasn't looking at me. I was looking at the Lord. I could see.

I read and studied Genesis and Exodus and learned that Christ was much more than a really good guy who taught honorably and died on the cross for my sins. The pre-incarnate Christ laid the foundations of the heavens and sculpted the earth. Prophecy in the books of Daniel and Isaiah of The Messiah blew me away. The gospels gave me a glimpse, what I need to know, of the life and ministry of the Son of Man. All of the epistles allowed for maximum encouragement and instruction when the accuser and his legions would attack my new faith. The Psalms and Proverbs showed me a taste of the mysteries of God and offered the wise, practical applications He has for life.

I learned the power of prayer and that, yes, God hears them. Many people had prayed for me and their prayers were answered. The more I read and learned more how to pray, the more I knew the Bible is true. Every single word of it.

I carried myself with a quiet confidence, the likes of which I had never known. I carried my Bible with me throughout the jail and was the target of "jailhouse religion" jeers more than once. I didn't care. My skin was tough and getting tougher.

In a phone conversation with my mom, we were discussing the possibilities of a harsher or lighter sentence.

She said outright to me, "Andrew, honey, you could have several years to deal with."

"I know, Mom. I know. I am not afraid. Good things are happening in my life."

She said, "I can tell and I thank God for what has happened to you."

Before we ended the conversation, we prayed together on the telephone. As much as anything, I could sense Mom was experiencing something good about me. Some peace, perhaps. Oh, how happy that made me.

The inmate garb in the Sumter jail always kind of reminded me of a clown. It was a one-piece jumpsuit with buttons up the front, and large green and white stripes running horizontally from bottom to top. I always quipped when they slid the bars open to let us out for chow that we looked like a bunch of rodeo clowns running into the ring.

There was this little guy, about four and half feet tall, sitting by himself one day and I sat next to him. His armband said, "John Doo."

"Hey man, I'm Andrew. So, you're John Doe," I said with a smile.

"No, John Doo," he said with a thick South American accent. This is how I met Miguel.

Miguel was from Ecuador and had no family in the United States. He was here illegally and had no credentials to show the officer who had pulled him over for a traffic violation. He had no one to call and no idea how long he would be there. The objective he had was to send money home to his family.

Miguel was Catholic and we read the Bible together often, discussing what we had read. He wrote the cardinal numbers from 1 to 100 out for me to learn in Spanish. We walked together like two women in a mall. Simply walking back and forth from one wall of the common area to the other…about 60 feet. We did that for hours at a time. As was common in these types of circumstances, he was having a tough time with a girl he had been seeing. I encouraged him and listened.

Miguel travelled around from county fair to county fair or festival to festival and sold his wares — T-shirts, caps, decals, CDs, etc. He sold Zamfir CDs and played his own pan flute to them, charming the passersby. He had his own minivan and could afford the licenses to sell at the fairs and festivals. We joked all the time how he could teach me the pan flute and we could take our show on the road.

Miguel had straight, thick, black hair. He attended a Native American festival once as a merchant. A requirement of the merchants was that they were Native American themselves. I have never laughed so hard in my life as when Miguel told the story of how he played his pan flute and a woman approached him. She watched him as he played nervously for 10 minutes or so.

Finally, between songs, she asked him what tribe he was from. Miguel was a little Ecuadorian. He explained to her he was a Cherokee. The only thing Miguel knew about a Cherokee is that it was a Jeep. The lady was from the festival committee and had him promptly removed. To hear him tell that story…I am laughing to myself as I write this.

I can hear him still, "Weel-keen-sohn." He told me about his home and "chupacabra," a small, mysterious animal that roams the countryside in Ecuador killing livestock and sucking their blood. He was fascinated to hear how it was for me growing up. I rarely shared with anyone about my life, but I did with him.

Miguel was an illegal immigrant. I was a convicted felon. I believe illegal immigration is a huge problem in our country. Miguel was not an addict. We put all that other stuff aside and took comfort in each other's company. That human connection is lost in all of our rules, labels, and prejudices. It is so rare in free society, and I witnessed it time and time again as I was incarcerated. Never before in my life would I have been friends with Miguel. I spent time with Miguel daily for over three months. "John Doo" was my friend.

Wherever he is now, I wish him well. There are many "John Doos" out there.

I had been in Sumter County for roughly three months when I was called to go to court in April of 2006. All of us going before the judge were chained together like kindergartners on ropes, and we walked across the skyway to the courthouse. We were placed in small holding cells and brought out alphabetically from our last names…A-Z. I was the very last one to go that day, and sat in the holding tank alone for a considerable time before they came for me.

As I walked into the courtroom, I noticed it was completely empty. It was late in the afternoon and only the judge, deputies, and court reporter were still present. I had no attorney as I approached the podium.

The judge asked me three questions: "Are you Andrew Wilkinson?"

"Yes, I am."

"How do you plead to the charge of violation of house arrest?"

"Guilty, sir."

"I hereby sentence you to one year and a day in Florida state prison. Credit time served. Have a good day, Mr. Wilkinson."

The entire exchange lasted about 60 seconds. I don't think the judge even recognized me. If he did, he didn't let on. That was it? I couldn't believe it. One year and a day and credit for time served! I had already been in for three months, so this meant only about nine more. This was a blessing, and as much as I could I skipped out of that courtroom in my clown suit and chains.

As soon as I got back to the jail, I called my mother with the great news. I'll never forget how she exclaimed, "Oh! Thank you, Lord! Thank you! Thank you for my Andrew!"

It was only a matter of days until, yet again, I heard, "Wilkinson! Come on! Roll your stuff up! You're gone!"

Inmates for transport are always called in the middle of the night. I don't know why. The lights are all turned on, and everyone stirs a little bit. Yelling and saying things like goodbye. I had made a prayerful effort to be gentle and humble as Jesus instructs us to do in my time there.

There was a guy who they say was an amateur boxer. I believe it, because I saw him put an uppercut on a guy he had been playing cards with and I thought was his friend. It totally jarred the guy's face. This fighter knew I had been intently reading my Bible, and one day he yelled at me, "Hey, Christian boy, why don't you go and fix me a cup of that coffee you got!"

As much as I could, I wanted to avoid fighting this man. I looked at him silently for a second and then proceeded up the stairs to my cell and fixed him a cup of coffee. The whole place was quiet. I came back down and walked over to him.

As I handed him the cup of coffee, I told him, "I will not do that again."

He took the coffee from my hand, and I was looking him dead in the eye. I had no clue what he was going to do, but I knew he could do whatever it was very fast.

He took a sip from the cup and said, "Thank you."

His cell was only a few down from me, and as I went by he said, "Hey you! You did your time well. Good luck."

I told him I appreciated it, and was on my way to prison. As the big bars were rolled back letting me out, I looked back one more time and could see Miguel's hand stuck up through the bars with his palm in the air.

They led me outside and put me in a van with row seats. I was the lone passenger. The engine was running, and the radio played as they went back inside to finish paperwork or something. The night was cool and the sky was dark blue with the moon and stars shining bright. It was a beautiful night in central Florida.

I sat there in peaceful silence for a few minutes taking it all in. It was real now. I was going to prison. Actually being taken there. On the radio came a song by Tim McGraw, "When the Stars Go Blue." It seemed like I was the only person on the planet and that song was being played solely for me. I was the only listener. Now, when I hear that song I am transformed back to being that only listener in the world. Even when people are around me who have no idea about me or my life, I still go into a mini trance of sorts. Funny, just something for me, I guess.

Chapter 17

In 2006, the state of Florida had two reception or "welcome" prisons — one in Miami and one in Orlando. On June 5, 2006, I was "welcomed" by the camp in Orlando. As soon as I and the other inmates stepped off of the van, it started. The van was pulled into a large area surrounded by the chain link fence and galvanized steel razor rolls you see everywhere on prison compounds. There were a handful of guards to greet us and they meant business.

Immediately the yelling and shouting began. We were formed along the walls in the shape of a big staple with the guards in the middle area looking at the "inside" of the staple. We were ordered to undress completely, turn around, bend over, and spread our buttocks…in so many words. It wasn't for only a moment. We were required to stay like that for several minutes as the officers examined all of us to determine if anyone was attempting to smuggle contraband onto the compound. Many criminals go to great lengths to be criminals. Placing items in the anal cavity is a common way for criminals to transport them.

As the examinations took place, loud statements were made concerning the characteristics of our anuses. For sure these actions are for security objectives, but there are other elements involved. They are intended to dehumanize and to degrade. To show that we are not in charge and in fact, they can literally be in our "asses" any time they choose.

The prison staff must establish control quickly. Not only physical, but mental as well. I have to say it is rather effective. There is a degree of debasement and vulnerability when one is forced to expose themselves in such a manner. All the arguments for why there is crime aside, the other men and I made the choices we made, and it was time to deal with the unpleasant consequences. This was punishment, and punishment is essential.

We, as a country, seem to do this part pretty well. It is called accountability and it is one of the major fabrics that hold a functioning, structured, and just society together. Rehabilitation is also essential. We, as a country, are still coming up way short on this one. Nonetheless, we were not free men. We were convicted felons moving into our new home.

The purpose of the reception prisons is to determine what the state has in terms of its new property. Here is where the convicts are given their Department of Corrections inmate number. Mine was DC U20203. This number is the method of identification, and we were required to clip it on our blue tops at all times. It was our ID badge. There we were issued our Class A uniforms, which were much different than the orange uniforms in the Sarasota County Jail and the green and white clown uniforms of the Sumter County Detention Center, These were a light blue short-sleeved shirt with a light blue pair of pants. A white stripe ran down the side of each leg.

We were also given a schedule of all sorts of activities for the following five days. The list included locations and times for simple intake procedures such as fingerprinting and classification as well as for medical and psychological tests. We were tested for Hepatitis C and HIV. The blood work takes a day or two for the results, which are returned unceremoniously by paper. There were some big, bad dudes walking around with more than a bit of apprehension in their eyes waiting on those results.

We were assigned to our cells. They were two-man cells, and I got the bottom bunk. The mattresses were basically like the gym pads we used to roll up in school and the pillows were long, hard, and flat. I remember my cellmate's name was Keshawn. Keshawn was a young, black kid and I remember noticing how handsome he was. We would stay awake and talk after lights out. There was no air conditioning and it was so miserable, sweltering hot. Getting to sleep every night took hours of tossing and turning in our perspiration.

We had a very narrow, tall window we could look out from. Keshawn would stare out the window and say how he missed his girl. He told me she said she would wait for him forever. Keshawn was serving a lengthy sentence for shooting someone. He had been a drug dealer on the streets of Tampa. I remember listening to his words. He truly believed she would be there many years from then.

He would always ask me, "Whatcha think Wilkinson, you think she will wait for me?"

I never had the heart to tell him the truth that, no, the likelihood of that happening was very slim.

I just would always say, "If that's what she told you, Keshawn, then I am sure she'll be there."

He was going to be in his mid-thirties when he got out.

The heat was a serious issue. There were large fans that circulated air in the larger, common areas, but inside the cells were humid to the point of being near unbearable.

My older cousin Michelle had written me a letter, and answering her was the first letter I wrote in Orlando. As I wrote, I needed to wrap my bath towel around my forearm. This was so the sweat from my arm would not smudge the letter to the point it was not legible.

Orlando also had a "jit" camp. In the state of Florida there is a "Youthful Offender Act." It was established to benefit young adults who would normally be prosecuted and sentenced in an adult criminal court. The concept was meant to introduce more flexible and less brusque sentencing guidelines. There are exceptions, but generally the act is for offenders older than 18 and younger than 21. The objective was to keep those designated as youthful offenders away from or severely limit their interaction with the more experienced and seasoned criminals in the adult penal system.

Orlando was also a reception center for them. Completely separated from the adult camp, we could see them being marched around on their yard as we were on ours. They were required to wear red hats rendering them easily identifiable. Ironically, society's effort to employ a softer, more compassionate approach to the youngsters has mixed results, I believe. It is a well-known and discussed fact on a prison compound how downright brutal and ruthless the jits are. It was quite common to hear those in the adult camp who could have been sent to juvenile exclaim out loud the relief they felt not being with the jits.

Orlando is also where I had my first job. I was assistant houseman to the regular houseman. A guy that we simply knew as "Bowleg." He was called that for obvious reasons. Bowleg was super nice, but apparently had a temper on him and I was told by a few of the other guys not to ask any questions. Just do what he told me and do it how he told me to do it.

The houseman in prison is responsible for the cleaning of common areas and more specifically, the bathrooms and showers. So, that was my initiation into prison life…scrubbing showers and toilets. Even as I cleaned a prison toilet every day, I wasn't discouraged. The Bible tells us to do all jobs and tasks, no matter how tedious or meaningless, as if we were doing it for Christ Himself. That is precisely what I did, and in return He gifted to me a positive, encouraged attitude.

If we show Jesus that we care for Him, that we try to understand constantly what He did and endured for us all, He is faithful and will return to us good, positive things to get us through. Over and over, Christ has shown me this in my life. We can absolutely trust Him.

The yard at Orlando was not bad. It had a large track running along its perimeter for running and walking, a large grass field in the center for games such as soccer or flag football, and it also had concrete ping-pong tables. This is one of the few prison activities I did participate in.

Years ago in high school, my good friend Pierce and I worked a summer together at a State Park. We worked in the recreation department and there were ping-pong tables there. We played a ton of ping-pong and acquired the ability to play a pretty decent game. So I took those skills to some of the guys at Orlando. I didn't win all my matches, but I definitely held my own and then some.

The commissary on a prison yard is something like a general store for the inmates. All types of merchandise can be purchased — soda, candy, chips, coffee, writing supplies, stamps, etc. Tobacco used to be available, but since 2011 all state prisons have been tobacco-free. Simple, little AM/FM radios with earphones were also available.

The ingenuity of some of the convicts was truly something to marvel at. They would disassemble the new, intact radios and collect bits and pieces of other materials found around the camp — shirt clips from tops of writing pens found in the dirt on the yard, aluminum foil from the kitchen, plastic from the bottles on the cleaning cart — and make things like other radios or tattoo guns. MacGyver or Ethan Hunt had nothing on these guys.

So many times I saw something remarkable from one of the men like a sketch or ink reservoir on a tattoo gun and wondered what if. What if their life had been something else? What could their life have become?

Of course, it takes money to buy items from commissary. An account is created for all convicts, and money can be put on the account of an inmate by family and friends from the outside. My mother would send me $20 or so a month. Many do not have anyone willing to help them with this. The other inmates often look for these unfortunate ones and take advantage of them. Or worse, prey on them.

This is how I met Tommy. I had noticed Tommy for a number of days in my dorm and out in the yard. The majority of the time he was by himself. He stuck out more than a sore thumb. In his early twenties, he had sandy blond hair, fair skin with freckles, and was chubby. He always had his pants pulled up around his belly. Tommy looked so lost and out of place. I felt sorry for the kid. The yard had a number of concrete foundations with roofs over them to provide shade.

One afternoon as I sat quietly, alone, observing, Tommy approached me. He walked up to me and waited. I gave him a nod to sit down. For several minutes we didn't speak until he broke the silence.

"I'm Tommy. I've seen you keep to yourself a lot. I don't know anyone here. How do you make friends here?"

"Sometimes you don't, I suppose," I answered.

All of us new guys had been, by this time, there for about two weeks. Enough time to get money on the books for commissary. For the guys without commissary, to spend their days watching those with the creature comforts of commissary is torture. They walk around with nothing, and are constantly seen meekly asking others for things and being told no.

Tommy cautiously built up the nerve to tell me the only person he knew on the outside was his grandmother. He had been trying for days to reach her with no success. If I spotted him a bag of powdered coffee, he would pay me back with two bags when his grandmother came through. Of course I had compassion for Tommy and was going to just give him a bag of the coffee, but I made him writhe and squirm a little bit by not answering him right away.

We broke into a little small talk and he said he was from a small town in Florida and his parents were gone. He was not the type you wanted to be seen hanging out with on a prison yard, but there was something about Tommy I liked. He was just a kid. I never knew for sure because he didn't flat out say it, but it seemed like he had gotten in over his head with a younger girl or girls on the internet and was convicted of a sexual predator crime.

Tommy loved the classic American gangster film "Scarface" with Al Pacino. In the film, Al Pacino's character, Tony Montana, is being warned by a fellow drug smuggler not to betray him. The line goes, "don't f——— me, Tony." The admonition is delivered by the actor with a calm, but very stern voice. Tommy loved this line and would repeat it often throughout the day. I had stopped cursing by then, especially taking The Lord's name in vain. I don't know why, but watching Tommy, in his character, walking around quoting that line was sometimes pretty funny. I guess you had to be there.

I had no problem talking with Tommy and would allow him to be around me. I didn't care what people thought. I kept to myself, stayed away from the betting and card games, and stayed real clear of the "buck" and drugs. But I was going to talk to or let talk to me anyone I wanted.

After a few days I saw Tommy, in the dorm and out on the yard, going around to people with the same sad story he had given me about him having no one and his grandmother would send money. The next time I spoke with him, I warned him to be careful. That there were bad dudes there and they would help him only to take advantage of him later. He assured me he was watching out for himself. Soon after, I was sent to another part of the prison to wait to be transported yet again to my "home" prison. I didn't see Tommy again.

Sure enough, as always, the middle of the night came when I heard, "Wilkinson! U20203!"

That was it, though. The voice didn't explain to roll my bunk up or grab my things. That was one of the big differences between prison and county jail. In county there was always an explanation. Prison wasn't that way. I can remember so many times I had no idea what line I was supposed to fall into or where I was supposed to go. Trying to stay cool or not look like a total imbecile was sometimes very difficult. There was a number of us from our dorm called out, and the exit processing took a little time. We were all gathered with our belongings at a large port area with tables. Our transport vehicle was there. It looked like an older school bus painted totally black with no identifying marks on it.

Finally, our group boarded. We were already on for a few minutes when another group boarded. After what seemed like an hour the bus pulled out. I had been in Orlando about three weeks. Now I was on my way again in the middle of the night. None of us had any idea what the destination was. Nodding in and out of sleep I leaned forward and rested my forehead on the seat back in front of me. That is how I slept until the sun began to rise in a couple of hours.

"Andrew? Is that you? Andrew?"

I opened my eyes and raised my head. I knew that voice. There was Tommy in the seat in front of me. All the passengers boarded in the night and we were not allowed to talk. I had not seen him. I rubbed my eyes.

"Yeah, Tommy, what's up? You all right? You have any idea where they're taking us?"

"No, no, I don't know."

Something was not right. I could hear in his voice something was up.

He went on, "I'm hurt real bad. They hurt me real bad."

That's when he told me. Tommy had found someone, a real nice guy, to help him out with commissary. He told Tommy it was no problem and just to get him back when his grandmother finally got the money on Tommy's account. A couple of days later, the man came by Tommy's cell one evening before lights out and asked if Grandma had taken care of the money situation. When Tommy explained not yet, but he thought soon, the man went into his cell.

Two other men stood guard right outside of the cell while Tommy was violently raped. His attacker held him down and told him if he didn't stay still he and the other two men would beat him.

I listened in heartache and disbelief with my mouth wide open.

The event was so violent it ripped Tommy's anus. As he told me of his beyond horrifying experience…as he sat there…he had stitches in his anus. He had to be closed up. The next day he had limped out of his cell to the control center. They took him to medical. He never said a word about who had done that to him. The man told Tommy if he talked to anyone he would kill him.

"Oh God, Tommy. Tommy, Jesus, I told you not to do that Tommy. I told you not to do that, man," I told him in a hushed voice.

"I know, I know, I'm sorry," he whispered.

"Tommy, listen to me, listen to me real careful and this time listen to me. Do not tell anyone about this. Do you hear me? Listen to me…no one. Do you understand? Tell me you understand! When we get where we're going you keep this to yourself no matter what. Tell me right now you understand exactly what I'm saying to you."

As he looked me in the eye I saw a soul that was to suffer the remainder of this life. A kind of suffering that is the deepest of despair. Only God could help Tommy now. No psychological tool of man is truly equipped or capable of offering peace for that level of hurt.

"I understand. I won't," he said. "I'm glad we're on this bus together."

"Me too, Tommy, me too."

Neither one of us said a word the entire rest of the ride. After about six hours of riding, the bus pulled into Franklin Correctional Institution in Carrabelle. As we stepped off the bus for the "you're not in control anymore so bend over" act, Tommy told me he hoped were in the same dorm. We were not assigned to the same dorm. I would see Tommy sometimes at a distance through chain link fences and wires. Then came the day when I didn't see him anymore.

I think of Tommy often. How I hope he found his way to The Lord. That he knows the acceptance and restoration of Jesus. This world is fallen. Bad things happen here. Bad things happen because of sin in us…not God. God wants us so much to choose Him. He waits for us to choose to love Him. Love cannot be forced. It must be given, but our pride and sin stand in our way. We want to know "Why this and how that?" all the time. Like God must answer to us. All we have to do is go to Him and admit we need Him…admit we need a Savior.

Chapter 18

It was the beginning of July 2006. I was at my final destination. Franklin Correctional Institution was my home camp. It was built in 2005 and sits in the panhandle of Florida close to the town of Carrabelle. It houses only adult males, with security grades running from minimum to closed. The only higher security classification is maximum. Maximum security prisons hold prisoners that have been sentenced to death. There were inmates at Franklin serving life sentences without parole for brutal crimes they had committed. There was an armed perimeter with armed guards and a watchtower situated directly in the middle of the compound. The service of canines was utilized, and like many other prisons, Franklin was out in the middle of nowhere.

The prison was opened in 2005. You could still smell the newness. The hierarchy and "game" of the inmates had not yet been established. There were two cell housing units and six open bay units. An open bay unit was a huge room with a control center in one corner. All around the perimeter of three walls were gray painted steel double bunks. In the middle of the room were single bunks in rows. On the fourth wall was the open entrance to the bathroom facilities. There was a smaller, common room on the other side of the wall that the control center was in the corner of. At the beginning of my sentence, I was in a cell unit, and later was moved to an open bay. There were several hundred prisoners in the open bay dorm. Again, I was lucky and was assigned a bottom bunk.

It was lights out at 10:30 p.m. and they came on again at 4:30 a.m. Monday through Friday. Diabetics and persons with restricted diets for whatever reasons were the first to be called out for morning chow. Then the general population was called out. A "call out" is when the guards in the control center notify the inmates that the doors are rolling back and allowing movement in and out of the dorm for a specific reason. There were many reasons for a call out — medical, administrative, laundry, etc. A call out could be for many people or could be for one individual.

We generally had 15 minutes to take care of our personal morning business — that is brush our teeth, shave, and use the toilet. The razors we signed in and out were cheap and orange. They had one single blade and routinely tore my skin into pieces. I never verified it, but the story on the razors was they were unsellable, defective blades donated by the manufacturer.

There was a female guard who always seemed to enjoy having some fun with the morning ritual. Right before call out, she would yell at those of us still on the toilets to, "Hurry up and pinch it off and go to work or I'm gonna start writing!"

Writing referred to a DR — disciplinary report. For any type of rules infraction or conduct problem, an inmate would receive a verbal or written DR. A prisoner with too many DRs is not eligible for early release, and can actually lose the time off their sentence gained through working and good behavior. I never received a DR.

The prison diet consisted of a lot of potatoes, rice, bread, and pasta. Chicken, hamburger, and pizza were common too. Bologna or peanut butter and jelly sandwiches were normally given for lunches on work detail. Drinks were powdered lemonade, tea, or fruit punch mixed with Florida hard tap water. Small pints of milk were also available and they were kept extremely cold. Dessert normally consisted of a brownie or cookie. I always traded my dessert off for an extra milk. Those little milk cartons were the best part of the meal to me. In fact, to this day when I drink an ice cold glass of milk I can close my eyes and taste those prison milks.

Black leather lace-up boots were issued to those of us with work assignments. Some guys got a pair of used ones, but I got a brand new pair. I was very excited about that.

My first job was working on the chow line in the kitchen. It was so brutally hot in there. Around 1,400 inmates were being fed three times a day, therefore, the chow line moved pretty quickly. I was on the line with five or six other guys. The trays would come sliding by, and we would slop the food on.

We had to wear plastic gloves that ran a bit of the length up our arm. In a short time, our hands would begin to sweat profusely. Sweat became pooled in the fingers of the gloves and then would run down our forearms and drip from our elbows on to the tray of food. Sometimes it was so bad it trickled like a slow leak. There was absolutely nothing we could do about it, and it happened to all of us. We all have to eat. After a while we just accepted it as part of our sentence and got on with it.

I was staying to myself and keeping clear of the hustlers and cons. One of the biggest rules of prison life is to always show respect. It doesn't matter who it is. Anybody could know somebody that could, and would, put a hurting on you in a second. You always deal with people cautiously and with the utmost respect. If you are known as someone who does not follow this code, then it is only a matter of time until you are dealt with in the harshest ways.

One Saturday I had already eaten morning chow and had returned to my dorm for a relaxing, hot shower. Then, I always returned to my space quickly to finish my personal preparation. One of the main, designated walk paths was obstructed. Without thinking, I ducked in and around two inmates' bunks illustrating my complete lack of prison acumen and returned to the main walkway. My first mistake was not thinking. If you don't think before you act in confinement, the probability of a very bad result for you is exponentially increased. The second mistake was invading the space of an inmate notorious for his threatening demeanor. Still wrapped in my towel and in my plastic slippers, I was dripping water.

Immediately I heard, "Get your cracker ass back here right f—ing now!"

The voice was loud and it startled me. I looked around and so did everyone else in the vicinity.

"I'm talking to you, you little motherf—er! Get your cracker ass back here now!"

Yelling at me was an African-American inmate that stood about 6'4" and appeared to be somewhere in the 250 pound range. At the time I was 5'10" and about 160 pounds. I did exactly as he told me to. In a second I was standing right in front of him in my towel and holding my toiletry bag. By this time I had been around and had interacted with every race or ethnicity jail or prison life had to offer. I was cool with pretty much everyone, and they were cool with me. But as I stood there, my lips began to tremble. This was the type of man who knew violence. It was all over his countenance. I understood clearly that unless this guy was threatening my life I was to sit there and listen to him. Period.

I had dripped water in front of and around the corner of his bunk.

He pointed down to the water drops and yelled, "Wipe that shit up!"

I removed my towel and wiped it up. I stood again, this time naked.

Then again, "You listen up you punk ass whitey! The next time you come through here I don't care how f—ing long you have to wait! You f—ing wait until you can walk over there!"

He was pointing at the main walk terminal. He stopped yelling and was in my face staring at me. Breathing on me. I didn't know if I should say something, walk away, or stand there.

After what seemed like an eternity I said, "Excuse me. I didn't know I had done that to your space. I did not mean to do that to your space. I'm sorry for that. It won't happen again."

He held his stare for another moment and then let me go. Literally, he let me go from his stare. I could feel the release as he turned away and sat on his bunk.

There is a moment in Kevin Costner's timeless film "Dances with Wolves" when his character, Lieutenant Dunbar, is terrifyingly accosted by a magnificent Indian warrior. He stands there with his pistol pointed as the warrior yells at him relentlessly. The Indian then grabs the mane of his horse and races away. Lieutenant Dunbar turns to walk and makes it only a few steps before he faints from the experience. I might as well have been Lieutenant Dunbar. As I walked away from that man, my knees were shaking. It was actually hard to put one foot in front of the other.

It was a total smack down. All I can say is that prison is a different place, and not like the real world. I was not humiliated or embarrassed. I was wrong in what I had done, and I had to sit there and take it — and I was terrified. Would I show respect? Was I smart enough to know I was beat? Or was I a cracker with a loud mouth and no respect?

I never violated that inmate's space again. We didn't become friends or anything, but every time I was close to his area again he was okay.

He would even say, "What's up?" or ask me how I was doing.

I was not threatened by him anymore. In prison it is a lot about how you handle yourself when something goes down. At the moment it might be brutal, but people are watching you. You can actually gain respect by taking whatever it is that's happening.

There is, without question, an inmate's mentality and vocabulary. For instance, a convict is someone who does their time and holds the codes about respect and not rolling over to the authorities. An inmate doesn't do their time. Their time does them. Inmates are not to be trusted and do not command respect like convicts do.

There was a guy at Franklin named Mike. Mike was built like a Mack truck. He stood about 6'2" and his shoulders were broad like the side of a barn. His forearms were the same size as my thighs. I used to think what kind of hurting some poor soul would be in if Mike hit them head down, full speed on. Mike's claim to fame was that he had served time at Attica Correctional Facility in New York State.

Attica is a super maximum security facility known to house the worst of the worst. There was an infamous riot there in 1971 that killed 43 people — 33 convicts and 10 guards.

He loved to talk about how tough it was and how Franklin was a playground compared to it. "Convicts? There ain't no convicts here! I'm the only convict here! The rest of you suckers are just inmates! That's it," he said over and over in a thick New York accent.

It got to the point we would just roll our eyes when he started. The other way, naturally.

Mike had hands like cinder blocks. They were literally like sledge hammers. There was a sand area in the yard with a volleyball net. Mike, in his Class A's, could jump and spike a volleyball like no one I had never seen. The team that had him won every single time. Picking sides for a match was the only time anyone liked Mike.

I was approached numerous times by men thinking about sex — ones who referred to themselves as heterosexual only doing what they had to do on the inside to satisfy their sexual desires, and also "punks." In prison a punk is a man who is openly homosexual and feminine. It is not necessarily a derogative term. To a large degree they are seen as the women of the compound. Sometimes punks would acquire and take hormones resulting in the development of female breasts. With a woman's breasts they were viewed by some as more sensual and desirable.

I was referred to as "cracker". I was referred to as "gringo." I was referred to as, "Hey, dumb ass!" With so much emphasis on political correctness and sensitivity today, I often wonder to myself when I overhear someone complaining. It is not only prison. It's poverty-ridden countries. It's war-ravaged areas. There are whole other worlds of survival and struggle out there that are extremely harsh. Places like Facebook and Twitter are full of commentary by people who seem to think the only world that exists is theirs.

I have spent a lot of time with a lot of people who would love to experience the luxury of complaining on a keyboard at the end of a day. Actually, if you have time to worry about all these types of emotional, sensitive issues, then my argument would be that you have a pretty darn good life. In my opinion, the more comfortable and struggle free our lives become the more frivolous and numerous our hang-ups and "wounds" can be.

I soon identified a couple of other guys who seemed like they were loners too. I don't remember who approached whom, but the three of us kind of migrated together. I never knew his real name, but everyone called him "Godfather." He was an older guy and looked the part. I don't know a lot of gang history, but apparently he had been a big wig with the Simon City Royals gang out of Chicago. He had killed the man who his wife was cheating on him with.

Then there was Wing Ki. Wing's full name was Wing Ki Chi. Everyone called him Wing except for me. I called him Wing Ki. Like so many he, too, was only a kid. He never liked that I said Ki because he felt like it didn't sound tough, but he got used to it. Wing had been a heroin "runner" in New York City. Runners are the guys who deliver the dope for the dealers. Wing decided one time he was not going to deliver a sizable package, and cash out to keep the money for himself. He thought he could stay hidden in the city, but he was wrong.

Word got out that the dealers were not only looking for him, but his family as well. His whole family moved to Miami to escape. Some guys came at him one night in a club, and he unloaded the clip of a handgun, shooting a couple of people. We talked many times about it. He knew what he had done was very wrong.

Like me, he wanted desperately to change his life. I can still see the three of us walking the circle of the yard. Round and round. Wing put together a training regimen for us and we were in very good shape. No weights, but a whole lot of resistance training: push-ups, sit-ups, pull-ups, squats, etc. Godfather didn't want any of that. When the training started, he always needed to go talk to someone about something important.

Then came the first surprise inspection. Inmates hate inspections. As a prisoner all you have is your tiny little world of personal things in just a tiny little area of personal space. Most prisoners keep their belongings neat and organized to the T. I did too. Toiletries, toilet paper, letters, writing supplies and stamps, a Bible or books, DOC paperwork, articles, drawings, coffee and sugar, and little packets of spices and condiments generally was about all there was. This was our bubble, and most of us took pride in it.

When the guards would come in, they just went into everything with little or no regard for our efforts at organization and cleanliness. Not all guards were that way. Some would attempt to conduct the search with order and respect, but that is hard. But if they were decent like that, we could tell and would reciprocate with a show of respect or appreciation.

Normally, by the time the inspection was over, all of our things were piled up messes — including our bedding and sheets. In just a matter of minutes the whole dorm was pretty much turned upside down. Then the guards would just leave, and we all would start putting our things back into place.

Items that they routinely found were homemade knives or shanks, drugs, and cell phones. People would have cell phones smuggled in with pre-paid minutes on them so they could place calls to the outside.

A punk was my neighbor for a few months. On one particular inspection he was busted with a razor blade wrapped around the end of a pencil in one of his socks. He was arrested and taken to jail. That is prison speak for he went to solitary confinement. As they took him out, he was yelling and saying he was framed. The word was he had been having a relationship with a "straight" man in secret. They had had an argument, and the other man thought the punk would talk about everything. So, the razor blade was planted to have him removed.

On weekends we were allowed to go back to sleep if we wanted after breakfast. While most of the others would sleep, I would sit at the tables in the smaller room. It was the quietest time a man could find in prison and I took advantage of it. I read my Bible, prayed, and wrote letters. There were no cell phones. Nothing ringing, beeping, or vibrating all the time to distract us. Man can be close to God in prison if he chooses to do so. A human being does not enter and exit prison remaining unchanged.

There is an admission or awareness that things must change and a person either tries to change or delves deeper into the pit of criminality. This is why rehabilitation is paramount. There is a crossroads in the life of convicts. It is society's job to head them off at the pass and help them choose and travel the right road. Due to the newness or some other reason, there was no substantial effort of rehabilitation at Franklin. At the time, there was an AA group and the Sunday religious services with the chaplain, John Hope. I know, great name for a chaplain.

Chaplain Hope and his wife were there every Sunday to lead us in service. In my opinion, they were very genuine in their faith. When we sang praise songs and hymns, Mrs. Hope would play keyboard and Chaplain Hope would sometimes have a tambourine in his hand. Inmates played other instruments that belonged to the couple.

I completed a 12-week extracurricular Bible study course that Chaplain Hope taught. The Chaplain also baptized me. In one of the clearest and undeniable shows of what the love of Jesus Christ can do, I was baptized with 11 other men. As we stood in a waiting room in our underwear, I looked around. I saw the signs and results of lives carried on without God — huge scars, piercings, pagan tattoos, and gang tattoos boasting of violence.

Before being called out individually by Chaplain Hope to the baptismal tank, we all came together with our arms around each other. We stood in a circle and prayed. We were white, we were Latino, we were black. Some of the men were crying tears of thankfulness and joy. You see, it is a sinful world; it is fallen man that takes Jesus Christ and turns Him into something divisive and hateful. The Savior of the world forgives, heals, and brings us together in unselfish love. I know that for a fact. I experienced it. Those that believe they don't need God, and I certainly was one, can't understand the beauty and freedom in Jesus and what He willingly endured for us. Human pride is a huge stumbling block to not seeing what God has done for us through Christ.

Chapter 19

So time goes by in prison for all the men. Hour after hour, day by day, month by month. I was privy to hearing some monster beats and rhymes from guys with big dreams of going from prison to the top. Some of those cats had real talent. Some really did not.

There was a small light with a red cover that burned all through the night. Night after night I would stare into that light thinking about my life and the lives of the men around me. As we laid there in the darkness it complemented the sadness and regret we felt in our hearts. I don't know if it was a poem or a song or what. I wrote about those days that always ended the same — with me staring into that red light. I called it "Underneath the Red Light."

"Another night alone
Underneath the red light
Another guilty night away from our home
We all know what we did was wrong
We all know we're where we belong
Underneath the red light."

Eventually I was taken out of the kitchen and placed on outside work detail. There was a greenhouse we maintained that grew pumpkins and tomatoes among other things. My work crew also pulled weeds in the "rabbit run" — the sand moat that ran the entire perimeter of the facility. On each side was a 12-foot chain link fence with razor wire on top.

If you cleared the near side you had a big, wide open space to cross before you could scale the far one. We cleared out large brush areas with machetes in the burning sun and, yes, we picked up trash on the side of the highway in our orange inmate vests.

In my life I had countless times driven by a roadside crew like mine and thought, "What a bunch of poor you know whats."

Perspective is such a huge part of our lives. The truth is, there was a small taste of freedom associated with leaving the compound for those jobs. It felt pretty darn good.

I had one visitor the entire time I was at Franklin. Robyn drove up from Sarasota a few weeks before I was released. My mother had informed me she would not be visiting. I accepted that and never asked any questions. Looking back, I believe Robyn had something she wanted to tell me, but couldn't muster the courage in a face-to-face meeting. She was distant. She was not Robyn. There is a saying in prison that many guys only learn the full truth when they are just weeks from being released. Then comes what they call the "short-timer's letter." Short-timers are inmates getting out in the near future.

It had been a couple of months and I wasn't receiving letters from Robyn anymore. In the beginning I would get one a week or more. On one of my quiet mornings I wrote her a letter half-jokingly asking if she remembered me and I reminded her I was getting out soon. Right on time, about 10 days before I was scheduled for release arrived my short timer's letter. Robyn acknowledged that she had met someone and it was a very serious relationship. When I came back to Sarasota she wasn't going to be around.

It didn't surprise me. I had let Robyn down so many times. Over and over she forgave and trusted again. She kept hoping. She stood by me and kept believing without cause for a long time. In the beginning, Robyn and I had been much different. We truly enjoyed each other's company and were always close. We had a lot of good times. Those days had long been over, and she did what she had to do. I was not angry and I wished her happiness in the future.

Initially, at the least, I felt I deserved a more proper, personal goodbye from her. In time I came to accept that, no, I didn't deserve anything from Robyn. I responded and let her know if she didn't make it to the Greyhound bus depot upon my return I understood. She answered that she would be there.

November 9, 2006 is the day I said goodbye to Wing and Godfather. I was released 45 days early with gain time and good behavior. Godfather and I shook hands. I knew it was the last time I would see him. Wing and I exchanged contact information and both promised we would be in touch and pray for the other. He assured me he would stay in The Lord.

At last, the voice that had always meant captivity, one final time meant freedom…"U20203 Wilkinson!"

I grabbed my bag and turned to look a final time. I won't forget the eyes of those who remained as I walked to my freedom. Many had been in long before I got there and would remain long after I departed.

At my exit interview I signed numerous papers, received a Greyhound ticket from Tallahassee to Sarasota, and was given a $100 gratuity discharge. In 2006, Florida would give a stipend to an inmate that met certain criteria upon release to assist in their journey. I changed into the new, fresh clothes my mother had sent me. She had not included shoes, so I continued to wear my blue cloth "Gilligan" inmate slip-ons. It did not bother me one bit.

Exiting the rolling bar and lock-clicking metal doors, I just stopped. I stood there and breathed. I don't know what else to say about that. It is indescribable. The only single way to understand the feeling is to be released from prison. An actual shuttle from the prison drove only me the little over an hour it takes to the Greyhound bus depot in Tallahassee. I had a few minutes to kill before my bus departed. As I sat there with my inmate slip-ons and my bag of belongings it was abundantly clear who I was. A man just released from prison. I made it. I made it through alive, sane, and in one piece. Thank you, God. Thank you!

I had never been on a Greyhound bus before. It was the finest eight-hour ride of my life. As we rolled south across the land and through the small towns of the countryside, the world looked different to me. Everything seemed more alive than I had ever noticed before. I was ready. I was prepared to start my life anew. I literally was born again. I was embarking on my second chance at life, with a clean slate and with God. I knew things were different and it didn't matter who didn't believe they were. I knew and that was enough.

A little after midnight the driver pulled the bus into the small Sarasota depot. A lone light pole lit the small parking lot. Underneath the light was my mother in her car waiting. Stepping off, I noticed another car over in the shadows and someone getting out of it. I walked a few strides, and then I was still. Robyn walked out of the shadows and up to me. For only a moment we looked at each other and then we hugged. She whispered something in my ear and I answered her. She let go, turned, and walked away. Her car started and was soon gone. That was that.

Mom, my blessing in the car watching, just smiled and motioned me to come on. She was excited and actually did believe things were going to be different. How much of that was due to the fact she was my mother and how much was because things really were different I don't know. I do know that mothers have a hope, a power to believe when all others have given up. It is so in the Bible as well. Women always had a special place in the ministry of Jesus. Generally, they are not as prideful as men and, in many cases, their faith is markedly more steadfast and consistent.

Mom and I were just thrilled to be together again. As we walked in the door to her house I smelled the welcoming aroma of her homemade banana bread. Always one of my favorites, Mom used perfect texture ripened bananas and a little extra butter. Glenn, too, had lost everything and was living with Mom. I didn't see him that night.

She had prepared the bedroom for me and the crisp, fresh sheets on the bed were turned down. We stayed up half the night talking. Both of us were giddy. We created an inside joke just between us that stuck. Prison was not prison. We would always refer to it as "the resort." The sentence I served was the extended stay I enjoyed at "the resort." Every so often she would ask me if I had gone online and rated my experience there.

Mom, as much as anyone I ever knew, could take a really bad situation and find something to chuckle about. I would say something about "the resort" and she would stop whatever it was that she was doing and look at me without saying a word. Not even blinking.

Only a couple of hours before the sun began to rise we laid down. As I slid into the cool sheets and stretched out, I acknowledged how blessed I was. Many, many people, men and women, are released from prison every year and don't have a mother at the bus station. They have no one. They have not been properly prepared, and it is only a matter of time until they falter and return to things they know. Through temptation, through rejection, through marginalization, through many things. Then society points their collective finger at them and says, "Ah-ha! See, we told you so! They are bad people!"

I am not a bleeding heart. I certainly believe in accountability and punishment. There are people in prison who absolutely deserve their sentences and sometimes more. People that have committed heinous, evil, unimaginable crimes. But there is a real segment of the prison population that through whatever actions or turn of events in their lives they now sit in prison. They want to change. They can change. They need help. I know for a fact they are there. I saw them all around me. These people are not lost causes…they are lost — in spiritual and worldly terms. There are fixes to both of these problems. Christ is the solution to one, and our genuine attention is the solution to the other.

I woke up the next morning with sunlight coming through the wooden blinds and the smell of fresh, real coffee in the air. I had not slumbered past sun up in many months. To roll over and be alone, to not smell the smells, to not hear gas being passed — it was a dream. It was a wonderful, splendid, blue sky and white puffy cloud dream.

I rose to get a cup of coffee and Mom was in the kitchen tinkering around with a list. She had a white terry cloth robe on and a pair of prescription sunglasses. She wore her shades of a morning when she made her rounds watering her plants outside. I told her she looked like Roy Orbison.

"I can sing like him too, honey," she said as she hugged me.

We sat and talked in the kitchen for a long time. Then we refilled our coffee and made our way out to the front porch. We sat there for a while. She updated me on everyone — Aunt Kathy, Uncle Gene, Mom Stafford (Lucille, my mother's mother), and the dogs. She didn't speak about Glenn and I didn't press it.

Glenn emerged from his room to tell me welcome home. We didn't even hug. It was only a few minutes until he returned to his room. He was where I had been. It's like a language. Once you've been there yourself, you can speak it. Today I see people all the time that are in a lot of trouble flying beneath the radar of unsuspecting family, friends, and colleagues. I see it in everyday life as well as television on celebrity awards shows, late night shows, concerts, and things like that. When I see it, I hear it; I am fluent.

Personal hygiene wise, I felt like The Lord had called me home. Well, not really, but pretty darn close. Dad and Mom had always been very particular about their appearance and so was I. I also had grown up the baby of all the cousins. All of the cousins on one side were girls. Being around Michelle, Carol, Myra, and Sarah had taught me all there was to know about physical appearances. I had been a guinea pig a time or two also. I knew the creams, lotions, cover-ups, the home remedies for hair care, and the ins and outs of hair removal.

In prison I had been denied pretty much everything outside of the "Big 3" — showering, shaving, and brushing teeth. A couple of times a month I could checkout a nail clipper and return it once I finished. Now, I had a bathroom full of concoctions, tools, and devices — a complete arsenal in the fight against bad personal hygiene! I had not so much as tweezed a hair or washed my back in a year. I went to work, and it was a glorious thing.

I was committed to making the most out of being home. I was released early, but I still had to report to a parole officer for the number of days taken off my sentence — 45. About nine days after I came home, I wanted to show my mother and my parole officer that I was serious. I rose very early in the morning, and drove my mom's car to a day labor agency in Bradenton, about 10 miles from Sarasota. The doors opened at 5:00 a.m., and I was there early. A man unlocked the doors and let us in right on time. There was cheap coffee brewing in a grungy little brewer…brown water. There were about 30 to 35 of us. He asked us all to listen up.

"All of you with a felony on your record please hold up your hands," he directed.

I have four. Along with close to half of everybody else, I raised my hand.

"Okay, we don't have enough today for everybody so we're gonna let you guys go on home. Thanks and try again," he told us.

I look at my life in clearly defined phases, chopped up stages. There are no real gray or overlapping areas. There has been around seven or eight of them. For pretty much all of them, I can recollect a moment when the outgoing phase shut for good and the incoming phase opened wide. I never have been adept at easing in and out of things. This was one of those moments.

It is probably hard for some folks to understand when I say I was a bit naive coming out of prison, but I was. I felt like the worst part was over now. I got in trouble. I went away and did my sentence. I faced the truth about myself. There will be some bumps ahead, but for the most part the storm had passed.

Being a Christian does not mean our lives all of a sudden become problem and suffering free zones. Quite the contrary. What it does mean is that we have The Source and The Power to endure anything that comes our way…absolutely anything. The Holy Spirit has more than what we need to survive and thrive in this world. Problem is, we don't always let Him in. And although He certainly could, He doesn't force His way in.

It was still before six o'clock in the morning. I couldn't even get a temporary labor job for the day digging a ditch or whatever. The money situation was a bummer, but the real damage was psychological. As I drove south back down Tamiami Trail, I realized, yes, the prison ordeal was over, but I had a whole new road before me. A road of rejection. As a convicted felon, getting back in the game of life and becoming a productive member of society again was going to be quite a bit tougher than I originally had believed. For the first time I was scared. As I drove back to my mother's house, my eyes were opened and I was really scared.

I turned in job application after job application — restaurants, retail shops, a couple of hotels close to where I lived, and more. I wasn't hearing from anyone. Twice I stood on the street corner dancing around with a sign for eight hours. There is not a single time I drive by a person doing the same in the abusive Florida sun and am not reminded of what it took. I don't pity them. I wonder what they're clawing their way back from or to.

When I did get the chance to speak with someone, obviously they always wanted to know why I had checked the yes box by the question, "Have you ever been convicted of a felony?" That was bad enough, but when I explained my charges were four felony counts involving drugs I could see in their eyes my chances fly out the window. I was discouraged and was praying about everything. I had read much more than the Bible at Franklin Correctional — books from contemporary Christian authors such as T.D. Jakes, Max Lucado, Chuck Colson, and Billy Graham. The Bible I had read was the New American Standard Bible (NASB). I am by leaps and bounds no Bible translation scholar, however from what I could ascertain the NASB is the purest and truest American Bible translation to the original Greek and Hebrew texts.

I had gathered a sense of Christian denominations and their strengths and weaknesses. Denominations are not of The Lord. I believe denominations grieve Him. They are of man. Not to say if you are a part of a denominational church you are not or cannot be saved. Only that Jesus is about unity not division.

However, from my learning and studying I concluded that Baptists were really close to what the Bible was saying. In other words, doctrinally speaking, Baptists adhered closely to the true Word of God. The word on the street, as they say, is that Baptists are a bit legalistic and judgmental. I was willing to deal with that in the name of receiving the Word as it was meant to be received. One day I just opened the yellow pages and started looking at churches. I found a Baptist church in Bradenton. I wrote the address down. The next morning, I drove there.

It was an established church with several hundred members. I walked in, introduced myself, and asked to see a pastor. Soon a man emerged from an office and introduced himself to me. He was Assistant Pastor Dean and asked me to follow him back in. Pastor Dean asked me what he could do for me and so I began. I gave him the condensed, 30-minute version of my life and that I was a new Christian with all of the needs of one. Just like a child. As I spoke, I watched him. The same as he was watching me. He listened and didn't interrupt one time. I appreciated that very much. I concluded by explaining my wish to have real fellowship with other believers. Pastor Dean told me there are no coincidences, and I was there for a reason. He rose, thanked me for coming, and invited me to the upcoming service in a number of days.

I was ecstatic. Although nothing was working out yet on the employment front, I knew if I kept God square in my sights He would help me. I returned home and shared with Mom the great news. She also was thrilled. To see in my mother's eyes the hope and happiness she was experiencing over me was better than any drug I had ever taken. She was proud of me. It was as if I was a child again showing Mom how good I could be. Good things were happening and there was life again. I hoped so much that Dad knew. That he could see.

Glenn, on the other hand, was not a part of this. I noticed the pattern of his days. He was sleeping through the days and staying awake at night. He wasn't working. One of the biggest blessings God has given me is the ability to not allow my pride to stand in the way of my climb back up the ladder of life. I accepted in full the fact that all of the money, influence, and privilege were gone. Those things were history. That truth ran parallel to another truth that I was standing flat on the bottom of a huge crater I had dug for myself. I didn't have time for pride, and it was not going to stand in my way. I was willing to do, and did, just about anything to come back. Dad had this ability. So did Mom. Glenn never did. Glenn simply could not let go of what was.

Within weeks, I was involved in the church. The senior pastor was pleasant and seemed genuine. I was meeting other Christians. I got involved in the youth group. There was an addiction recovery program I participated in. I even started to work in the maintenance department of the church. There was a remodel underway. I helped install rows of seats, scraped up old tiles, picked up litter. I cleaned Pastor Dean's house for some extra money on the side. I was alive and positive and thankful. I had a ton of energy and it showed. I was sharing my testimony every chance afforded me and it did seem to capture the attention of others when I spoke.

I know I was a bit of a novelty. I always had been. Only before, it was because I was the son of the wealthy governor. Now I was the broke son of a former governor who had gone to prison.

Once as I emptied the trash can in one of the offices a church administrator happened by and she said, "Look at that, the governor's son is emptying the trash."

Of course this had a sting to it. But I had been stung so many times by then it was just another day in the life.

Through one of the Bible studies or church activities I met Scott. Only God knows the hearts of men. But as far as I could tell Scott was one of the godliest men I had ever met. He had been a baseball standout and serious athlete earlier in his life. Scott had run a marathon before and he asked if I wanted to train and run in the annual Sarasota Grouper Marathon together. For several months we got our training on. Early morning runs on the pier as the sun rose. Gradually increasing distances every week. We ran a cross-country 10K together in prep. Our last training run before the race was 19 miles.

A true marathon is 26.2 miles. I was concerned I couldn't make it the distance on race day. Scott assured me I could and would. Scott, his daughter, and I ran it in a little over four hours. The finish line of the marathon was at the famous Ringling Museum of Art in Sarasota. My mother's house was situated diagonally across the street from the museum. As I ran by, Mom was on her porch watching and cheering. I never told her how important that moment was for me. It was every bit as important as crossing the finish line itself.

It was only a few months and I started to feel the need to find my own place to live. Straight out of prison was one thing, but I began to feel some shame about it. Here was Martha with her two grown men boys hoarded up with her. Mom did not feel that way. She wanted me to stick around to balance out the Glenn situation. She was getting older and the years had taken their toll on her.

Glenn was more than a handful. He always had been. Power and fortitude were required to deal with him. Glenn was my older brother and I loved him. He was a good brother to me in many ways, but you needed to be on top of your game to withstand his prolonged presence. He could suck the power right out of you. And he was sucking it out of Mom. I noticed her drinking wine more and more.

Chapter 20

I was introduced to a man by the name of Bryn Mercer. He was the longtime friend of both the senior pastor and assistant pastor, Pastor Dean. Bryn was an evangelist and had his own association that conducted missions all over the world. At this particular time, he was spending time in Brazil and Germany. Bryn was like dynamite and loved The Lord. He also loved his Starbucks. His enthusiasm was infectious to me, and I gravitated toward him. I spent time with him and his family at their home. They spent their money on me. Bryn was real. He was all about Jesus, but he could connect on a very human level. When I talked to him about my life he understood or, at least, pretended to. He understood the difficulties and challenges of going from what my life used to be like to what it was now.

Countless times I had shared with another person regarding my life and the clear reaction, with or without words, was, "Oh, boo-hoo. We're not rich anymore and Daddy's not here to make it better. Guess what! You're at the back of the crying line."

And heck, that might have been true. But that doesn't change the fact I still needed someone to understand. I was grateful for that, and I shared with him often how I felt.

An opportunity arose for me to participate on one of Bryn's missions to Germany. I jumped all over it. I was able to raise some money to pay for it, but his association covered most of it. He wanted me to go, and I can't describe how utterly wonderful that felt to me. That I was a part of something about God, real, and healthy. Only a year before, I was shackled up in the back of a prisoner transport. In the church I was being included when everywhere else it seemed I was being excluded. In October 2007, I travelled to Worms, Germany as part of an official mission team.

I was flying high and was so happy I just wanted to hug everyone. The church in Worms had around 150 members. We were there for a little more than a week. A German couple and their youngest daughter allowed me and another member of the team to stay in their home and were very gracious. The four of us spent our time together talking about God, the United States, Germany, and eating. An older daughter would come to visit with her husband. It felt wonderful to sit in their home and be in a family setting. That had not been a part of my life for some time. The father learned I had owned two Mercedes-Benz E55 AMGs and he picked my brain often about them.

As I sat with them at the table or in the living room I could actually hear my voice in my head, "Please God, please, can I have this too one day? Will I be able to have this?"

Germans are very reserved, and I am not. Yes, they can be downright stiff at times. I am a hugger, a patter, a hand holder. I think they believed I was another type of animal at first. The sun was shining, and it was an early autumn day in Worms. The air was crisp and I was smelling fall in the air. The climate and landscape were incredibly similar to Lexington, conjuring up memories of the first weeks of school.

I was feeling completely blessed as I approached the church for the first full day of meetings. There was a German girl, a member of the church, greeting everyone as they entered. She wore a gold and pink scarf wrapped over an off-white sweater and her hands were gently clasped as she spoke, "Hallo, guten tag. Herzlich Wilkommen."

I was deeply struck by her eyes and smile…so warm and pleasant. They spoke their own language. Her hair was long and full of waves, vibrant and thick. Her nametag said

"Nadine," and I knew she was special. From that moment on I was quietly watching her, and if she wasn't around I was quietly looking for her.

One night I had the honor of sharing my testimony to the congregation through a translator. Numerous members of the audience approached me afterward and wished to talk. In a foreign land is where I realized the ability to deeply connect with people through God is a huge responsibility. God gives us all gifts. The ability to talk about my life and connect it to the lives of other people so we both feel it is what He has given me. It is an honor, a privilege, and a blessing.

This world will present us with pain and suffering. It has no bearing on anything at all what sex we are, where we come from, or what color our skin is. It is the same predicament for each and every one of us. When everyone around me has a mask on and I am supposed to wear one too, it is like kryptonite to me. That's why I find myself struggling sometimes in the workplace today. We are encouraged, in fact, expected to wear masks. Authenticity may upset or offend someone, so let's all put our mask on for eight hours or more. The interaction is so generic and bland. It is very difficult for me.

Worms is also the first time my eyes were opened wider about other Christians. The day after I addressed the congregation, one of the senior members of the team commented to me about it. "Andrew, your testimony was great, but everyone has a testimony. You need to go to seminary and get a degree. If you do that you will be lethal," he instructed me.

Lethal? My witness about Jesus Christ will be lethal? This guy was very learned in Christianity, and I looked up to him as an authority. My testimony was given in spiritual terms, and he was critiquing it like I was his marketing student. This was the first in a series of letdowns I experienced with the church and other Christians.

Throughout the week, I had sought out Nadine's company. Her English was broken, and I couldn't get enough of listening to her. My German was nonexistent. When there was another speaker, I would sit next to or behind her. During a meal I sat next to or directly across from her.

Behind the church was a neighborhood and a small park was not far away. We would walk to the park in the autumn sun. Words were difficult for us, but that was the wonder of it. Another level of communication, a deep connection, was preempting words. We sat in silence, not hindered or restricted by sound. Words can be misunderstood. I would learn this later.

Neither one of us really knew what to say, and different languages were not to blame. What was, neither one of us misunderstood. It was strong. It was real. We accepted the silence. For both of us a thirst was being quenched. It is very rare in life to experience that with another human being. Some never do. We did, together. The silence was not awkward for us. It was not uncomfortable. It was the way to feel what was happening. It was indescribable. Nadine and I were in love from the beginning.

Like always, the time flew by and before we knew it our time to leave was approaching. I had to decide how to say goodbye to Nadine. What was I going to say? How was I going to say it? After a long, personal deliberation, I decided I was going to go for it. It was the latter part of the afternoon our next to last day and I saw Nadine with some other girls on the main level. I asked her if she could come with me downstairs, as I needed to show her something. She suspected nothing. As we reached the basement level I grabbed her hand and we ducked into another room. I didn't say a word and planted a kiss right on her lips. I had to. I couldn't go home wondering. After a moment's hesitation, she kissed me back. It felt wonderful, but this type of thing was not what I was there for and I knew it.

The nine days wrapped up, and it was time to go. The team gathered at the church one final morning. I had said goodbye to my host family. Now, it was time to say goodbye to Nadine. We were both depressed, but also very aware of all the good things that had taken place. I lived in the United States and she in Germany. This was the end for now. We exchanged letters we had written, and I promised she would hear from me. At the time I was 35 and Nadine was 21. I can certainly see how, at the time, it might have appeared a certain way. But for Nadine and I it was a non-issue. I knew I was not going to be forgetting her.

During this time, I had been riding a KTM motorcycle back home as my mode of transportation. As convenient and efficient as motorcycles can be, they have their drawbacks. When the weather was foul or I needed to look nice for a church activity the bike wasn't getting it done. Pastor Dean had put the word out he wanted to help me find a car somehow. He had been praying about it. A member of the church learned of this need. He anonymously donated several thousand dollars to purchase a car from another member to give me. All of this took place as I was in Germany.

The night I returned stateside, Pastor Dean called me out to his home. He and his wife were there with several other members of the church. They presented me with this car. It was a gray Toyota Camry. Basic with no frills, but in excellent condition. It was what I needed. It was a prime example of when we get God involved through prayer He will make things happen. Needs will be met. I was blown away and wanted to express my gratitude to the man who made it possible with his donation. Pastor Dean told me that being able to a supply a need through God was all the gratitude the man had asked for.

In the meantime, Glenn had conceived a plan. He wanted to go to Australia and attend Bond University International Law School in Queensland. Mom had begun a relationship of sorts with a man she and my family had known for many years. His wife had succumbed to a battle with cancer and he lived on Siesta Key. More than anything it was two people gravitating toward another person they knew and respected. To have someone to eat dinner with, to talk to.

Mom had asked both Glenn and I if we believed Dad would have had an issue with it. We both answered no. Dad would be happy to know she was not alone. This man, earnestly wanting to ease the burden on Mom, had put forth a large amount of money to the Australia law school idea to make it possible. Maybe it was what Glenn really needed.

The collapse and his divorce had put him in a tailspin. He had been living at our mother's with no motivation, no plan, nothing healthy in his life. Maybe this huge blessing was the start of a new life. With silent trepidation, everyone embraced and supported the idea of Australia. Glenn was leaving in a few weeks.

Pastor Dean was highly educated in the Word of God. He believed in and practiced expository preaching. Expository preaching is to take a Bible verse or a particular text and explain its meaning word for word. It is highly regarded by true Bible scholars and those thirsting for the pure milk of Scripture. For doctrinally difficult and in-depth books of the Bible, it is absolutely necessary to exposit. For instance, the Book of Romans. In it, the Apostle Paul explains in precise detail God's plan of salvation through Jesus Christ for all of humanity.

Often, when asked why I believe the Bible is from God, I direct folks to the Book of Romans. For me, it is not possible that the finite mind of man could come up with something so intricate and detailed while simultaneously containing heavenly pureness and simplicity.

However, expository preaching does not sugar coat or water down what the Bible has to say about sin, Satan, and condemnation. Unfortunately, in many church services today people only attend to hear the fluffy, wonderful messages of Scripture. The Truth is not real popular. It makes people uncomfortable and offends others.

For this reason and the fact Pastor Dean had a bit of a dry personality, there were a number of people in the church who had a problem with him. Only a couple of months after I was back from Germany it came to an unbelievable head.

The senior pastor, along with members of the church management committee, informed Pastor Dean he was to be moving on. They informed him he had decided to resign and take his ministry elsewhere. In fact, not the senior pastor, or Pastor Dean himself, but a financial officer stood in front of the congregation and read a letter of resignation the church said Pastor Dean wrote. By that time I knew some things about Pastor Dean. How he taught. His style. That resignation letter was not from him.

I was truly in shock, but what made it even worse was that approximately 75 percent of the congregation also knew it wasn't true. Let me say it another way. Everyone knew what was happening was shady and not exactly the whole truth was being told, but they were going along with it. They wanted to see Pastor Dean leave.

What had begun as a small crack in my new fellowship in Worms with the "lethal testimony" comment from an authority figure was now a rip. Pastor Dean left the church, taking close to 100 members – including me – with him.

It was not a church split, but it sure was a splintering. I just couldn't believe it. Is this what it was all about? On the outside all about God, but on the inside exactly the same as the world? A country club? High school?

Chapter 21

I found work on a commercial landscaping crew. I was carrying a weed eater in the Florida sun for 12 hours a day wearing heavy boots, pants, and a long-sleeve shirt. It was brutal, but it was work. I moved into a small apartment over the garage of some members of the church. Nadine and I were in constant contact through the telephone or the computer.

There was a drama unfolding in a triangle between Bryn Mercer, Pastor Dean, and the senior pastor. Bryn and Pastor Dean had gone to seminary school together years ago. Their families knew each other well. Bryn had brought Pastor Dean to the senior pastor when the church had been looking for an assistant pastor.

I had been close to Pastor Dean and I was close with Bryn. Pastor Dean immediately decided he was going to start his own church. Bryn wasn't necessarily convinced, along with others, that was wise. The whole model of church and fellowshipping Christians I had been introduced to blew up like a case of TNT.

I would drive to Bryn's home and stay for the weekend. Bryn hadn't let me down, but the situation had put him in a very awkward position because his evangelistic association was still connected to the church and the senior pastor. He would ask questions if I knew what was going on. I would return home and deal with questions from Pastor Dean about Bryn and what was going on. The two of them and their families weren't speaking. I turned into a go-between. Sometimes I felt like a spy.

I had compassion for Pastor Dean. It was a very bad development in the life of a church and believers. I saw a bunch of faithful followers of Jesus Christ being tested. I saw a bunch of faithful followers of Jesus Christ failing. Including me. Gossip was pre-imminent. It was an ugly situation, and it rubbed off on every single one of us it touched. I was a new Christian, and I didn't know what to do or think. I was very confused. The joy I experienced at prison and upon coming home was gone. I felt like I had been very naïve, the same as when I came home from prison.

I was a part of the start-up. Pastor Dean is the one who had taken me in when I first went to the church. I felt a loyalty to him. I scheduled an appointment with the senior pastor. On the day of the appointment we sat in his office together. I gave notice of my leaving the church and going with the other defecting members and Pastor Dean.

He asked me to forgive him regarding the surrounding circumstances. He also warned me not to follow any man. It was imperative to always keep our eyes and hearts on Jesus. People can let us down, betray, and even forsake us. There is never disappointment in Jesus Christ and He will never forsake us. I understood this and still do. Still, I was beside myself at the level and amount of worldly behavior by darn near everybody. It was widespread.

On a worldly basis I knew exactly what was happening. I could see some things develop beforehand. It was a game. The same game as is played in business and politics all over the world every single day. Actually, I felt the temptation to get involved and coach some of the players.

On a spiritual basis, I was floored. Although more than seasoned in the ways of the world, I was a child in Christ. I didn't have maturity in Him and I felt abandoned. Everyone had been tainted on some level. Bryn had done so much for me, and in my heart I knew he was a good man. Pastor Dean had taken me in and listened when no one else was willing. He too was a good man. I just believed I would see different ways of dealing with things. For such a young Christian to witness so much stumbling so early on in his faith was damaging. My faith was damaged.

The trust issues I struggled with from the collapse were again front and center. I was present and participated in the activities and happenings of the start-up church by Pastor Dean, but inside I was pulling back. I began to see all around me through the lens of cynicism.

An elderly man slated to be an elder in the new church, in my opinion, was difficult to deal with. We had batted the ball back and forth at a number of meetings, and it was no secret we both needed Christ to accept each other. He did not care for me, and I did not like him. It got to the point where we didn't speak unless it was necessary. This was happening among believers in the body of Christ.

Although the circumstances in the church were a disaster, corporately speaking, God did place those people in my life for good things too. Sin, the flesh, and the world are so powerful. They can creep into the life of even the "strongest" Christian. We can't win without Christ. Attempts at living a Christian life without the power of The Holy Spirit will fail. And letting The Holy Spirit do His work in us is a daily endeavor through prayer.

Frank, his wife, Terri, and their two daughters became friends of mine. They shared in the discouragement and disillusionment over the church and fellowship with me. However, all the times I sat with them in their home produced its own fruit. We read the Bible, prayed, and I watched the entire family take care of one of the daughters who was handicapped. They were a remarkable family. I look forward to seeing them again one day.

My buddy, Wing, and I had been staying in touch through letters. He wrote me that someone had challenged him and he was in a fight. He asked me please to not be mad at him. I knew exactly what that was like.

Jesus says in the gospel of Luke when someone hits us on the cheek not only to not retaliate, but to offer the other cheek as well. How difficult that is in free society is one thing. Oh gosh, it is difficult to state how impossible that seems in prison. Our flesh screams at us all day every day in there, "Protect yourself! Only you can protect yourself! If you have to fight then fight!"

Wing had given me an address in Miami where his mother lived. I sent a letter to the address and it was returned. On the envelope someone had written, "Wing is not here. Don't send again." That is all I know about him.

I allowed my prayer life to be seriously affected. Not only was I seeing other Christians as hypocrites, but also I felt like one. Before going to prison I had smoked cigarettes for years. Members on both sides of my family going back generations had smoked. I like the flavor and smell of tobacco — cigarettes, cigars, and smokeless tobacco all taste good to me. I know, disgusting.

Tobacco is addictive as everyone knows. Cigarettes were for me time killers, a nervous habit — something to do to deal with the stress of the moment. At Franklin, tobacco was available, but I had given it up. Now, I had picked it up again. I wasn't supposed to smoke in my apartment. After dinner and before bed, I smoked and blew the smoke out of the bathroom window. I was becoming weak to the world once more.

I had, by this point, travelled to Germany twice to visit Nadine and meet her family. During the months in between, we burned the phone lines and webcams. It was her turn to come to the United States. It was August 2008, and she was flying in for three weeks. It was time for her to see my home, who I was here, and meet Mom and Glenn. It was not opportune as I had to be at the job site every day, but the visit needed to happen. Both of us felt like a decision needed to be made about what we were. Were we a fun, international splash that was exciting, or were we taking it all the way?

From time to time I would stay at my mother's house just to be near her. I needed to wake up around 4:30 a.m. for work. Mom would get up to make coffee for me and chit chat for a few minutes before I left. That morning she was in the kitchen and just the oven light was on.

I walked in, boots already on, and announced, "Mom, I'm going to marry Nadine."

I thought she was going to spill her coffee as she pulled the cup from her lips. Her eyes were wide open.

"Mornin,'" she said.

I grabbed a banana, gave her a kiss, and headed out the door.

"Mornin,'" I said over my shoulder as the screen door shut.

The day before Nadine was flying in from Frankfurt to Tampa, I went to the dollar store and bought some construction paper and markers. I wanted her to feel welcome and comfortable here. She had been to the United States several times with her family as a child, but this was her maiden voyage alone. I made a sign to hold up so she would see me as she and the other passengers got off the shuttle from the terminals. In huge red letters I wrote, "My Nadine" on a white piece of paper.

The next day, on my way to the Tampa International Airport, I purchased a red rose. I had been to Germany several times and the two of us were very close by then. But this time was different. She was coming to my country, to my home. I have travelled to many places all over the world. I believe when we voyage away from home there is a small part of us that always stays behind — a part of our spirit, who we are. Nadine was going to see this part of me for the very first time.

As the shuttle approached, I made my way to the front of the group of others who were also waiting. It was not my style to hold up a sign with a rose. I would have always labeled someone else who did that sort of thing very corny. And I did feel corny. But as she walked toward me with her carry-on bag, I held that sign and rose up to be as visible as I could. I guess this is what love does to us.

Nadine was staying with Mom and Glenn, as I worked during the day. Mom was happy to have her, and Glenn was within a couple of weeks of leaving for Queensland. There was a side of Glenn that was kind-hearted, charming, and fun. This is the side Nadine saw, and the two of them formed a friendship quickly.

Mom was a bit older and continuously busy with her chores and lists. While I was working, Glenn took Nadine on errands, showed her some things locally, and generally spent time with her. It was a big help, and meant a lot to both Nadine and I. Although, admittedly, I was sometimes anxious during our separation in the day. Brothers can share things they don't always need to.

My landlords were kind enough to plan a dinner for Nadine and me at their home during one of the evenings of her stay. They were members of Pastor Dean's new church. Along with Pastor Dean and his wife, several other members of the church were invited. Nadine was 22 years old — certainly old enough to attend a dinner and answer normal questions about her life. Undoubtedly there was curiosity about her family, her homeland, and her Christianity. I knew and understood this, and I approached my landlords about it.

My concerns were that I wanted to make sure normal, curious questions didn't morph into a situation where Nadine was uncomfortable or felt as though she was under interrogation. I had been around long enough to know my concerns were valid. People get carried away sometimes in their curiosity. I was assured everything would be fine.

The evening of the dinner arrived. My landlords had an older daughter and a younger son. I had spent time with both of them and they were good kids. As other guests were arriving, Nadine and I were hanging out with them. Finally, all guests had arrived and everyone took their places at the table. My mother was also there. All in all there were about 12 people in attendance.

Grace was said, and everyone grabbed some bread and filled their plate. Then the games began. Perhaps two or three bites had been savored when the inquiries pumped out in rapid-fire succession.

"So, Nadine, how long have you been a Christian?"

"Is your family Christian also?"

"Tell us about your church. What exactly do they believe?"

"And your Pastor, where did he study or train?"

"What is it you believe about Jesus?"

Precisely what I had hoped would not happen was happening. Nadine graciously accommodated all questions and did her best to answer them. It was difficult for her and I tried to help. But it became too much and I began to sense her frustration. They were not vicious attacks by any stretch, but the questioning parties couldn't help themselves. Proper consideration was not given to Nadine as new to the country and as a guest. I felt bad for her.

To make matters worse, Mom had also shown up less than herself. She was clearly under the influence of alcohol or some other substance. I knew at the time she had a prescription of Xanax that a doctor had given her for anxiety. Whether it was wine, Xanax, or a combination of both, Mom was not fit to be there and the others recognized it. As she sat at the table, my heart was breaking for her.

An eternity later, the dinner was finished and the plates were cleared. I don't recall anyone being interested in coffee or dessert, and after proper thanks were given everybody left. Over three hours had passed and I allowed Mom to drive her SUV home as Nadine and I followed directly behind her. It had been a bad evening.

Between the many questions of Nadine and the embarrassing situation with my mother I had only sat there waiting, praying for time to pass. I too was a guest in someone's home. I handled it poorly. Between Nadine and Mom, I regretted not, in a respectful way, taking a course of action that would have been helpful to both of them. Whatever that might have been I don't know, but it would have been more than only sitting there watching everything.

All of my life I had seen the strength of my mother. Countless others had also bore witness to her foundation. In fact, she was known for it. The years of turmoil and the cost of unconditional, sacrificial love were taking their toll on her. Like flowing water over limestone, her surface was being eroded. It was vanishing. Always a picture of underlying happiness and health, my mother was losing weight and beginning to appear older than she was. She had been enabling Glenn and the constant strain, financial and otherwise, was tremendous.

Glenn was simultaneously in a very dark place and preparing to go to another continent. In his darkness, he had done things he normally never would have done. The same as I had. He had taken things that didn't belong to him and accrued debt that he couldn't cover. Mom couldn't take the heartache of another travesty and felt trapped by her love for Glenn. She could not forcefully send him on his way, and she was a prisoner in her own home because of it. The boxes of wine were being replaced in the refrigerator every couple of days.

Around this time I began having dreams about my father. Nightmares. Dad was always a few feet in front of me. I could see only him. Everything else was black. He wore a white tuxedo, but it was tattered and torn.

He would motion me to him with his arm and speak, "Come on, Spruder," and "Spruder, come on. Again…we'll go again."

Flesh and skin were hanging from his bones, and through the rips in the material I could see his skeleton. It was always the same.

I would tell him, "No, Dad, we can't go again. It's over. There's nothing to do again."

He would continue stronger and stronger, "Come on…come on…come on!"

As I began yelling, "We can't, Dad! No!" I would awaken.

The image of my father was so bad —and his voice. I had never experienced anything like these dreams. When I had them, they stole the proceeding day from me. I was having them once or twice a week. I would struggle throughout the entire day with them.

During the weeks preceding Nadine's visit, I had been saving all the money I could. The week before she was to fly in from Germany, I went to a small, old school jewelry store in downtown Sarasota. There I bought Nadine the best engagement ring I could afford. It was a simple, classic 18K yellow gold ring with a .5 carat diamond set on top. My purchasing power was greatly diminished compared to years earlier, but my reason for buying it was high-end. I was proud of that little sucker as I walked down Main Street to my car. I hatched a plan to spring it on Nadine.

Straight up the coast from Sarasota is a small, old Florida town called Homosassa Springs about 75 miles north of Tampa Bay. Throughout the area are some of the state's awesome freshwater springs. To experience swimming in one on a sweltering hot Florida summer day is remarkable. They are fresh and pure. The water runs crystal clear and maintains a low 70-degree temperature even during the hottest months.

I have been to a lot of luxurious, fancy destinations — The Danieli in Venice, The Dorchester in London, Hotel Bel-Air in Los Angeles, The Pierre in New York City, to name just a few. But I have always been the most comfortable in the more real spots — the lakeside motor lodges, the state park cabins, the 100-year-old bed and breakfast, or in the forest waking up in a tent and grabbing some straw for the horses.

I found a little retreat lodge on the Homosassa River that had that feel to me. There were cottages and a small wooden boat dock with a fuel pump and a solitary dock light with a metal shade that burned in the night.

Glenn had interacted more with Nadine than anyone else in years. She really liked him, and it fed her heart to help him that way. Nadine has the purest, most genuine heart of any person I have ever met. She has a special, powerful way of drawing those in pain to her. Underneath the levels of pain and disillusionment, Glenn also had a tender heart. I believe that innerness connected them in a meaningful way. It made me happy to witness that some of what was making Glenn alive again was the person I loved.

I had been working still and we were just a couple of days past the not-so-great dinner. The time had come for Nadine and I to spend time together just the two of us. We packed up the car and headed up the highway to Homosassa Springs. August is storm season in Florida, and there was a tropical storm dancing around in the Gulf of Mexico looking to come ashore somewhere in the Tampa and Saint Petersburg area. I knew about it from weather reports I had seen, and the rain and wind were becoming more intense by the mile as we drove.

By the time we arrived at the lodge, the water levels were rising rapidly and the wind gusts were dangerous. I remember driving in the parking area through at least 10 inches of water. It was bad and getting worse by the minute. We called the front desk and learned the cottage I had reserved was already not accessible. There were a few rooms connected to the main lodge, which were being approached by the rising tide of the storm surge. The owner, anticipating our arrival and worried about us, had an employee open the door to one of these rooms. Nadine and I checked straight into the room.

Our drive time had been greatly increased by the tempestuous weather. It was probably six or seven o'clock by the time we were in the room and wondering what we do next. I had originally booked two nights at the lodge. The night of our arrival I had planned to take Nadine to a small, intimate restaurant with candlelight and red and white-square patterned tablecloths. There, sitting in a corner with light flickering in our faces, I was going to ask her to marry me. Admittedly not terribly fancy, but I had love, the ring, and the girl. I was going to make it work.

The following day we would check out one of the springs and soak in our newly acquired, mutually agreed upon "engagedness." All very simple, but simple has so much to it. The realness doesn't get lost or cluttered up. Focus and emphasis stays fixed and doesn't shoot off in a million different directions. Plus, I was broke.

Now this plan had been blown to smithereens. I didn't know what the heck I was going to do. Here we were on the Homosassa River at this lodge and a tropical storm was right on top of us. Power was out and our source of light was candles the proprietor had supplied. Although visibly concerned, Nadine was being a good sport about everything. Germany doesn't see many violent storms — hurricanes, tornados, or otherwise.

As we sat in the front room of the small suite, I opened the door to the outside. The wind had died down, but the rain was still coming down strong.

I was thinking, "Okay Andrew, what do you do? Do you do it now or hold off? Do you tell her what the plan was? Do you wait to see if tomorrow night is an option depending on flooding from the storm? Great…just great."

Then out of nowhere we heard a tiny, little "Meow." We looked at each other. Then another "Meow." A moment later a tiny, wet, gray kitty cat came into the room. Its little fur was matted down from the water. It wasn't more than nine or ten weeks old. We grabbed a towel quickly and the three of us sat on the floor in the middle of the room to dry it.

As Nadine and I were preoccupied with it, we heard yet another "Meow" followed by a whole chorus of mewing. As we watched, about seven or eight very vocal kitties flooded the room. Just like that we had singing critters all over the place.

I love animals — cats, dogs, horses. As a family we always had something around, but the first animal I called mine was an orange cat from my grandmother's farm, Fuzzy. You have to work with cats for their attention. They don't dish it out for free. I always loved the game of winning a cat over.

Just as Nadine and I were beginning to wonder worriedly where the mother was, she came in as well. The high water had pushed the mother and her brood out of their nook.

So, here we were in the middle of a storm in old Florida. The rain was pouring down and the power had been interrupted. Nadine and I sat in the middle of the room with a displaced family of cats that sought shelter with us. I took it as a sign. I acted.

On the carpet with a bevy of meows and little paws all over us, I produced the ring and asked Nadine Claudia Ortlieb to be my wife. It was such a simple moment. There was a type of meaning that those little kitties and their mother showed up with.

In our hurry to impress, to fit in, to be a part of what is acceptable or expected, often times we trample all over these meanings. They go by completely unnoticed. Not in a million years would I have ever imagined that is how I would have popped the question. I am thankful it happened that way, and I am thankful Nadine's answer was yes. For Nadine the thrust of importance was that I loved her and wanted to spend the rest of my life in her love. Where and how I expressed it was not as important.

She is by no means a pushover, but Nadine knows what she is looking for. When she finds it she is satisfied. Everything else is a bonus. Zero pretense is in her makeup, and that is definitely a love language for me. We still talk about those cats. A storm, cats, and a proposal — sounds like the title to a bad romantic comedy.

The storm passed as one always does, and we bid our cat family farewell. There was still flooding in some areas, but the skies were blue. When we got back to Sarasota both Mom and Glenn were home, and we shared the news. Both of them knew it was coming or at least acted like they did. They both congratulated us. Glenn and Nadine continued hanging out that night, strengthening their buddy status. Nadine was flying out the following day returning to Germany, and Glenn was set to leave in a couple of weeks for Australia.

As we drove to the airport, Nadine and I discussed how her family was going to react to the engagement. They would believe things were moving too fast, or to say in German style, moving too aggressively forward. The United States and Germany is not like a long distance relationship in the same country — say, Florida and Kentucky. We were separated by an ocean and felt it. Our hearts ached.

Sometimes we had both been so sad in our separation we could just sit on the phone or on a video call in silence. It was terribly difficult and both of us wanted it no more. Things were moving fast, and would soon move even faster. We began to focus on ourselves more and more, and less on God. We were looking at each other and not looking at Him.

(From back to front, left to right.) My father, then-Governor Wallace Wilkinson; my brother, Glenn; my mother, Martha; and I in the Governor's Mansion in Frankfort, Kentucky, 1989.

Andrew Wilkinson

My parents at the inauguration of my father for Governor in the Kentucky State Capitol Rotunda, 1987.

Glenn, left, and I at the inauguration of my father for
Governor in the Kentucky State Capitol rotunda, 1987.

(From top to bottom, left to right.) My brother, Glenn Wilkinson; my father, Wallace Wilkinson; my uncle, Gene Rubarts; my aunt, Katherine Rubarts; my uncle, Gary Stafford; my aunt, Paulette Stafford; me; my cousin, Michelle Rubarts; my cousin, Sarah Stafford; my mother, Martha Wilkinson; my cousin, Carol Christ; my grandmother, Lucille Stafford; and my cousin, Myra Stafford. Photo taken in 1986.

"Greenbrier" – home base for the Wilkinson family for many years. My childhood home that, ultimately, my mother and I walked out of and locked the door behind us.

Since I was a kid, our family spent Thanksgiving in New York City. Mom and I in 1998.

Dad, Mom, and I in Palm Beach, Florida, 1993.

Andrew Wilkinson

"The Cousins" — Myra, Carol, me, Michelle, Glenn, and Sarah. Palm Beach Gardens, Florida, 1983.

My family's Bombardier Challenger business jet before the collapse.

Me, aboard First Lady in 1994. Nonetheless, I was "lost" at sea.

Me, Dad, and Glenn in Mexico, 1992.

Mom and her cabin. Leaving behind things like that took things from my mother on the inside that never came back.

Glenn, with Dad and Mom, at his high school graduation in 1988. It is still hard to believe they are gone.

Myra and I today.

Dad and Mom, the way I remember them.

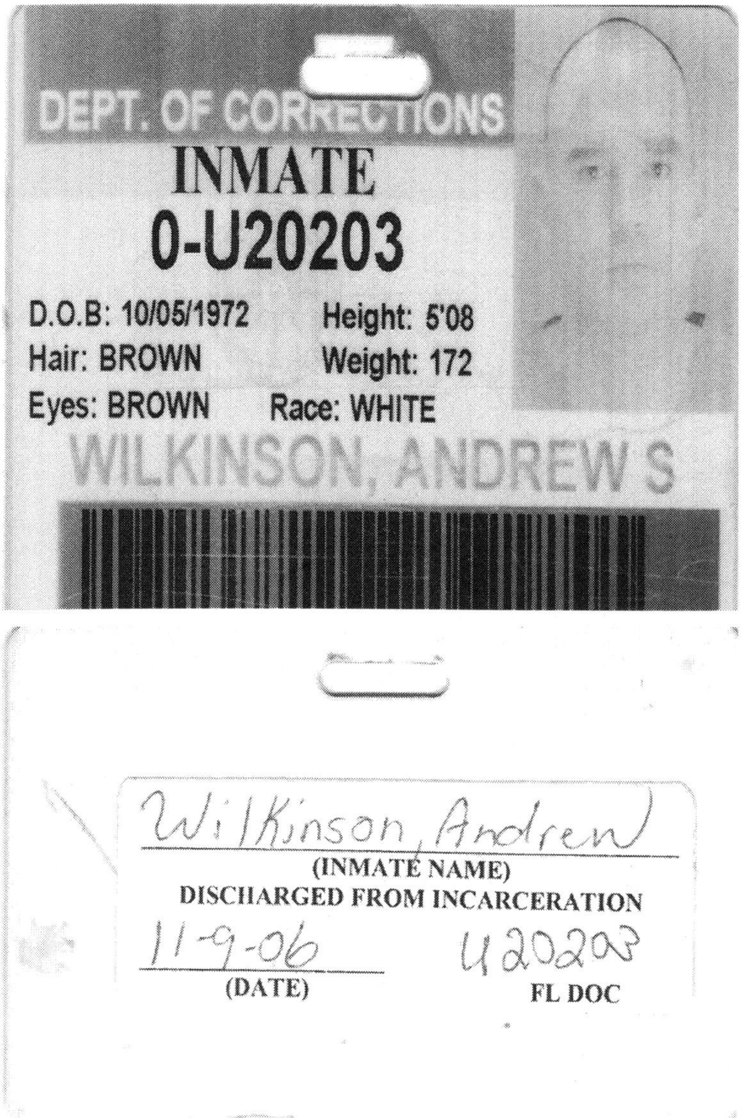

DEPT. OF CORRECTIONS
INMATE
0-U20203
D.O.B: 10/05/1972   Height: 5'08
Hair: BROWN   Weight: 172
Eyes: BROWN   Race: WHITE
WILKINSON, ANDREW S

Wilkinson, Andrew
(INMATE NAME)
DISCHARGED FROM INCARCERATION
11-9-06   *U20203*
(DATE)   FL DOC

My Florida State Department of Corrections inmate badge.

Nadine, Melina, and I in Bensheim, Germany, 2011.

Nadine, Carola (meine gute Schwiegermutter), Melina, and
I. Luisenpark, Mannheim, Germany, 2011.

Me and my German family in 2009 at Weihnachtsmarkt (Christmas market) in Baden-Baden, Germany. From left to right are Melina, Nadine, me, cousin Annabelle, mother-in-law Carola, Aunt Sabine, Aunt Karin, Uncle Ruediger, Aunt Netty, Uncle Eberhard, and cousin Gina.

My brother, Glenn, alive again after years of darkness.
Panama, 2014.

Nadine and I, today, as an awesome team.

The state prison in Carrabelle, Florida where I served my one-year-and-a-day sentence in 2006.

My two "American Girls."

Glenn, Melina, and Ro six days before Glenn died
November 20, 2014 at the age of 44.

Nadine, Melina, and I in a diner in the Blue Ridge
Mountains of North Carolina, 2014.

Melina and I on her first day of kindergarten in the United States, 2014. She was very brave.

"Familie Wilkinson", Siesta Key, Florida, 2015.

Chapter 22

It was September and I had been promoted at my job. Originally just a body carrying a weed eater for 12 hours every day, I was named the crew supervisor. This meant driving the truck to work sites and riding a mower instead of walking all day. In the context of the job it was a huge move up. A couple of weeks after I had been back on the job, I was sitting alone in the shade under a row of trees eating my lunch.

The crew I was supervising had been working together for a while. It was an all-Hispanic crew, and I never could fit in with them. Normally I had no problem at all mingling with other groups or people I didn't know, but these guys didn't accept me. Every day I sat by myself during break. Solitude is something I had grown accustomed to, so it wasn't much of a problem for me. As I savored a bologna sandwich and a pickle, my cell phone rang. It was Nadine calling from Germany.

"Hi sweetheart! How are you?"

Immediately I could hear Nadine crying on the other end.

"Hi Schatz," she answered through broken, crying syllables.

"Schatz" is German for sweetheart or darling.

"Nadine, are you all right? What's going on?"

"It is a something," she said.

I couldn't see her face and I wasn't looking into her eyes, but I knew instantly what she was about to tell me.

"Yes?" I replied.

She paused for what seemed like a half a minute.

Then it came, "Um, I'm schwanger."

"What do you mean? What the heck is swanger? What does that mean, swanger?" I asked rather impatiently.

Then it came in a much more understandable form. "I have a baby!"

And she wasn't talking about a baby that was sitting on her lap and goo-gooing some 4,500 miles away. This baby was in her belly and it was a direct result of our "storm kitties" engagement night.

I was not in shock. In fact, I enjoyed hearing those words after I understood what they were. As is most often the case when a pregnancy begins, Nadine did not start her menstrual cycle on time after she was back in Germany. Concerned, she had purchased an early pregnancy test. After a positive reading, she followed up with a doctor's appointment. It was official.

Nadine was distraught on the telephone in the beginning of the call, and I totally understand that. As a few minutes passed, she understood my relative calmness. I assured her everything was fine. This news was going to have a tremendous impact on whatever our original plans were going to be, but it was manageable.

As I had sat in prison, a man of 34 whose life was by all measures in free fall and dire straits, I had often contemplated my life. Would I lead a productive existence back in the game of life? Would I have a family? Would I have the chance to not fail at something important in life? I had failed so much. Nadine answered many of these questions.

As my lunch break ended, I needed to get back to work. I assured Nadine we were going to be okay.

Just before we ended the call she asked in her German accent, "Are you happy to hear?"

"Yes, Nadine. I am happy to hear."

"I am happy too," she said.

I finished the afternoon cutting grass on my riding mower at a huge mobile home park. I felt very happy. The news that I was going to be a father was wonderful and I welcomed it. There was just one problem with everything. Nadine and I were Christians. Although it is commonplace today among Christians, the Bible teaches sex outside of the marital union is a sin. Nadine and I understood this, and we both had discussed our wishes to honor God and our union by abstaining from sex. We had sinned.

Yes, it takes two to tango. Yes, we were both there. But I was 36 and Nadine was 22. I should have taken the lead for us together on this important aspect of our faith and relationship. The truth is, I had been pretty much the instigator. Even worse, when I for a moment had clarity of thought, I didn't stop us. I failed Nadine with this. And I failed God.

In the early evening I returned home, and my mother was in the kitchen. I joined her as I opened a can of La Croix sparkling water. A very cold can of La Croix after spending all day in the Florida sun is so crisp and refreshing to me. Mom knew that and kept the refrigerator stocked. I wasn't nervous and didn't waste any time. I told her about the call from Nadine.

"I'm going to be a father, Mom," I said rather proudly.

She walked over to me and put her hands on my shoulders and gazed upon me for a moment. Then she too asked if I was happy and glad to learn of the news. I didn't hesitate and replied that I was as she continued looking in my eyes. What she said next is why I loved my mother so much. What she said next revealed the very essence of who she was and how she looked at the world — her belief system, her code.

There was no question about if we wanted the baby and had we thought about all the options. She had no inquiries about how we would support it and where we would live. She didn't have any negative comments thinly veiled with questions of my certainty that I was the father. I only felt love and wisdom.

"You know you have to go to her, Andrew. You have to go to Germany to be with Nadine," she said tenderly.

I nodded my head up and down, "I know, Mom."

Nadine is the only child and her parents have been split up since she was very young. They are cordial and involved in her life. She did have a stepfather for a time, but he and her mother divorced. Although I had been treated with respect, I knew Nadine's family and friends in Germany were skeptical of me and my intentions. Here was this much older American who had come into Nadine's life. What did I want? Why Nadine? Was I going to take her away from Germany? Germans are excessively analytical like that. But I can't say that I blame them. Our relationship was not really normal. Nadine was young, and a pregnancy is a big-time game-changer. She needed to be at home with the people who loved her and where she was comfortable. If Nadine had come to the United States, it would have been a terrible mistake. Mom knew this and so did I. One of the biggest questions that needed to be addressed was settled. I was going to Germany.

I had been to Europe five times before — a couple of times before it was the European Union and a few times after. The first time was in the early 1980s with my family. We traveled to London to board the world famous Venice-Simplon Orient Express that had been restored to its former glory. My father knew the man who had taken the project on. We boarded a dining car train in London that carried us to the English Channel. Once we reached the channel, we ferried across to France. From there we rode the Orient Express into Paris, then through the Alps of Switzerland, continuing to Milan and beyond, finally arriving in Venice.

The journey lasted two days and it was phenomenal. I was 10 years old and even then recognized what a special trip it was. Liza Minnelli was a fellow passenger, and on the first afternoon I ran into her. There was a bit of fanfare around Glenn and me due to the fact we were the only children aboard the train. She was sitting in a chair and asked me to come to her. I didn't know who she was. I went to her and she motioned me to sit in her lap, which I did.

There were news cameras filming and she asked me, "Have you ever heard of murder on the Orient Express, little boy?"

No, I hadn't and that totally freaked me out. She then inquired what I thought of the train.

This is how I answered, "I think it's great. We don't have trains in Kentucky."

What? A day later as we checked into our hotel in Venice, Glenn and I turned on the television and there I was explaining to Liza Minnelli that in Kentucky we didn't have trains.

At a beautiful family dinner one night beside the Grand Canal, Dad gave Mom a very special pair of gold ruby and diamond earrings. They are Nadine's now.

I spent three weeks during the summer of 1989 at Oxford University's St. Andrew's College. For a time my Dad had an interest in some lumber companies with Italian and German partners. He even kept an office in Hamburg for several years. On one occasion Glenn and I, as teenagers, visited the "Reeperbahn" without Dad or Mom knowing.

The "Reeperbahn" is Hamburg's red light district full of lostness and all sorts of indicators of the dire state that is man's dilemma. Certainly it is no place for teenagers, and if either one of them had found out it would have meant big-time trouble.

France is where my mother and I had been when Dad was kidnapped. So, I wasn't a stranger to traveling abroad. But I knew enough to know that visiting and living are two completely different animals. My ticket to "Deutschland" was one-way.

The Book of Exodus in the Old Testament tells the story of how God freed the Israelites from bondage under Pharaoh in Egypt. The Israelites had been enslaved there for over 400 years. God chose Moses to be their point man as He led the way to the Promised Land of Canaan. The 200 and some odd mile trek should have taken only 11 days or so for the millions of freed journeyers. However, due to disobedience, disrespect, whining, and a whole host of other surly attitudes, God denied them. He let them wander around for 40 years in the wilderness before He allowed them to enter the land of milk and honey He had promised to their forefathers.

The moral of the Exodus story and many others in the Bible is that if we only believe and trust in God all things will work out for good. But we make things much harder and worse for ourselves through fear, doubt, and disobedience. We are the ones who introduce misery and hardship into our circumstances, because we are weak in our faith and don't believe His promises to us. In other words, He's got our backs. Things don't have to be so bad. This is absolutely true, and Nadine and I were about to prove it.

It was autumn 2008 and Glenn had left for Queensland, Australia. Everyone was hoping and praying for the best. Maybe to be far away and just a student from the United

States was what he needed. Perhaps he would hit his stride after eight really bad years.

Everyone involved wholeheartedly accepted the decision of me going to Nadine. I gave notice at my job, and Nadine and I began the paperwork process of getting me into Germany. This meant I needed a visa based on the fact I was going to be married to a German woman. It was a document-intense process. I had to submit all sorts of identification, my birth certificate, and wages earned in my jobs prior to leaving just to name a few. Plus, everything I turned in needed to be translated from English to German.

Simultaneously, Nadine started to plan the wedding in Worms. There would be a marriage recognized by the state at the "Standesamt" — the local registry office. Then, we were having a ceremony for ourselves, family, and friends at the church where we met. Things began to be stressful and rushed. On top of all the documentation we translated and provided, there always seemed to be something extra needed that we weren't told about. Or the paperwork was not prepared correctly and was returned for resubmission. And then, of course, there were the fees and costs associated with everything. I had no idea translators could charge so much for their services. Nadine, pregnant and 22, along with her mother, Carola, were handling many details. There was a huge amount of everything happening at once.

Somewhere in all of the craziness the decision was made for Nadine and me to stand in front of the church in Worms and share what was going on with us. It was November, and I flew to Germany for a week. On a Sunday after the service, Nadine and I stood together in front of the congregation to address them. I spoke, and there was a translator to assist me. I explained that Nadine had returned from the United States with more than just a ring, that I would be returning in January to marry her, and we would commence our life together in Germany.

There were about 100 members of the church listening to me. To this day, I still don't know exactly why we did this. As I was speaking, I regretted doing it. Immediately after I finished, we left the stage together and joined the others for coffee and tea. Most came to us offering their support and understanding. I was extremely uncomfortable, and had the feeling everything was way out of control. I told Nadine that I thought it was a mistake, and we quarreled about it. But it was more than just that. We were beginning to realize we had taken on more than we could handle.

The dates for the weddings were set. The first wedding was to be January 21, 2009 and the church ceremony three days later on the 24th. I returned to Florida for the remaining two months.

In hindsight, it is so clear what I should have been doing. I should have been focusing on The Lord, asking for His forgiveness and compassion, asking for Him to draw me closer to Him, and that He would please bring both of us back to focusing on Him. This is the glorious beauty of Jesus Christ. He understands our weaknesses. He forgives us. He became one of us — weak and in the flesh exactly like we are. But He never faltered. He used precisely the same power that is available to every single believer.

I have had countless conversations with unbelievers who say they find it unacceptable that a person could commit many terrible, heinous acts and still be forgiven by the Lord if they accept Him as their Savior while at the same time a "good" person by worldly standards will not see heaven unless they choose Him.

My response is the same every time. They have it backwards because of our human pride. This forgiveness from God is exactly what we must be eternally grateful for. We have all sinned and fallen short of the glory of God. Every last one of us. The Pope, the apostle Paul, Mother

Teresa, our pastor, our favorite Sunday school teacher — all of us.

What the world says is good, or even holy, doesn't come to close to what we need to be in His presence. We are talking about the holiness of heaven and our Creator from days of eternity past. The standards of this world don't cut it. Our brains can't fully comprehend His greatness and holiness, but our pride sure can stand in the way of us ever experiencing it.

Bryn Mercer and his wife drove down a couple days before I was scheduled to leave. We went to lunch together. I had spent a lot of time with them. Nadine and I had spent a few nights with them at their home. We had been to Orlando and taken in a show together. They were so unselfish, and receiving marked just about everyone's experience with them.

Normally, we could enjoy ourselves and have fun together. It was a subdued lunch. I was not myself, and they knew it. They knew I was not strong enough for a voyage I needed to be very strong for. They were also disappointed in me. I know they were. As they dropped me off at home, I got out and stood looking at both of them. I was sad about everything, and they were too. It was not difficult to see that Nadine and I had taken on so, so much. For both of us, the table had been wiped completely clean, and we were starting from scratch in countless areas of our lives.

So January 17, 2009 finally arrived. The day I was to begin a new life. My mother, with a show of pep and enthusiasm she hadn't had since Glenn had left for Australia, helped me get my things together the night before. We talked about her and Dad in the early years. How they endured many lean times before their work paid off. How Dad was always on the floor or in front drumming up business or sales while she was in the back taking care of the books.

She talked to me about commitment and hard work — two fields she was an authority in. She also expressed her belief in me. We held hands and sat at the foot of the bed. We prayed together. I would be seeing her again in a matter of days at the church wedding.

I was moving to Germany with two bags and a suit carrier. My pocket had a little more than two thousand dollars in it. Soon I would be a new husband with a new wife expecting a new baby in a new land with a new language at a new job. And I was embarking on this dramatically new life at much less than 100%. My new, joyful faith had been wounded by the fiasco in the church. My force had been diminished by my own sin. I was not prepared for what was going to be required of me. Plain and simple.

Mom drove me to the airport the next morning, and we said our goodbyes. I always enjoy going through airports when I'm traveling. This is especially true in the international terminals. I have the feeling of being on the move. Like I am going on an adventure. Like I'm alive. This time was no different, and it definitely was a big league adventure. I was true to my form, but there was an excitement apart from the other emotions.

Whether real, imagined, or both I had been living with this "Wilkinson drama" cloud directly over my head for years. I left that nuisance at the airport in Tampa. I was going to Europe, and this meant nobody was going to know who I was. It also meant there would be no phone calls and messages bringing up the past. I could be at the market or in the city and know for certain when I came home there would be no unannounced visitors telling me for two hours about their history with my family.

At the same time, I was thrilled to be seeing Nadine in a matter of hours. To board that plane and feel it thunder down the runway until the wheels came up felt good. No, it felt great.

I got into Frankfurt the following night because Germany is six hours ahead of American Eastern time and the eastward flight over the Atlantic is straight into wind. This is nice flying home the other way, because the tailwind hacks about an hour off of the flight time.

As discussed, Nadine was there to meet me, and it was wonderful to see her. Many times I had and still would ask myself what the heck I was doing. Was I crazy? But I never did ask about Nadine. I doubted the decisions were so rushed and frantic. I doubted our favor in the sight of The Lord at the moment. I doubted myself. I never did doubt Nadine, her heart, and who she was. I sometimes wondered if we had just screwed it all up, if we had put more on top of us than two people can handle.

As I came to her, we kissed and hugged. I felt her belly in the second trimester on my belly. We both looked at each other.

"Ready or not, here we go!" was the emoji for both of our faces. I remember that look very well.

A couple of friends of hers had driven her to the airport. In Germany, like most of the EU, many citizens drive tiny cars for fuel savings and space limitations. They had such an auto, and as we drove about an hour to Nadine's apartment my luggage, Nadine, and I were stacked one on top of the other. Her apartment was in Pfeddersheim. Pfeddersheim was a "Dorf," or village, some a mile and a half west of Worms.

It was the dead of winter in Germany, and it felt like it. The air was cold and sharp. By this time, I had been in and out of the country half a dozen times or more in my life. That night the differences between our countries, conspicuous and subtle, were extra pronounced to me as never before — the air, the water, road signs, electrical outlets, gas heaters, window systems, toilets, kitchen appliances…everything. Germany consists of 16 federal states. The one in which we lived was Hessen. Ironically, the landscape and climate of Hessen are remarkably similar to the bluegrass region of Kentucky.

Nadine and her mother, Carola, had made great progress with the plans for the weddings and everything else that came with them. I recognized immediately how hard they had been working on not only the wedding schedules and details, but also the visa documentation process. Everything was in motion, and although I was thankful for that I did not feel involved.

I am the type of person who is normally very plugged in with issues concerning me. I like to buy my own underwear and socks. I absolutely have to pack my own belongings. I have opinions on just about everything.

As soon as I got there, through no one's fault, I was put on the sidelines. During the first few days, I sat silently through countless conversations others were having in German.

Then after five or 10 minutes of silence someone would say, "Ah, hallo Andrew."

It was by no means a lack of etiquette. Life was going on and there was much to consider and work through. As much as they could everyone was making an effort to help me feel welcome, especially Carola and an aunt of Nadine's, Karin. It was just the nature of the situation. I understood it then and I understand it now in reflection. I was worlds away from even a hint of my comfort zone.

The official wedding took place on January 21. Members of Nadine's family attended. We were married in a small chamber room, and it was very matter of fact. Nadine had a witness. I had a witness. We both recited a couple of sentences and placed the rings on each other's fingers. We received our "Heiratseintrag," which was the marriage record.

Three days later, January 24, was our personal ceremony at the church in Worms. The choir assembled a special presentation for us. One of my favorite songs is titled "In Christ Alone," and they performed a beautiful rendition of it.

Nadine was showing in her pregnancy, but she still looked just beautiful. All throughout the time with Melina in her belly, she looked fabulous. Pregnancy agreed with her, and we all noticed it.

Again, her family was in attendance along with close friends and members of the church. My mother was there. She was my only guest and although we never really spoke of it, I know it created a level of sadness in both of us. She wore a classic, earth tone green and gold suit she found on one of our many afternoon outings in Manhattan through the years. She wore it only twice — for my brother's wedding and mine. It was beautiful on her.

It was the middle of winter. The skies were cloudy and grey with a bite in the air. Everyone was doing the best they could. Through no fault of anyone's, I was feeling pushed. Everything seemed so rushed, because it was. Nadine and I were talking, but we were not communicating. We hadn't really learned to communicate the way two people need to for beginning a life and a family together.

The afternoon after the wedding, we went to a centuries old royal residence and grounds for photos to be taken. It was gloomy, cold, and wet. Mud was on the ground, and as we stood in it, our clothes became wet and stained. The hemline of her dress and my tuxedo pants and favorite ever pair of tuxedo shoes were filthy. Although not ideal, it wasn't the end of the world. Though it was symbolic in nature. What was and should have been beautiful and thrilling was cold, wet, and messy. Nadine and I started our life together this way. Getting to the warmth of what God intended for us was cold, wet, and messy.

One day in the future I will sit down with Melina, and explain to her the hardships her mother and I made for ourselves. We didn't do much right, but we had a deep love that we were going to need to power us through. And it did.

As is customary after the wedding, a dinner party was thrown. Nadine and Carola had orchestrated a nice event for all to enjoy. Aside from the dinner there were toasts, games, music, and dancing. The evening did give me a respite from all of the other emotions I was experiencing.

My mother and Nadine's grandmother were seated next to each other, and seemed to enjoy themselves. This in spite of the fact neither one of them understood a single word the other muttered. There was alcohol served, and some people noticed the amount of red wine Mom was drinking.

At some point during the night, someone became sick in the restroom. Vomit was splashed everywhere in one of the stalls. Some people attending suggested it was my mother.

After the party, I walked her less than a mile to the home where she was staying. She was tipsy. She was also proud of me and sad that she was leaving me the next day. Mom knew that it was going to be very difficult for me there. By her behavior and her clothes, there was no indication she had been sick.

As we live life and then have the opportunity to reflect, we become aware of so many things. Things that carried a tremendous impact, but we were ignorant of its value. As we stood at the door of the home, she took my face in her hands. As water gathered in her eyes, she looked into mine. Then she hugged me gently, reassuringly rubbing her hand in a circle on my back. This was the mother I had always known. I felt so loved and protected standing on that front step in Germany. With the sunrise she would be gone. That was the last time I experienced a moment like that with my mother.

Chapter 23

So, life began in Germany and the differences of my new home from my birth home were jumping out at me everywhere. I believe the United States is extraordinary. Not to be expressed in an arrogant way, but we were born out of something magnificent. Men and women committed to an idea, a hope, of real freedom. They fought and died and sacrificed everything for it. The courage and perseverance it took to create our nation is the likes of which the world has never seen.

American grit is a very real trait, and it is in our genes. I too love the idea of real freedom, personal responsibility, and the pursuit of happiness. All people have far more potential and capability than they are being led to believe these days. It is the government's job to create an environment where folks can stand on their own two feet and provide assistance when necessary. This is America. America was not founded to be a nation where a dependent class was created by the government.

Europeans didn't fight and die for freedom in a new world. They've never really rejected everything that is and gone to a new world to form an entire nation, and this shows in their personalities and culture. Activism is nowhere near the levels of the United States. As long as many of the social ideas are acquiesced, then folks are generally happy. They don't generally cultivate in their children the notion to go for it, dream big, or reach for the stars.

Now, it should be noted that war has ravaged Europe many times. Germany itself has been destroyed twice in world wars. The prevailing attitude of the German people is one of moving cautiously forward — playing it safe. There is also a dose of shame regarding the legacy of Hitler.

Germans are eager to show the world that Germany is not what it was. I empathize completely with that. Therefore a lack of concern for war (justified or not) and social programs being placed at the front of the line characterize their policies and positions. Words such as forbidden (verboten) and must (muessen) are heard in a steady stream of continuation on any given day.

It used to drive me kind of nuts to hear German children, whatever the activity, often exclaiming, "Ich kann nicht mehr."

The translation is, "I can't anymore."

I felt the urge countless times to bend over and look a strange child in the eyes with their parent beside them and say, "Doch, doch...du kannst!" or "But yet...you can!"

Germany is a democratic socialist country. No systems of man are without flaws. However, I am a proud American. I believe in the potential of a free people unhindered by big government. I believe far more in the benefits of creating opportunity as opposed to forced giving and obscene waste of government resources.

Nadine only understood the socialist approach to the world. Understandably, that is what she grew up with. Like in the United States, capitalists and conservatives are not given a fair voice in the European media. Nadine, through what she had always been taught, accused me of being things I was not. It was very hurtful and I struggled to deal with it.

In a glaring example of how systems of man separate people, Nadine, because I said I would rather own my own business than work for someone, concluded I was not a family man. One can imagine how this offended me given the fact I had just left my own country to be with her and our baby.

Today, because she knows me and I her, we laugh and talk about things that would have been the source of an argument when I came to Germany. The German people are not bad people. They are critical, analytical, and can be rigid. However, when you get to know them their walls come down and inside, quite often, you find a sensitive, big heart. The point to be made is the adjustment for me to the German way of life was one more difficult task on an already overflowing plate.

An uncle of Nadine's owned an organic nut, fruit, and vegetable import-export company. Admittedly there are some aspects of life that Europe is much farther ahead of the United States in. Mass transportation comes to mind. Their railway system is modern and superbly engineered. Organic farming and consumption are other areas in which Europe is farther ahead. In Germany the organic industry has been strong for decades. The largest organic trade show in the world, BIOFACH, is held in Nuremberg. I had the privilege of twice attending, and it was impressive.

Nadine's uncle, Eberhard, had realized a measure of success and offered me a job. Nadine's family had applied pressure, but I am sure he also wanted to help his niece. The original thought was that I might be able to bump up the sales performance by creating venues with more English-speaking markets. The folly of this notion soon became apparent. I had absolutely no experience in selling or sourcing organic agriculture. Also, I possessed zero contacts. After only a couple of frustrating weeks of cold calling, everyone agreed my efforts would be better served elsewhere.

So, I started in the production hall. The firm offered raw, natural products as well as processed items. The raw products were sorted and cleaned to extract abnormalities and foreign materials. Nuts were roasted for chopping.

There were hazelnuts, walnuts, cashews, pistachios, and macadamias just to name a few.

I knew nothing of the processes or the machines used in them, and again my ignorance showed itself in short order. On top of this, the day-to-day language was German. The other employees came from a variety of different backgrounds and nationalities such as Polish, Turkish, Slavic, and obviously German. They all understood I was Nadine's husband, and some of them made fun of me. I truly did not know what I was doing. I was the new American in town, and nobody was jumping up and down to help me. I was floundering, and very quickly I was relegated to doing the most basic of tasks. My days included eight, nine, 10 hours sorting hundreds of kilos of nuts. I also filled and sealed jars of herbs and spices.

When I returned home, I was exhausted by the work and the effort of communicating. I felt alienated and discouraged. I have experienced many long days in my life, but those beginning weeks in Germany were some of the longest. I was 36 years old with the life experiences I had had up until that point. Nadine was 14 years younger and pregnant. Her childhood and background were vastly different than mine.

In March, Nadine was hospitalized for almost three weeks due to severe contractions. It was serious, and the doctors were very concerned Melina would come early. I believe today the strain of everything going on was a contributing factor, if not the primary reason. She was on bed rest and literally in bed all day every day.

It is so clear now the pivotal moment this was for me. This was the moment I could reclaim my practicing faith in Christ. It was the time I could show Him, me, Nadine, the church, her family…everyone, that I was the real deal. After work and visiting Nadine, I could have reached out to the church and her family. I could have initiated necessary and meaningful relationship building with others. I could have spent time at the church. I could have enjoyed getting to know her family — my family — better.

But just as I had done all of my life, I veered from the wonderful path straight in front of me and went my own way. My way was stubborn, prideful, and destructive. I was afraid to let others see I was in pain and not as strong as I wanted everyone to believe. I was terrified of anyone figuring out I was a total mess inside. I rejected the blessings God had given me and took matters into my own hands. There was a corner bar in Pfeddersheim only a couple of blocks from the apartment. I had noticed it for some time. I knew exactly where it was. A number of times I had put my coat and scarf on to get some fresh air and just happened to pass by there. Finally, as the same old, tired story goes I didn't pass by. I stepped inside.

I knew what I was doing. I knew the imminent danger this posed for me. I was fully aware I was walking back to the person I was. I didn't care. I was overwhelmed and I needed relief. Some solitude, a stool, and a drink were what I wanted. This is how Satan gets us. This is how the world gets us. Yes, this is how we get ourselves. When we're tired, alone, and vulnerable. Cut off from the flock. The devil was using my distrust and hurt in other believers in a very effective way. I pretty much was rejecting the church in Worms. When someone had anything to say about me, inside my head I was hearing one single word over and over — hypocrite. I don't believe it is a sin for Christians to consume alcohol and absolutely they have every right not to in the name of their faith.

The first miracle of Jesus on this earth was turning water into wine at the wedding reception at Cana in the Gospel of John. We can even assume it was a spiritual allegory, and Christ himself was "The Good Wine." He still was at a wedding party where wine was being served to enjoy and celebrate.

There is a multitude of opinions on whether or not the cause of addiction is a medical or spiritual one. It is both. I believe God is my creator. I was created how He wanted to create me — thorns in the flesh and all. I have an addictive personality. It is spiritual because God didn't make us with anything we don't have the power through Him to overcome. It is medical because if you look into my brain, you will find whatever it is that makes people addicts. It is physically there in cells, nodules, or whatever.

Therefore, knowing what I know and definitely what kind of trouble it got me into, drinking is a no go for me. Drugs are the same. I never did enjoy the taste of alcohol anyway. Substances, alcohol or drugs, were always an escape for me. Always. This is what I was doing when I decided to walk through the door of that pub. It started the same as it always does. In the beginning, it was only a couple of beers during the evening…in the beginning.

Germany has an agreement with the United States and will honor an American driver's license in Germany for a designated time. Nadine's father, Dieter, was very kind and loaned me his favorite car. It was a Volvo station wagon. Over there, they call them a "combi." I experienced the famous German Autobahn right off of the bat, and yes, it is a heck of an adventure. People think the Autobahn is a single or a few restricted access, high-performance highways in the country. Autobahn translated is simply "car track." It is the German freeway system. There was an experimental Autobahn built in Berlin before the ascension of Hitler as "Fuehrer." However, the vast majority of Autobahns laid were during the Third Reich.

There are speed-controlled zones entering and exiting metropolitan and congested areas. But once a driver is out on an open stretch of the highway, he can lay it out. It is common to see a BMW (pronounced BM-veeh), Porsche, Maserati, or Jaguar blistering by at 135 mph or more.

I have always loved motorcycles, and they are also there. I too have pushed the limits on a few ill-advised rides in my time, but I have never flat out exploded like some of the riders I saw.

It is fair also to describe the Germans' detailed attention to safety and procedures. Riders are always decked out in full regalia — helmet, jacket, gloves, pants, boots, etc. Each auto's lighting and signals must always be operational and utilized. Driving violations are extremely costly, and a "Fuererschein" (driver's license) can easily be revoked.

One particular morning I was driving to work and stopped for gasoline. Unbeknownst to me, in Germany it is customary to pump the gas first and then pay for the specified amount. Of course, at home it is the other way around to minimize the occurrences of people not paying. I guess that clearly shows a positive for Germany that they can generally trust their populace more than we can.

Believing I was following the correct course of procedure, I entered the business to say how much gas I needed and to pay. The attendant started speaking to me and pointing outside to the pumps. I did not understand him.

I shrugged my shoulders and spoke in slower English like that is more understandable, "I…would…like…to…"

He became impatient with me. His tone went up a notch as others were in line behind me. I was showing him my money and begging him to take all of it. I began to dance around in my confusion. By this time the man was speaking very sternly and continued pointing outside. I thought he was throwing me out of his store.

"Please, please," I begged, "I'm just trying to get to work. I need gas!"

It was reaching a fever pitch when another customer entered who spoke English. He explained to me I needed to go back outside and pump. Then I would return to pay. It's funny now. It wasn't at the time. As I arrived late to work, I was flustered and already exhausted.

In a matter of months Nadine and I moved to Bensheim, 30 miles east of Pfeddersheim. Bensheim is where I worked and also where Nadine had lived in her childhood and teenage years. She had experienced a degree of unhappiness and difficulty there and was not thrilled about going back.

The members of the church in Worms expressed concern as well. They realized things were going to be tough for us and believed we needed to be closer to the church family that knew us. They were right. Piece after piece, stitch by stitch Nadine and I continued our way away from God and into the wilderness. We both starting pulling back and sinking further into ourselves. I believed Nadine wasn't showing me the love and appreciation I should have been receiving from her for coming so quickly to Germany and taking so many things on. I was constantly mentally exhausted and started to view being home with Nadine as reporting to a second job. Resentment and anger started to build.

Nadine, on the other hand, had needs of her own that I was not even coming close to fulfilling. Focusing on my own suffering, I was not reassuring her and nurturing her. I was not showing her I was happy to be with her. Yes, I had come to Germany and was willing to do all these things, but she wasn't seeing happiness and love in my eyes anymore. This hurt her very much.

We stepped right into the stereotypical mold of the tired, detached man and the upset, vocal woman. I would try to get away, and she would follow. We were both wrong and hurting the other. The breakdown in communication was so severe, I felt lonelier in my few first months there than I ever had in prison.

I looked for Narcotics Anonymous or another type of support group. Bensheim was small and the only thing I could find was an all German-speaking group for teenagers. Nadine and I were not partners by this time. We weren't even friends. We didn't understand each other to the degree that sometimes daily communication happened and sometimes not. Forced, uncomfortable silence became a portion of our daily lives. It was just horrible for both us.

In this time I started to wonder if I had made yet another massive mistake in my life. Nadine sensed this and naturally began to question my commitment — was it to her or to our unborn child?

We replaced discussion of important matters with fighting. Without God in our lives, we continued to hurt each other while languishing in our pain. Words became our weapons, and we used them to slice, cut, and stab the enemy — each other. That is what we so quickly became under the immense pressure we had put ourselves in without the Lord. We turned on each other and it could be vicious.

We fought over each other's family, language, country, and customs. How long would she stay at home with the baby? What immunizations would the baby be given? Where would we live in the future? That is my favorite one because we weren't even dealing with the current days, let alone the future. I was a resentful, angry man bitter at the world, and she was immature, naïve, and only concerned with her own feelings. This is what we had reduced each other to in our minds.

My focus and concentration were so affected that I was struggling at work and learning the language the way I should have been. I had actual physical pain from the stress and tension. Years ago I had injured my shoulder in a motorcycle accident on our farm. Sometimes the dull, throbbing pain in this shoulder was intolerable. I was battling with the nightmares about my father two or three times a week. I completely stopped all forward movement and progress. I was flailing around it seemed at every single thing I did.

I took the train to and from work every day; it was about a 10-minute ride one way. The solitary walks through town to the train station in the early morning and evening became my favorite parts of the day.

Finally, Eberhard called me to say he had a matter to discuss with me and could he come over? Disappointed by my performance at his company, he believed he was not getting enough return on what he paid me for wages. Beginning immediately I would be making fewer Euros per hour than what he had originally agreed to. I can't say I really blame him. Later we would develop a personal relationship that continues today, but then he didn't know me well. As we stood and shook hands, I told him I understood.

In a matter of months my marriage was in shambles, and I was forced to take a pay cut for picking nuts and filling jars. The victor caged and shackled in the back of that prison transport van was nowhere to be found. Instead, an alone, exhausted struggler had arrived at still another low point. The very afternoon I learned my pay would be decreased, I went to the liquor store and purchased a bottle of vodka.

King David of the Old Testament cries out to God in the Psalms many times. He cries out in fear, distress, and seeking protection from his enemies pursuing him. David also cried out, feeling abandoned and forsaken in seemingly hopeless situations. David knew and loved his Savior, but had sinned in going his own way. In response, God allowed David to feel His absence. He pulled back from David, allowing him to experience utter loneliness.

There is so much talk today about how Jesus is love and the church is love. Everything is about only love. While love is a massive cornerstone of who God is, it is simplistic and misleading to leave it there. In love, God disciplines and corrects. In love, Christ commanded the disciples to go out in the world and be fishers of men. He has expectations of us, and they are called fruits. Our salvation is not based on them. We have only God's grace and mercy to thank for that. He is our Father, and we are His children. When we need to learn a lesson, He will teach us, and it doesn't always feel good.

God had given a deep, instantly recognizable love to Nadine and I — a beautiful, wonderful gift. We took this gift and immediately selfishly delighted in each other, placing Him on the bedside table for prayers at night. Other than that, we were too busy with ourselves. Well, just like David, He was letting us remember what life is without Him. Before we know The Lord, it is not a problem for us to not feel His presence in our lives. We are numb in our senses and sensitivities from the sin in our life. The more we sin, the better it feels until we don't even realize we are doing anything wrong. It feels perfectly normal. But when we turn to Him, the Holy Spirit comes rushing in like a raging river wonderfully and lovingly filling us up with God.

Caverns that sat unknown and empty throughout our previous life are suddenly pumped up with life and God. It is miraculous and unmistakable.

So too it is when He pulls away from us, basically saying, "So you want to have Me in your life, but only on your terms? Well, why don't you see how this feels when I turn you over to your faculties and ways of understanding?"

It is a crash.

On May 10, 2009, Nadine gave birth to our daughter, Melina Myra Wilkinson. Melina was born on Mother's Day and was the perfect gift to her mother. Nadine had been to the hospital a day earlier with another episode of major contractions. When they released her, they sent us both home with the advice to pack her bags and place them by the door. The next time would most likely be the big one.

After we got home, I helped Nadine settle in and be comfortable. Then I ran around packing clothes, toiletries, and whatever else a person might need for giving birth. I ducked in and out of the bedroom asking if she needed this or needed that. I felt close to her, and I wanted her to know I was there to play my role. That is to say, experiencing everything with her as much as I could. Her father and mother were not in Bensheim, and if Melina came it was going to be just the two of us.

Sure enough, in the late evening Nadine knew it was time to go and notified me. I got her to the car and then grabbed everything. Off we went. Even though I felt far away from God, I prayed as I drove that car the five minutes to the hospital. Other than the contraction episodes, pregnancy suited Nadine very well. Her belly was big, round, and beautiful. Everyone constantly commented upon seeing her how lovely she looked. One saw the incredible bond between a mother and child even as Melina was still in her stomach. I remember it well, and it was something so nice to sense.

Bensheim is a small town with around 40,000 people. Their hospital is an acceptable facility, but by no means large. It was a Sunday night and the atmosphere was markedly quiet. Even the corridors were dimly lit. As we sat in the hallway not sure what we were doing or what was going to happen next, the only sound we heard was of another woman in labor. They were not pleasant sounds, and the two of us turned and looked at each other with wide eyes. We still laugh about that.

A nurse came and took Nadine from me. I sat with my heart pounding as I heard them preparing the room with her in it. After a few minutes I was allowed in, and Nadine was in position on the hospital bed. The doctor was not there, and the nurse left the room. This is when we turned it on.

We were partners. We were teammates and we were in it together. I grabbed her hand with both of my hands and told her I loved her. I was right there, and I was not going to leave. All of the stress and tension between us was gone. It was replaced with reciprocated trust and love. This is who we were meant to be. This is what God gave us for each other. Why were we messing it up so bad absent giving birth to a baby? We all have seen movies where the expectant father is in the room during birth and he is basically getting in everyone's way and helping nothing. I was determined not to be that. I wanted to give Nadine a picture of calm, steadfast support during the most physically painful moment of her life.

The doctor arrived and immediately both of us felt he was aggravated. It was unnerving. He was short in his speech and rather unpleasant. It was as if he didn't like that we were there — or that he was. It is impossible to know the reasons why, but our hopes to be with a professional, reassuring doctor soon faded. He and the nurse were moving quickly in and out of the room and speaking in broken sentences. Melina was giving notice she would be coming into the world soon and the heavy contractions returned.

Without a spoken word, Nadine and I understood there would be no comfort or support from the professionals there. In those terms it was going to be just us. As Nadine had to start pushing, her pain became intense. She did not take an epidural, and I was impressed by that. She did not want to, but we both agreed if the pain was unbearable to have it administered. She was in extreme pain and I believed she would ask for it, but she never did.

After almost three hours, the doctor impatiently decided Melina was not moving fast enough and took a number of steps to facilitate the process. If Nadine and I could go back to that moment in time we would have stopped him. What was done caused significant pain and discomfort for Nadine for weeks after Melina's birth.

Around four hours into this unfortunate hospital situation Melina showed herself. Nadine was pushing incredibly hard. I was holding her hand and telling her I loved her with my squeezes. The miracle of childbirth is awesome. I gained a whole new respect for life in that moment. Nadine's breathing was controlled, but she was struggling.

At one point she exclaimed out loud, "M-E-L-I-N-A!" As if to say, "Melina, I love you, but don't stop moving!"

Both of us have shared this story with Melina. Melina made herself known, but stalled like she was having second thoughts about leaving the safety and warmth of her mother's body. Once again events were not progressing rapidly enough for our good doctor, and he utilized a tool to grab Melina and pull her out. If labor had dragged on hour after painful hour, there does come a point with modern medical advances that acceleration is acceptable or even necessary. But as Nadine will explain, she still had a lot of fight in her. She wasn't ready for these things just yet. Finally, and I say finally because of the experience, not

Melina, our baby girl was out. And boy did she let us know.

The moments following were some of the most profound of my life. Watching Nadine take her in the arms and observing the immensely powerful moment of a mother, exhausted and filled with love, hold her newborn. Then, as a new father, getting to hold my sweet baby girl. In all of life's experiences it comes down to a few times that showcase what life is about. Childbirth takes its place with authority in that list.

We have a very private photograph of Nadine's face immediately following the birth — the beauty, the exhaustion, the strain, the dignity of motherhood. Wow. Just wow. I was overjoyed with the reality of having a daughter.

Months before when Nadine had told me on the telephone the gender of the baby, my response was calm. "That's great news, honey. But, you know, whatever the baby is I am thrilled just the same." In the privacy of my room, I was bouncing off the walls!

It was around 5 a.m., and I made my way outside to call my mother-in-law. I was so proud of Nadine. I told Carola all about it. It was a special time. After the birth Nadine was dealing with extreme pain, and was not ready to go home for several days. Melina was beautiful and healthy. I used the time to ready the apartment for the homecoming of mama and baby.

The day arrived when it was time for everyone to come home. I had parked the car at the front of the main entrance of the hospital. I pushed Nadine, holding Melina, in a wheelchair to the vehicle. Even though our time in the hospital wasn't pleasant, there was still a sense of security. If something did go wrong, there was somebody somewhere who knew what to do more than we did.

As Nadine and Melina watched, waiting, I struggled to properly secure the baby seat. Minute after minute passed, and I could not figure the thing out. Still tired and in pain, Nadine gave me Melina, stood up, and struggled with the baby seat. I'm holding the baby, Nadine can barely walk and is wrestling around in the car, and people were happening by. After numerous long minutes, the seat was installed and Melina was secure. It was a small demonstration of how much life had changed and that we still had a lot to learn. It was only day #1. We went home.

The joy of such a moment is so large everyone feels it and it elevates itself above everything else for a while. In Germany, they have "Hebammen." These are midwives that offer pre and postnatal care. The midwife assigned to Nadine initially visited her several times per week, and her presence was beneficial. Both Nadine and I were grateful when she concurred with us regarding the activities of the doctor we were discouraged about. She helped Nadine very much. My mother and Glenn had been in touch and things seemed as if they were good on both fronts — in Sarasota and Australia. I returned to work.

I was determined to do something about the pay cut at work. I thought long and hard how to counteract it. My knowledge (or lack of) of just about everything was a negative for me. It was May, and I had been there a little over a year. I kept asking myself what I could do to change my situation. I did the only thing it seemed I could do. I went in earlier and stayed later. I worked on Saturdays and sometimes Sundays. I constantly pulled 11 and 12-hour days. I started asserting myself even about things I wasn't so sure about. Basically, I went for broke. If I was going to fail, I was going to go down swinging.

I started showing up on the loading dock to receive drivers and their cargo. Looking back, I still don't know how I did it sometimes. Drivers came from places all over like

Azerbaijan, Spain, and Russia. In the past I had been afraid to take paperwork into the office due to my inability to communicate. I was taking paper from people and marching into the office with it.

I would stay after hours into the late evening learning the ins and outs of the company's computer operating system. The head of the production department, although German, had spent a number of years in Alaska earlier in his life and spoke English. I took the initiative to start following him around. I started shadowing Eberhard, Nadine's uncle, to get a grip on scheduling and how to make samples for customers. I replaced anxiety with motivation and determination.

Although fruitful on the work side of things, I was returning home extremely tired every night. Saturdays I could normally make it home at a decent time in the afternoon, but I was worn out and impatient for the rest of the weekend.

Production and transportation are fast-paced and rough around the edges. Schedules are changed, orders are adjusted, compromised raw product is delivered, communication breaks down, people are sick, and the list goes on. Some days, the chaos takes over completely. Then after a matter of minutes on a train, I needed to walk in the door to my family and the challenges I was facing there. Where I had seemed to find the right equation at work, it was a totally unbalanced approach and inadequate for home life.

In her mother's belly, Melina felt the unrest that was our lives. She had definitely been negatively affected by the stress. Sometimes she was distressed. She would cry with no apparent remedy that Nadine and I could find. It was not a simple baby's cry, but a guttural, deep cry that kept everyone awake throughout the night. There too were normal baby episodes, sicknesses, and events, but I am convinced part of her was reacting to the absence of general tranquility in the prenatal period. Many nights all three of us were awake until two or three o'clock in the morning and I needed to wake for work at five. This was the lead into many arguments. Nadine was worn out too. It took six to eight weeks at home for her to be fully functional and without pain.

In some of our earlier arguments, Nadine and I said some very hurtful things to each other. Neither of us had forgiven the other, and we carried this hurt and anger with us into each subsequent battle. We argued the same argument over and over again with every new occurrence driving the dagger home a little deeper.

There was a pub, "Kneipe" in German, in the town square that was on my way home every day. I had started frequenting it after work. On one particularly memorable occasion, I was within 150 feet of the apartment and I heard Melina screaming. Without hesitation, I turned around and proceeded straight to the bar. True to form, the hideout I had found wasn't enough by itself for long. Soon I was bringing bottles of vodka home with me.

During this time were the worst arguments of our marriage. A strained marriage was being pushed farther by a screaming baby and my alcohol use. Nadine breast-fed Melina, and the natural mother-child relationship developed very quickly. Neither Nadine nor I had been married or had children before. We learned as we went along, the same as most people do.

In the immediate months following the birth, Nadine and Melina were spending vast amounts of time together. Nadine had been a physical therapist before, but was on maternity leave. Between the two of them I soon began to feel pushed to the edge. I didn't feel like I was an important part of the circle.

There was a time when Nadine and I were standing at opposite ends of a long hallway in our apartment. Melina had only recently begun to crawl and emerged from the bathroom almost halfway down the hall. She saw me and looked at me. Then she turned to see Nadine. Without hesitation, she went to Nadine. I can still remember how the pain felt in my heart. She clearly chose to go to Nadine. She chose against me.

Everyone understands the mother-baby relationship as special and strong. But I had walked away from The Lord. Therefore my peace and understanding were gone. I was tired and I was coldly alone. I had never experienced anything like that in my life when someone I loved had so obviously illustrated my importance to them as less than that of another. It took the breath out of me. It hurt so badly. Of course, Melina didn't choose against me. Our sweet girl instinctively was going to the presence of her mother. However, in the winter season of my cold heart it was an ice storm. I was close to the threshold of not being able to take it any longer.

The truth is Nadine and I weren't frequently getting into arguments. Our life together had morphed into one long argument with some breaks here and there to eat, sleep, and breathe. We had several blowouts that were out of control. There was pushing, shoving, and a kicked-in door. Mothers are mothers, and I had given reasons for my mother-in-law to turn her back on me. She never did. Carola always, while loving Nadine, did her best to try and understand me. I love her for this and today we are very close. One weekend Nadine and Melina had gone to Carola in Iffezheim. I was alone at the apartment after finishing my Friday at work.

In active rebellion to God, without my family, no support at church from a prayer or accountability partner, and no friends, I had succeeded one more time at what I do so well. I was at the complete mercy of my two enemies — the flesh and Satan. Unprotected and alone, they closed in on me. I stood no chance. Miserable and feeling sorry for myself, I drank four beers in less than two hours.

I called the one person I knew who spoke English and told him I was coming over. I didn't think twice as I grabbed the keys and headed out of the apartment. Feeling relieved and anticipating a nice, normal conversation hanging out with someone, I looked over to turn the radio on. Turning my eyes back to the road, I saw the flashing blue lights of two police cars parked hood to hood in the road. It was a roadblock at one of the busiest intersections in Bensheim. It was a trap, and I drove straight into it.

There were two automobiles in front of me being stopped one at a time. Each check by the police lasted two or three minutes. I knew I was going to be arrested. I didn't even turn the radio down or look for a piece of gum. I sat quietly behind the wheel and waited my turn. The officer motioned me to drive forward and I rolled the window down. At that point I knew enough German to understand the question he was asking me.

In English I answered him, "Yes sir, I have."

The car was parked and I was taken to the police station where I was administered a Breathalyzer. I was not twice the legal limit, but I was well over what German law considers sober enough to operate a vehicle. The officers were nice to me and asked me questions about the United States. I would not be losing my visa, but I would lose my driver's license. After processing the paperwork, the police very kindly drove me home. One bright spot, I thought as I stepped out of their car, is that I wasn't spending the night in jail.

However, the bright spot went black before I reached the door to the apartment. As I entered the apartment, with the keys still in my hand, I went for the refrigerator. I started drinking again. I couldn't sober up and face what had happened two hours earlier. I sat on the sofa with a floor lamp burning in the far corner of the room. I was numb.

Between the misery and the alcohol I couldn't feel anymore. I had gone into numbness autopilot. I woke up with the sunlight of the new day flooding the room through the huge window in our living room. Denial and self-deception are hugely powerful. Without much of an internal debate, I decided I was going to go on about my business and pretend like it didn't happen.

That is what I did, until a couple of weeks later a letter arrived from the police detailing what had happened. One doesn't have to use much imagination to understand how disappointed Nadine was. Nothing was ever said to my face, but I am certain her family was wondering how in the heck everything could work itself out at that point.

To tell the truth, my feelings and emotions were shot. I did not stop drinking. I only existed to go to work and provide income for my family. I was not being a good husband, and I was not being a good father. I wasn't even in the same universe of what God wanted for me.

At the expense of my family, I continued the full court press at work. It was much easier. It does not require much effort to be cold, matter-of-fact, and all about business. However, I began learning a lot. My confidence, knowledge, and German all started to grow a little each day. I didn't shy away from conversations or a pushy driver from another country. Although I was not in a position of authority, I was acting like I was. In the bank, grocery store, or on the platform at the train station, I was talking. People I would see every day started hearing something from me, whether they liked it or not. Slowly but surely, I started to open up again instead of being trapped inside of myself all the time.

One day the leader of the production department left work and didn't return. About two weeks later he called Nadine's uncle, Eberhard, to say he was in Austria at his mother's house dealing with personal issues. He said he would be in touch. Eberhard believed him and wanted to help instead of making more problems for him. Eberhard owned and ran the entire company as "Geschäftsführer." That is to say, the leader. His wife, Sabine, was the head accountant or "Buchhalter." Both of them came to me and asked if I could step up my game and fill in as director of production. They would be there to help me.

I was not ready for this, and I think they knew it. But I also believe they saw something in me that allowed them to make that decision anyway. This decision of theirs is what I can look back on in this time and say it was the defining tide-turner. Even if it was only temporary, I was now the "Produktionsleiter." I had gone from sorting through nuts with my hands to running the entire department. My, oh my, how good that made me feel.

I would love to have been a fly on the wall watching some of the morning schedule and production meetings. The whole multitude of the production team members spoke, what I will call "factory German" — German, sprinkled with English and hints of our mother language. It was foundational and got the job done. However, it was certainly not good for detail and beauty. The meetings would sometimes last a little longer than they should have.

I spent a lot of time wrestling them out of habitual, counterproductive activities. They were not laughing and looking at me any more though. I was standing in front of them and authoritatively laying out the business of the moment or day. Personal relationships began to develop. I still think of them often — Victor, Henok, Michaela, Huso, Tomasz, Adam, Melake, and Iwona.

I also had enrolled in a German language course offered by the region's "Volkshochschule" (people's high school). It was two times in the week on Tuesday and Thursday nights. It was two and a half hours long with two 15-minute breaks. I was always strong in the first half, but I would fade in the second due to the previous day's work.

I would yawn or nod off and the teacher would constantly say, "Gute Nacht, Andrew Lloyd Webber!" Meaning, "Good night, Andrew Lloyd Webber!" — the awesome English composer.

There were about 20 students from all over the world in the course with me. This is where I really noticed something. In many places throughout the globe, it is popular to criticize the United States. I heard it all. But it was also the same people who would come back around and listen gleefully as I answered a question they had asked me about the United States.

This time also saw me returning to yet another habit. I started to read my Bible again. Before bed in the evenings I would spend 20-30 minutes or until I fell asleep going through the gospels. I have always said that Luke is my favorite. I like the way the physician and the companion of Paul wrote. His style, I should say. He also penned, with inspiration from The Holy Spirit, the Book of Acts.

Acts had infused me with real power in prison. This is a time when the disciples and believers, only a short time earlier marked by fear and misunderstanding, came forth with immense courage and resilience in the face of colossal adversity. When people ask me about my belief in Christ and what He did for us all I answer them with a question. Do they want me to answer spiritually about what I have experienced in my life or do they want me to respond intellectually? When they desire an intellectual explanation I always go to the Book of Acts.

Before the crucifixion there was a rag tag group of followers that high tailed it at Jesus' arrest in the garden of Gethsemane. After the crucifixion they, as Jesus always had, stood defiant against the Roman authorities and Jewish leaders that threatened them with death and imprisonment. Something with unbelievable power had transformed them.

They had seen the resurrected Lord. They had seen the miracle that Jesus had promised them. He spoke with them. He walked with and ate with them. They were changed. They knew what they knew and nobody was going to tell them otherwise. They weren't believers anymore. They were knowers. The church grew, with Paul and Peter as leaders, from this group of glorious people. They endured it all. All disciples went to their death standing firm on the forgiveness of sins by and the resurrection of Jesus Christ. God bless them.

Only John, appointed by God to write the Book of Revelations while exiled on the island of Patmos, lived long enough to see length of days.

While I say Luke is my favorite gospel, it is just as easy for me to be blown away by the power, truth, and imagery in any part of scripture. In the gospel of John, Pontius Pilate is interrogating Jesus and asks Him simply, "What is truth?" Here, Pilate is beholding The Truth of all time and things. Oh my gosh, what a scene in history is that? Pilate's unbelief blinds him so completely he cannot see The Truth as it stands right in front of him. This is the tragic dilemma of mankind.

Also, when Jesus is hanging on the cross after willingly suffering brutality we can't even fathom, and he proclaims, "It is finished." Are there three other words in the history of man that carry as much meaning as these? Indeed, it is sometimes difficult for me to stick to one part of scripture because I like to picture all of these scenes in my mind.

Another one is The Lord explaining to his proud of themselves followers not to get too big for their pants. Seventy of them had returned from casting out demons in His name and were feeling pretty good about themselves. To place them back into the proper perspective, He reminded them He was there watching Satan fall like lightning when God expelled him from heaven. I can't even imagine!

For those of you wondering how I fell back to drink alcohol after coming to The Lord, my answer is simple. The awesome apostle, Paul writes that if anyone is in Christ he is a new creature. New things have come and the old things have passed away. In that statement everything hangs on the very key two words "in Christ."

It is not enough to one day say we accept Jesus as our Savior and then all is good. We must go to Him. We must include Him in our daily lives. The relationship has to be built on prayer and willingness to follow Him. Not perfection, but a sincere willingness that goes directly against our nature, our flesh.

Before Germany and in Germany, I had not followed Him. Christ tells all of us who are weary and heavy-laden to come to Him. Give Him everything, take His yoke, and learn from Him. In return we will have peace and rest that surpasses all understanding from The Holy Spirit.

I love to pretend how strong and capable I am. I love to show how much control I have over things. I took absolutely everything and placed it on my shoulders. I tried to carry it all. And I failed.

People think that Christians are supposed to be perfect. Quite the contrary. We know that we are far from perfect. We know that we need help. In fact, we cannot live the life we are supposed to on our own. We must submit and let The Holy Spirit guide and hold us up.

I heard a sermon the other day from our pastor that justification in Christ is immediate when we accept Him, and sanctification is a process going forward in our walk with Him. Me being called back to the Bible was a part of my sanctification. The Holy Spirit was tugging at my heart. I had grieved Him enough and He was pulling me back. Thus, my sanctification began again.

I was reading my Bible, and Nadine was reading hers. Nadine also began earnestly going to God with all of the problems we were experiencing. Life began to calm down. As parents we learned, and home life actually started to take shape. We started to understand each other more. So many of our arguments had been about misunderstandings. Melina became a little bucket of sweet and happy most of the time. Time together was more about pictures, planning to paint her bedroom, and firsts.

A partner was taken on at work that significantly increased our output. They were a company out of Switzerland that processed macadamias. Their product specifications were serious. They sold to world famous chocolatiers in Germany and French ice cream producers. In other words, we had to step up our game.

I accepted the extra responsibility with eagerness. I desired so badly to showcase what I was capable of. The two men who ran the Swiss company had personalities from opposite ends of the spectrum. Both of them had high expectations and were infamous for an ambitious production schedule. They were equally as infamous for coming to me with new and additional orders once we had set our production schedule. I learned the fine art of keeping flexibility organized during this time.

Chapter 25

Mother seemed to be doing well in Florida, and Glenn in Australia. When I talked to her, she was much more herself than she had been in years. She and her friend were going out for lunch and dinner throughout the week. The sense of humor was there and I could tell that it was directly related to the fact I was in Germany and Glenn was in Australia. Mom needed a break from us. Both of us.

I was good with Mom and we were whole again, but I was a man and needed to be out from under her feet. Glenn was not whole and Mom had gone along with Australia just to get him out. Her hopes and prayers were hanging on the fact that something would turn around for Glenn down there. Glenn had written letters and emails to people relaying how well things were going for him in school. He loved it in Australia, and it was exactly what he needed. Everyone was in a state of suspicious acceptance to hear such good reports from him.

Then one day the phone rang. It was Mom calling. She was beside herself and distraught. Glenn was not in Australia anymore. Glenn was sitting in the Fayette County Detention Center in Lexington, Kentucky. A half a world away from where he was supposed to be. He was in jail in our hometown.

Apparently, he had been in Lexington for several weeks and had been bouncing around staying with different people. The rental car company he had a car from reported it stolen when he had not returned it on time. The police had located the car in a hotel parking lot and then Glenn in one of the rooms a few minutes later. He had no money to pay the hotel bill and was close to being homeless. The whole ordeal had been reported on in the media. His mug shot was posted everywhere and it was devastating how bad he looked.

I have tried to imagine how my mother must have felt learning of those developments and seeing that photo. I can't. I can't imagine what that moment was like for her. To see, to learn, to know yet again that another God-awful situation had publicly unfolded.

Glenn had, in a matter of months, completely messed up his opportunity in Australia. He had blown through his resources and was suspended from school. Glenn had qualified for financial aid, so that was a huge problem and ultimately his student visa was revoked. He knew he could not just go back to Mom's.

In desperation he sold everything he could to get enough money to fly to Lexington. There he was going to try and work everything out. Perhaps he thought he could get his hands on some more money. I think of him, my older brother, on that plane flying for 20 hours. The scheming and lies he was concocting to explain the unexplainable. The darkness and deceit he must have been rehearsing over and over in his head. How alone he must have felt. Like an animal gnawing at its limb to get out of steel jaws. How I wish I could have somehow been with him on that flight. I would have hugged him. I would have held him.

So, here Glenn was in jail in Lexington. Australia was an afterthought. My mother could see clearly where his next stop was going to be when he was released. She did not bail him out. It was not so much tough love. She could not bear the thought of having Glenn back in her home the same as before. She also believed, at that point, Glenn could not make it on his own.

There are countless parents and loved ones who have faced this horrendous dilemma. It is so easy to sit back, look at a situation like this, and say what should have been done.

The reality is worlds more difficult. Enabling is like a prison for the enablers. It is misery and pain galore, but it is somehow better than having to bury someone. Thus began the slow, tortuous decline for my mother that would be her road until the end.

Glenn was incarcerated for around 90 days. The theft charges for the rental car were lessened to some type of misdemeanor by the company it belonged to. He was released, and a dear friend and former employee of ours took him in for a couple of days to feed and clean him up. Then she drove him to my mother in Sarasota.

Everyone knew the whole Australia situation was smoke and mirrors. But hope was piled upon hope that it was the shove Glenn needed out of the nest to fly. Still, no one was quite ready for it to end like it did. So suddenly, dramatically, and back to square one.

As the bottom had fallen out for Glenn, life was continuing to improve for us in Germany. I was more professional at my job. I was managing everything much better. Therefore, I wasn't bringing it home with me nearly as much. Production and transportation will eat you alive if you let it. There is a ton of stress involved on a daily basis. I had learned how to go home and be with my family. Work will be there waiting for me tomorrow.

In the Gospel of Matthew, Christ Himself teaches us not to worry about tomorrow. First, we always need to seek His Kingdom and the rest will be added to us. In other words, tomorrow will always have its troubles. We must stay in the present and focus on what matters.

I had a moment while I was at home by myself one day. I actually went to the life size mirror we had in our bedroom.

I basically looked at myself with disgust and said out loud, "Andrew, what are you doing? Stop drinking alcohol. You are better than this, man. Come on! Come on and get it together. No more drinking for you. Look what you have. You have life. You have a family. God will help you. So, let's go. That's it."

And that was it. I stopped drinking.

Storms will pass. I have endured a fair share of them and they always do. Indeed, I have gone from seasons of them to other seasons of them. The key, the trick, is to hang on when they are right on top of us. When there is no end in sight and the cold, dark wind is blowing, we have to take refuge in God. All the attributes of Him can be discussed for eternity, but the one that has consistently pulled me from the brink is His understanding.

I was in the Bible pretty much every night and other times throughout the day. Proper perspective flowed into me. Nadine noticed the difference and she was reading hers as well. We both had had enough of what life had been for us. We knew that we loved each other with an extremely special love. I think most people would have called it quits a number of times in the beginning for us. We stuck those times out and, today, I am very proud of that fact. We learned a lot about each other in our storms. Knowledge that serves us well today in our marriage.

There is more to Christian life than reading the Bible, but it is the place to start. Its power as a catalyst for change in a life can never be underestimated. Plain and simple, the Bible shows up with power and pushes other things we have held high on a pedestal out of the way.

Whenever I am feeling sorry for myself, I need not look any further than the life of Jesus. This world is super saturated with statements of "me, me, me" and "now, now, now." He came here willingly to understand us and use the same power we can to endure until the end. Today, people quit, they whine, they lie, and they become a victim. Not

Jesus. There has never been a real deal like Him. He came with a mission. He never deviated even though He knew full well the fate that awaited Him at the hands of man. In the garden, He could barely function from the knowledge of what He was about to suffer as He prayed to The Father.

Show me someone like that today. Show me someone like that ever. He took it all the way. And He loved all as He took it there. Absolutely, He alone earned His place as King of Kings and Lord of Lords.

So, our lives separately and together were elevating. I settled into my role at work. I never did necessarily love the work I did. I was in a warehouse all day every day. The same machines surrounded me hour by hour. Trucks and their normal problems showed up at the ramp continuously. I yearned for more human interaction.

However, the blessing was I learned how to learn. I learned how to adapt. I learned how not to give up. I learned to appreciate a job or task well done when I was the solitary soul that knew what I had done. Yes, there was a time I was ridiculed openly, and the only one who believed in what I was doing was me.

I persevered and many times I thought about Dad and would he be proud of me? It was never my objective to become fluent in German, but with that said my ability to understand and communicate became very functional. Today, with a little more work I certainly could be fluent. If you found yourself in Germany and needed someone to help you, I could get you wherever you needed to be. And throw in some helpful tips along the way.

We started exploring, and went to places like Frankfurt, Mannheim, Darmstadt, and Heidelberg. On one of my voyages back to Germany after Nadine and I had met we found Heidelberg. It is not hidden and, for sure, is well known, but we found it for ourselves. Both of us loved

Heidelberg. Situated on the Neckar River in southwestern Germany, it is home to Heidelberg Castle and the oldest university in the country — still going strong with about 30,000.

However, Heidelberg is much more than an old building and a school. It is Old World charm, romance, and beauty at its best. I always found a sense of mystery and nostalgia when we walked the gorgeous fountains and squares. Nadine and I walked arm in arm as we strolled through the "Altstadt Marktplatz" and across the "Alte Brucke." We would sit for coffee or tea and watch the bicycles streaming around town with students and tourists on board. It was there that we separated from everything that seemed to separate us. Without question, memories were made in Heidelberg.

Melina grew and grew and was becoming a little person from the wrinkly little sack of a baby. I never had a problem caring for her. Changing her diapers and washing her were a chance for me to get in on the action. Indeed, a lot of the bonding that shaped our relationship later happened as she lay on her back looking up at me. She was like a little bug. Her little arms and legs in constant motion like she was trying to flip herself over, but never could. There was nothing like it when she would look at me and smile as I smeared some salve or lotion on her.

But the real bonding came as she became around two years old. Then she was very mobile and we could communicate. It was quite funny, actually. Melina was born in Germany, so her mother tongue was German. She was a perfect little practice partner for me. I learned much from the children's books and stories I read her.

Nadine, on the other hand, wanted to improve her English. So, we often had this smoothie of a language going on at our house. In German, Germany is called Deutschland and the language is Deutsch. Therefore, we called our Wilkinson family language "deunglish."

Months passed as we walked together further down the road of being a family. A sense of trust replaced the corrosive and toxic, hurtful things we had said in the beginning. Nadine's family, especially Carola, were thrilled and things really began to fall into place. We were getting to a place I knew we could be, and I was starting to feel whole. It was great.

However, I knew what the situation must be like in Florida. When I talked to Mom she would over and over again tell me how well Glenn was doing. Everything had happened in Australia and that was that. Now he was in Florida and going to enroll in school again. Also she said, he was helping with chores and around the house all the time. She only gave me her prepared "talking points." Anything outside of them she was never willing to discuss. I never would hear from Glenn himself. Always the reports would come through Mom.

As the weeks went by, I noticed a clear shift in her demeanor. For some time it seemed she was not drinking anymore. Or not drinking nearly as much. But the thick tongue and slurred words had returned to our conversations.

Sundays at 16:00 hours (4:00 p.m.) German time was our standing weekly appointment to talk. More and more, our conversations began with what she wanted to tell me or spend her time on. Pretty much the same as the week before. Naturally, I was always excited and eager to talk about how good things were in Germany. There was a clear lack of interest across the Atlantic Ocean on the other end of the line. One word responses or sounds such as "uh-hmn" were pretty much the extent of her participation in the conversation. It hurt me to hear her. But I never became angry. I always had a sound understanding of why Mom had become so and the choices she made. She had been burned badly and I too had thrown fire on her. I always extended my unconditional love and understanding to her.

Chapter 26

We had begun a new year, and it was 2012. In Germany the tide had turned. Nadine had returned to work part time as a physical therapist. We had a "Tagesmutter" (day mother) for Melina we were happy with. The stress from my work was not grinding me down as before. A structured, real life had formed in and around us. Nadine began to show herself as the prayer warrior of our group and I continued reading every day in my Bible. We needed more, but this was sustaining us.

Our lives together were bearing fruit. I did not feel as alone and my communication skills were greatly improved. Therefore, I participated more in conversations and others began to learn about and understand me more. I know that both Nadine and I numerous times had considered throwing in the towel. I know too that both of us thank God we did not. We have put so much of ourselves into our marriage. So much that neither one of us were willing to quit on the other.

I know it sounds crazy to say that I am grateful we struggled so incredibly like we did. Today we are even more committed to us. Nadine and I will look at each other and still see that love we felt that autumn day on the park bench. That love would not and did not let us down. That love was a gift from God.

Mom's struggles at home became more and more evident. Seldom did I hear any semblance of happiness in her voice. I rarely talked with Glenn. The thought of returning home began weighing heavy on my heart. To be with Mom and support her. To let her see her only grandchild grow. To help my older brother. Somehow, some way Glenn had to change things. I knew where he was and how long he had been there. He was in serious danger. No, he had been in serious danger for a long time. I was in the world and alive. Maybe, just maybe, Glenn could see this in my life and decided he wanted some for himself.

I went to Nadine and expressed my thoughts of going home. She understood without too much convincing how concerned I was. She also believed, as I did, taking Mom's only grandchild to her and letting her participate in the growing up process could provide much needed light again. We never discussed it, but I think Nadine also thought about my well being if something tragic came to pass with Mom or Glenn and I was in Germany.

We agreed to plan and save our resources for a return to the United States. As earlier stated, Nadine is an only child, and her family was not exactly thrilled to hear the news. The potential reality of her leaving understandably shocked them. However, we had made our minds up. That was the plan and we were sticking to it. We applied for Nadine's green card. I know initially they were hoping that somehow our strategy would be thwarted. As weeks, months, and a couple of seasons passed, however, it became increasingly clear our determination was solid. So, the attitude transformed from one of hesitation to acceptance. This is a natural progression. I understood it. When this happened I was very happy for Nadine because I knew she was dedicated to our decision no matter what.

After much round tabling and looking at the calendar we put something together. The three of us would fly together to Florida in December 2013. Nadine, Melina, and I would spend Christmas together and with Mom and Glenn. On the first day of 2014 Nadine and Melina would return to Germany, leaving me behind in the States. I would have four months — 120 days — to set up shop. That is get a job, find a place to live, buy a car, find a school and a doctor, secure health insurance, and engage in countless other activities vital to success in our new home.

The "man-provider" gene is strong in me. It comes straight from my father and I cannot deny it. Maybe sometimes it is a little too much. Nonetheless, I jumped at this opportunity to prove myself to my wife and child…and myself.

There was one vital piece of negotiation that emerged. Melina had decided that she would require something. In exchange for leaving her friends in kindergarten, she would need acknowledgement of her sacrifice. It would have to be in the form of a furry little critter. A kitty cat would suffice. She was clear. It was not to be done after her arrival. She expected to arrive at her new home with a kitty cat inside of it waiting for her. Nadine and I agreed and the negotiations were final. It was full steam ahead for Familie Wilkinson.

During one of our Sunday conversations, I told Mom what we were doing. We were coming to the United States. I was not so shocked to ascertain a bit of ambivalence in her response. She said it was great and was happy for me, for us. Those were her words. Her voice told me something else. There was no excitement. Just flat.

A few days later, she called me back and wanted to talk about a concern Glenn had. Was I sure coming back was what I really wanted to do? Had I looked enough into the possibilities for me to support my family? Due to my four-time convicted felon status would it be possible for me to secure the work I needed? It might be better for my family to stay in Germany.

That phone call was devastating. My father was a fighter and always believed. My mother was right there along with him. My brother had the same blood I did and it was supposed to be full of against the odds fight. I knew then I wasn't dealing with the mother and brother I always had. I wasn't sure what was waiting for me in Florida, but I knew it was nothing like what I had known. There were two different people there.

Ironically, as the time neared to return to the United States I was taking stock on Germany and what it had done for me. It was more difficult for me and Nadine than I ever had imagined.

In prison I was forced to deal with the person I had become and how I had destroyed my life. Prison was structured and distractions were limited. I could do the "book" work on myself. Germany was altogether different. What I had learned and faced about myself I had to put to the test. And Germany was a test. A very hard test. In the process I stumbled, but I did not give up. Neither did Nadine.

The man I am today was sculpted in Germany. I am still being chiseled, but the recognizable form began there. It was, for me, the hardest and the best thing I would never want to do again. In many ways Germany was more difficult than prison. That statement is a reflection on my time, circumstances, and experiences there. Not the land and people of it.

Our departure time of November inched closer and closer. Autumn arrived and I received a phone call from Mom. Her mother, my Mom Stafford, had passed away at the age of 92. In the course of a decade I had missed the funerals of several important people and family members. I was not willing to do that again. I made hasty arrangements to return to Kentucky. I flew out the next day.

In Lexington, Mom and I stayed with my Aunt Kathy and Uncle Gene. When I saw my mother, I was taken aback. She appeared malnourished and her walk was not a healthy stride. Rather a beleaguered shuffle. She appeared 15 years older than she was. My worst suspicions were confirmed.

The day before the funeral, Aunt Kathy pulled me aside and asked if I would be willing to speak at Mom Stafford's funeral. Me? Was she being for real? By that time, everyone at home knew what life had been like for me. The struggles, drugs, prison…calamity after calamity. That moment was of major importance for me.

I felt like a man who had been restored with his family. Indeed, the people of Israel had sinned against God over and over again. In Psalms one can find many examples of the people asking God for restoration. Restoration to Him, for sure. I couldn't help but feel this applied to me with my family just the same. She might as well have been robing me and putting a ring on my finger. I was the prodigal son. Aunt Kathy has no idea how grateful I am to her for that. She could have asked 10 other people who declined. It didn't matter at all. She asked me. She was willing to place her trust in me.

Mom Stafford was a fervent Christian, and we all understood she was in glory with The Lord. As she had gone on to eternal life I took another step back to life in this world. I consider it the highest of honors to speak of someone and their life at a funeral or memorial. I'd prayed and hoped my grandmother would be pleased as I spoke of her. God gave me very clear thought that day as I remembered the grandmother that I had many memories with as a child and young man. Life had torn me away from her. I knew speaking, as she watched and heard, that she had forgiven me.

It was October, and I returned to Germany to prepare to return to the United States. At work I began the dedicated teaching of my responsibilities and duties to Henok, my second hand. The reality of my leaving began to really set in. Although I knew I had other roads to travel, I was feeling the sadness. I had grown close to the people there. They were good, hard working people that I had forged relationships with. They had seen me at my best and at my worst. Somehow they still held me in high esteem. I held them also in high esteem and continue to today.

All countries and cultures have customs people not from there find peculiar. In Germany, when one has a birthday or a send off, it is customary for them to supply the cake or other items to be enjoyed by all. Eberhard and Sabine informed me of the date of my going away party at the office.

Sure enough, I showed up on the designated day with nothing but a healthy appetite. Sabine, who I had shared several very personal conversations with, was kind enough to quickly throw together something to eat. I was thankful to them for the undeserved chance they had given me. I spoke of my hope that I had served them well. With the others, memories and stories were shared a final time. I was sad to leave those people, but it was time to go.

Finally, the days came right before our departure. It was late November 2013. Nadine, Melina, and I drove to Carola's in Baden-Baden to stay a few nights. I left in two days and they were leaving later in the week. Nadine and Melina were returning to Germany after the New Year. They would live with Carola while I worked my list for 120 days. In a loving, supportive way Carola and Nadine's other family members were telling us that if things didn't work out in the United States we could always return. We would have a home in Germany.

I knew things were going to be okay. I was going home and bringing my family. I was fit and strong and felt good. Nadine was confident in our decision and that was so critical. As I do often, I looked at her and thought what a wonderful wife I have.

Early my departure morning, we all drove to the airport. I was flying out. Nadine and Melina were following in several days. Goodbyes are always sad. In prison I had to face the truth. I decided I was going to fight back. I accepted Jesus Christ as My Savior. Germany taught me who Andrew was…the man. When I look in the mirror I know that person. I know how to face down fear and get back up because of Germany.

The Apostle Paul mentored a young man named Timothy. In the epistle by the same name, Paul instructs Timothy that God did not give us a spirit of fear. Rather, a spirit of love, power, and of sound mind is what He has freely given us. As is normally the case on a flight crossing the Atlantic, I became restless.

As I walked the aisle in the large, dark cabin of the airplane, I was in prayerful thought. I was not afraid. God had taken fear from me. I didn't know what exactly the future held, but whatever it was I wasn't afraid of it.

In the United States, Glenn and my mother were at the Tampa Bay airport to drive me home after the flight. Again the sight of Mom was painful. The level of thinness she had reached was extreme to the point of her clothes hanging off of her. She looked old and tired. There was no warmth in her brown eyes as all of us had always known. Glenn was detached and politely asked some obligatory, general questions about my flight and the change in weather. Both of them were pale white.

Basically, I sat in the back and got my first close-up of Glenn, in the driver's seat, and Mom, on the passenger side, and the situation. They spoke short to each other and argued about directions. A couple of times I just sat in the back and listened to them while they ignored I was there. They talked like they were on a ride to the post office. Not like they had just picked me up from living out of the country for five years.

When we walked into my mother's house in Sarasota I felt the isolation. I could literally feel oppression, pressure. It was not a happy home. No life was detectable, only existing. Glenn headed directly back to his room on the far left side of the house. Mom hovered between the kitchen and her bedroom on the far right side. There was no show of happiness I was home. I knew this was not time to be selfishly in pain. I even knew it wasn't personal from either of them. Still, it was a blunt force pain. I cried that first night back.

The Book of Romans tells us the Holy Spirit will intercede for us and will pray with moanings too deep for words. In other words, He knows what we need to pray and what is in our hearts sometimes better than we do. I was thankful for this as I prayed in my bed.

Returning home to my mother and brother in such shape was sobering. Their relationship was dysfunctional and Glenn was being enabled. He was overbearing, and Mom didn't have the power to deal with him. I recognized Mom was a miserable prisoner in her own home.

I was awake a couple of times in the night to use the bathroom and to get a drink of water. I noticed light from the computer screen and television through Glenn's window paned bedroom door.

In the morning I made coffee alone as the others slept. I went to the beach to work out and swim. The water was chilly, but I like it that way after a nice sweat in the sun. Even on the first day I found myself not wanting to return to Mom's house. Glenn finally did stir around three o'clock in the afternoon. He had enrolled again in school and was taking online classes. They didn't communicate unless they had to.

A few days passed and it was time to drive to Tampa and pick up Nadine and Melina at the airport. This was my chance to talk with Mom alone. I would tell her how everything was going to be all right. I was home and felt strong. I would find a good job or get something going. I was going to get in the game. Good times were bound to come along again with hard work and God. Glenn would see me out in the world and be motivated to do the same. I would help him. Nadine and Melina would also rub off on him in a productive, positive way. Absolutely everything was going to work out.

I was a little boy again high in a tree. "Mom! Mom! Look at me! Look how high I am! I can go even farther! Do you want to see?" I exclaimed.

She would answer, "Oh yes, I see you sweetheart. Look at you go! You are so strong and brave. Just be careful and don't fall!"

I longed for this mother. This mother was not there anymore. The person I was talking to didn't care one way or another as she watched the passing gas price signs in the window. On that drive I resigned myself to the knowledge that Mom was gone. The mother I had known all my life and the Martha everyone else knew was only a memory. In silence, I accepted this as I drove north on I-75 with only the headlights in front of me to look at. We picked the girls up at the airport.

Once the four of us were back at the house, the conversation elevated somewhat. Nadine and Melina generated more chatter than I had. I was okay with it. Just to have some sense of normal conversation was such a relief.

Glenn seemed to come alive with Nadine and Melina. He genuinely had a heart for both of them and they for him. I could see it. What they provided him with he needed desperately. He was overweight, smoked, and did not exercise. In fact, he had transformed into a hermit. The functioning teeth in his mouth only numbered around seven or eight. Glenn was severely depressed and was only enrolled in school to prolong his inactivity in the real world. He had offered an elaborate explanation to Mom about what had happened in Australia. I knew it was not the truth. I also could recognize he believed his own lies.

Glenn was very sick. He had lost his ability to naturally interact with others. Other than two or three very short stints, over 10 years of unemployment and focus on the past had rendered Glenn listless. Repeatedly he had taken my mother's credit cards and pawned some of her belongings. He did not appear to be using illicit drugs.

However, he had many prescription medicines. Glenn was skilled in representing situations a certain way so doctors would initially follow suit with the recommended medication. When the professional figured out his game, Glenn would find another one.

Often he would repeat the same strategy he, Mom, and I should have used with the creditors after Dad had died. According to him, we could have still walked away with millions. It was not connected to reality. We were out-lawyered, out-gunned, and out-resourced without Dad. It was a blessing how we ultimately did get out. Glenn could not live in anything but the past. He believed the best of his life was behind him. How very tragic. Mom, on the other hand, did not dwell in the past, but she had no power left for going forward.

As I looked to the left at him and the right at her I saw how they both still needed Dad. Dad had been gone for 11 years. It was just me there. I didn't even have a job yet. I would be lying to say I never felt completely overwhelmed in those first days back as I realized where Mom and Glenn were. I still looked at the three of us and wondered at what had become of us all — Dad, Mom, Glenn, and I — what had happened to our family. Dad gone. Mom and Glenn in total disarray and consumed with serious afflictions. Much water had gushed under their bridges and catastrophic levels of flooding were happening in front of my eyes.

Then there was me, a convicted felon and former state prison inmate. I have no description for the sad heaviness. Knowing things from afar is vastly different than being immersed and understanding. I was immersed and I understood. Being back from Germany and coming to terms with these very hard truths was profoundly difficult. It was all way too much for me. God was the only one with the power to get me through. Alone I stood no chance.

It was a blessing that Nadine and Melina were there for the holidays. Although his schedule did not change, Glenn enjoyed their presence. Still very much in his shell, he would at least poke his head out from time to time. Whether it was watching cartoons with Melina or discussing global current affairs with Nadine, it was something other than the day-to-day monotony he experienced with Mom.

Mom took no visible joy in anything. Melina, her only grandchild, failed to produce pleasantness in her. Those were strange days. On one occasion Mom was particularly offensive in something she said about Nadine and Melina being there. I defended them, and I did it in an ugly way. She needed to hear what I had said, but it was another reminder of how things were.

On Christmas morning, Nadine, Melina, and I were the only ones by the tree and presents from Santa Claus. Melina, thrilled the cookies she left were gone, was five years old. She could definitely sense that something was amiss. Although it was a long time, I was ready for Nadine and Melina to fly back to Germany for four months. I needed the process to start. Sitting around over the holidays and watching all of this was borderline brutal for everyone involved. When they returned on May 1, it would be so much different and better; I knew it.

On January 1, 2015 the girls flew back to Germany. At the airport, I was particularly proud of Nadine. We were in sync about everything going on — their visit, Mom and Glenn, the weirdness and the sadness, everything that we had to get done.

It was not a mushy goodbye. It was a grab your face and look you in the eye goodbye. It was a long, firm hold goodbye. It was a "We're in this together, let's do this" goodbye. Melina was strong too. She felt what was coming from her parents. I appreciated that drop-off from both of them so much. That partnership I felt when we said goodbye is what I had fought to save my marriage for. I'm pretty sure it's the same for Nadine. My mother, in the car watching, saw what we were saying to each other without speaking.

As I was in the car buckling up she remarked, "That was a good goodbye," while she patted my leg.

"I know," I said, thinking of the reflection she might have been having on her own life and years long gone by.

In little, brief moments Mom could still show me she was in there somewhere. I took it with a grateful heart.

So began the clock on 120 days. I prayed about it all. My to-do list didn't fit on one sheet of paper. The first order of business was work and my need for it. First, I needed work immediately to keep money coming in, whatever the amount. Second, the search for long-term employment had to commence.

I spent a couple of days putting together what I called the "Andrew Packet." It was a collection of items I assembled with the intention of explaining thoroughly to a potential employer who I was and why they might benefit from taking me on. It consisted of my resume, personal and professional character references, and a "disclosure" letter, as I called it, about my felon status. Too many times I had waited for the convicted felon issue to come up and I was forced to defensively deal with it. I figured I would lay everything out in a proactive style and see where that got me. I had nothing to lose. I prepared a dozen of them in manila envelopes.

Chapter 27

I knew in my heart how important it was going to be for us, my family, to find a church home. Because of my history and my nature, I can shut others out of my life with ease. But this is contradictory to what the Bible tells us about fellowship. It is paramount to a Christian's life. We do not exist alone on an island with The Lord. We are commanded to love and fellowship with one another.

In fact, a true follower of God bears fruit and one of these fruits is the desire to be around brothers and sisters in Christ. One can open the New Testament randomly and find a verse or statement about Christian fellowship. Paul, Peter, James, the Gospel writers…everyone wrote of and stressed its importance. Christ Himself took it a step further with His second greatest commandment to us of loving all others how we ourselves want to be loved. It is second only to the commandment of loving God with all of our hearts, souls, and minds.

I did not start knocking on church doors immediately as I had before. I acknowledged and accepted the truth of fellowship in my heart and prayed. I trusted Him for this. Then I went about my business of preparing for my family to return to me. I didn't waste any time. Within a week I had a job delivering food. The company specialized in delivering food from restaurants that don't deliver. The following week I picked up another part-time job driving rental cars to the locations where they were assigned. Bottom of the rung deals, but that wasn't the point. Moving from one country to another is very expensive. The longer I didn't have a job, the longer we saw our funds flying out with nothing coming in. After a couple of more weeks, I was in the office assigning orders to available drivers in the field.

I preferred driving much more to being on the telephone. There were little tricks here and there I learned to enhance the driving experience. For instance, no one ever wanted to drive on rainy nights. I was always available to drive those shifts. Why? It was a chance for me to channel my inner performer. I would simply make sure the customer could see how unpleasant it was for me out there. Additionally, I assured the diners I had kept the food nice and warm. Maybe a little extra shivering on a cold night or my clothes being completely soaked, and my tips consistently performed better. No problem. I drove every rainy night.

For the other work, many times a van would carry 10 or 12 of us to a single location to pick up pool cars. Sometimes the ride in the van would last a couple of hours. A Russian immigrant and I had a spirited debate about the United States. Whenever someone is demeaning the United States, I have to step up and get involved. Particularly when it has to do with the whole capitalism/democracy versus communism/socialism debate.

Not only am I a true believer in setting a broad parameter with proper restrictions and then allowing businesses to flourish, but I also experienced the day-to-day frustrations of a manager operating with socialist oversight. In Germany I lived and worked it. There is absolutely no question about it. Socialism restricts and constricts business. Costs are severely high. Scheduling and human resource issues can be so difficult, it doesn't seem real. I scratched my head a lot in Germany. Maybe that is why I have no hair left.

I identified numerous companies in and around the greater Sarasota area to make inquiries. I had submitted five or six "Andrew Packets" in the first three or four weeks. Of the companies were two natural/organic foods retail chains and an organic fruit and vegetable distributorship.

Mom was not drinking anymore. There was no alcohol in the house. I never asked her about this. I accepted it as a blessing. But her days were just chores, busybody jobs, and making a few phone calls. She did not meet with her friend anymore. Their relationship was basically three or four check-in calls throughout the day to talk about the news or the stock market. She was so frail. When I, in a loving way, talked to her about her weight she would not discuss it. And had she been to the doctor? Yes, was the answer. Any time we came close to either subject she would turn cold and matter of fact. She made it abundantly clear those areas she did not wish to go to.

Sometimes I got the feeling Mom was communicating, "I'm Martha; don't you do it! I've earned the right to behave how I want and to not be questioned."

I understand how she felt that way.

I was video calling Nadine and Melina at least once every two days. The days before video calling must have been torturous. I was doing my due diligence on schools, a home, doctors, health insurance, tax matters, and everything else. Nadine and Melina were in Baden-Baden with Carola. There was a measure of items and concerns in Germany that remained to be tidied up. Everyone was busy…in the daylight hours. The evenings and nights quickly became long and lonely for all three of us.

Maybe close to halfway through the four months we had an episode on one of our calls. Melina seemed normal and fine the first few minutes. I consider myself to be in tune with these types of things. In fact, I was looking for signs of anything because of the stress on the family.

Melina was silent for a few moments and then out of nowhere came, "Pa-pi!" as she broke down crying.

Not a spoiled or a silly cry. It was a pain cry. To hear it and see her, but not be able to grab and hold her was a type of punishment torture. It wasn't just Melina. All three of us love each other big time. We were all feeling it.

The situation with Glenn's teeth was a very big problem. As a child he had all of the dental technology — the retainer, the headgear, the braces. His mouth had always required attention. Twelve years of no dental care, bad oral hygiene, and corrosive drug use had rendered the health of his teeth null and void. There were massive problems front, back, left, and right.

He had researched total mouth extractions and implant surgery on the internet. The cost of the procedures he needed in the United States was in the multiple tens of thousands of dollars. He could have the same professional solutions for less than half the cost in India. Mom was an enabler, but this had to be done for Glenn's mental state, outlook for the future, and his health.

Yet again a personal, family item from years past was sold for some quick cash. These 16 years had seen some of our most precious family items go away. Some of the things I would have not believed in a million years would ever leave our family. I have seen so much lost that now only a few rare, private things have my attention and protection for my family going forward. Everything else is all the same. Sure, I understand, a blessing in a very real sense.

I learned blessings can be very painful. I enjoy quality and nice things, but the truth of it is rocks are rocks and metal is metal. Man-made value is not real. Our self worth and identity don't depend on these things. That is shallow. Believe me, I know. There is a whole other level out there that is real and deep.

From the settlement after Dad passed away and a couple of the real estate deals early on in Sarasota Mom was, with her very practical needs, secure and comfortable with some left over. Although still secure, the years, and more recently the Glenn situation, had eroded a significant portion of her resources. This went directly against her nature and caused her a great deal of strain. She resented it, and it ate her up inside. She did not know how to stop it.

It was an unending circle. There are two ways to interrupt circumstances like these — prayer and serious, deep intervention. I was alone in Sarasota, and I didn't have contacts or resources. I had a pre-determined amount of time to prepare for Nadine and Melina. I prayed so hard something would give on the Mom and Glenn front. I am a man of action, and it is not always to my benefit. Life can and will present us with times when prayer is the only thing that can be done. I had to learn and accept this. Actually, The Holy Spirit has had to work with me on this on numerous occasions.

After three months I had purchased a car, rented a decent house, secured insurance for the three of us, found a doctor, located an acceptable kindergarten, distributed my "Andrew packets" far and wide, and was working two part-time jobs. I was in get it done mode. It was high stress, but I was sleeping at night. I have had real difficulties getting the proper amount of sleep in the past. Sometimes I still have several consecutive nights when I struggle to sleep. I signed a lease and was staying at a house that was in the same neighborhood as Mom's. On April 12th, two days before his birthday, Glenn left for India to have his entire mouth filled with tooth implants.

I drove him to the airport with his travel visa in order. I didn't press him on anything. I was tired, but I wanted my brother to experience the joyful time of his mouth reparations. The appearance of his teeth had become shameful to him. There were many other areas that he needed to focus on. However, I was going to allow him to take in the whole adventure in and not feel like his little brother was interrogating him. I was happy for him. He was, naturally, excited and looking forward to his trip. I did ask Glenn about Jesus Christ. Did he truly believe The Lord was his personal Savior and He stood resurrected after the cross? He looked over at me and assured me he did. I dropped him off, and told him I would be praying for him and the whole process. Glenn thanked me.

Chapter 28

I returned to Mom's house to visit with her. It was early in the evening. We chatted for a few minutes, before she crawled into bed explaining how tired she was. She fell asleep almost immediately, and I went home. The next morning before I had to go to work, I went back to check on her. She was in exactly the same place and position on the bed as I had left her. A little concerned, I gently stirred her to ask if she was okay. She said yes she was, but she was exhausted. During my shift I called her, one time speaking and another leaving a message. She called me back. That to me was a good signal. But this behavior continued on for two more days more. I observed her closely and it genuinely appeared that when Glenn left the property, her whole system just collapsed in fatigue. It appeared like she had been forcing herself to get out of bed and through the day. I know how to assess a dire situation, and that is what I was looking at. It was severe. I was seriously considering getting medical professionals involved.

Glenn had been gone three full days. I went to Mom's in the morning to tell her of my concern and check on her. There was no answer when I knocked on the door. I used my key and hurried to her bedroom. There she lay at the foot of her bed on the hardwood floor. I ran to her. Crying, I picked her up as gently as I could. Her might was no more than that of a child. She was barely conscious. I placed her on the bed, putting a pillow behind her head.

"Mom! Mom! Please hear me, can you hear me? Mom?" My voice was cracking intensely.

"Huh?"

"Mom, it's me! Andrew. Are you all right? Mom? What happened?"

"I…was…just…tired…"

After going back and forth for several minutes, I realized she had gone to the bathroom to use to the toilet. On the way back to bed, she simply lay down from exhaustion. She stabilized a little bit and was comfortable in bed with a glass of water. I called my job and learned I could not miss the shift. I had to be there. I was manning the phone and computer that afternoon at the food delivery job. I made Mom comfortable again. I showed her how to speed dial me and a neighbor. I prepared some grapes, cheese, and crackers for her to eat. I told her I expected a check in call from her before lunch. She agreed she could do that. I was a nervous wreck and left to organize food delivery for strangers. At the appropriate time I received the call from Mom. Oh gosh, was I relieved! I told her to hang tight until my lunch hour when I could return to her.

Two hours later I arrived at her house again. I didn't bother knocking and ran in. Again, on the cold floor, was my sweet mother. This time some things were disheveled. Blankets were pulled down the side of the bed and a couple of pillows were on the floor. Again, I ran to her.

"Oh God, Mom! I'm sorry! I'm so sorry," I said as tears blinded me.

I scooped her in my arms a second time for the day, "Mom, I'm sorry. I'm calling the ambulance now, okay?"

"No. No. No. Andrew, no!"

I didn't know what to do as I stared at her on the bed. "Mom, I have to. I can't take care of you the way you need. Please. Please let me call."

She grabbed my hand. "No, honey. Don't. Let me stay here."

I stayed with my mother the rest of that day and night. I took care of her, brought food and water, kept her clean, and helped her to the toilet. I sat on the bed beside her and we talked kind of like none of it was happening. Memories came up, mostly of Dad, and we even laughed together several times. We prayed. In the evening I brought her a cool, damp cloth. As she slumbered, I looked over at her.

By morning, I was calling an ambulance. I knew it was the last time Mom would ever stay in her own home.

The next morning as Mom still slept, I rose. I had a cup of coffee on the front porch. Then I dialed 911.

"This is 911. What's your emergency?"

"I need an ambulance for my mother, please."

I let her sleep until the medics arrived. I went to her and quietly woke her up.

"Mom, I've called an ambulance. They're here. I love you so much I had to, Mom. That's just all there is to it," I explained.

All she did was grimace, turn her head, and mutter "No" under her breath.

I allowed the professionals into her bedroom, and they took over. I followed them outside as they pushed her gurney toward the ambulance. I held her hand. She was quiet. They lifted her up, pushed her in, and closed the doors behind her. I thanked the driver and EMTs before I went back in the house.

I immediately called Aunt Kathy and Uncle Gene. They were preparing to leave for Florida within the hour, driving 14 hours straight. Then I called Myra. Everyone was shocked because it was a shocking situation. No one was actually surprised that it had happened. Myra was coming down the following day when she could catch a flight.

I gathered some things up for Mom. Her toiletries, clothes, and some items I knew she would like. Then, I raced to the hospital.

It didn't even occur to me to call Glenn. Years before, everyone had decided not to tell me Dad had been kidnapped when Mom and I were in Paris. I employed the same logic with Glenn. I didn't have any answers. Dumping everything on him while he sat in India didn't make any sense to me. Actually, it would have blown up into another matter I had to manage. I wasn't up for that.

I knew I was going to call Mom's friend, but first I wanted to learn what the results of the tests were and what the doctors had to say.

When I arrived at Sarasota Memorial Hospital they had already taken Mom to examine her. I waited, and a couple of hours later Mom was brought back to a room on the floor where I was. She was taken into a room with a curtain dividing her from the other half of the room and the patient in it.

Without hesitation I pulled a nurse to the side, "Ma'am, please forgive me for my insistence on this matter. I hope you don't…" I caught my breath.

"Please don't misunderstand me. I don't mean my mother is better than anyone. She is a former First Lady of Kentucky widowed for 12 years. The last decade has been a very trying time for her, my brother, and I. She has always been an extraordinary mother. I am asking you to please allow us her own room. Please."

The nurse agreed with tears welling up in her own eyes. A single room was prepared for Mom, and I was extremely grateful. She was barely conscious and from time to time would look at me and roll her head back over.

I checked in with Aunt Kathy, Myra, and reached out to her friend. He was in Louisville, Kentucky with a seriously ill brother and would be down in a couple of days. Then I waited.

Several hours later as I wet her lips with a sponge lollipop soaked in water, the doctor entered the room. The diagnosis was diverticulitis. It was in her intestines, stomach, and colon. Small pouches form on the inside walls of internal organs in the digestive tract when diverticulitis is diagnosed. Normally, it is treatable with antibiotics, rest, and a change in diet. However, it can be severe and the pouches become inflamed or infected. Mom's case was severe. Her insides were infected and perforated. Emphysema was also in the picture. They wanted to stabilize her, and then we would discuss going forward.

Before I left for the night, I helped situate her. As she slept there were tubes running in and out of her and bandages were everywhere. I noticed her big and second toes on her right foot were purple on the tips.

I stayed at Mom's house that night. I called Nadine and Melina when I got there. Obviously, the conversation changed the dynamic of their preparation for travel. Uncle Gene, Aunt Kathy, and Myra would be there in the morning.

In Mom's house, alone and quiet, I stayed up most of the night. I went through hundreds of pictures and documents she kept in the beautiful, custom, hand carved desk Dad used in the Governor's office. Dad had commissioned it to a loyal friend and supporter. He and his family, the Faulkners of Stanford, were wonderful people to my family over the years. I traveled down a thousand memory lanes before the sun rose the next day.

Uncle Gene, Aunt Kathy, and Myra came straight to the hospital when they arrived. Mom was in and out of consciousness, but knew everyone who was there. Aunt Kathy's oldest daughter, my cousin, Michelle, was also flying in from Nashville. She would be there that evening.

Diverticulitis is a common condition, and I believe it relieved all of us to hear it was the problem. The hope was that a strong program of antibiotics and some rest would allow Mom to go home in several days. I knew, as we all did, this was going to be the beginning of a new, advanced phase in Mom's life. A lot of changes would need to be made and I needed to start the search for someone to help her. The emphysema was a concern, but it was in its beginning stages.

The brother of Mom's friend in Kentucky had passed away. Now, he was coming to Florida to see Mom at the hospital. It was an extremely trying time for him.

All of us stayed with Mom in her room for several hours. Then we started to take breaks. Mom was asleep and we all went to her house. All of us were exhausted and in need of a shower, but our spirits had been elevated somewhat by the prognosis. It was very serious, but there was hope for a return to some type of normalcy.

Myra, Michelle, and I went through all kinds of things and took a collective trip down memory lane. We were melancholy, but we also laughed and cried. Uncle Gene and Aunt Kathy helped with anything that needed doing. We all shuttled to and from the hospital two more days.

Then, Glenn returned from India after his teeth implant surgery. I went alone to pick him up at the airport. He looked as handsome as I had seen him appear in years. It had nothing to do with anything physical. I hadn't even seen him smile, and I knew a big piece had been fixed. There was much more that needed to be addressed

233

concerning things unseen, but I let Glenn have his earthly joy and newfound confidence. When Glenn was fit and put together, he was exceptionally handsome. I was happy for him, and we smiled as we walked to the car.

I waited until we got to the interstate to explain Mom's condition. Growing up, we always heard that I was "Martha" and Glenn was "Wallace." That didn't change in the years that followed.

"Listen, buddy, we need to talk. It's Mom."

He turned his face and shoulders to me. For a moment it felt like I was looking at and talking with Dad.

"She is safe and in the hospital, but there are issues. Her insides are a mess because she has not been taking caring of herself properly. And we haven't known the extent of what's going on. Well, now we do and this is the wake up call," I explained.

"Why didn't you tell me?" Glenn asked with a touch of anger in his voice.

"Because I made the decision not to," I told him sternly.

By my countenance and posture, he understood exactly what I was communicating to him. He stared at me for a second, trying to figure out how he was going to react, and then he just sighed back into his seat.

Something passed in that moment between us. I'm not sure exactly what or even if all of it was passed, but a transfer took place. We both understood it.

"Is she going to live?" Glenn asked.

"I don't know."

"Are we going to the hospital now?" he asked.

"Yes, we are," I answered.

The rest of the way, I explained diverticulitis and the nature of everything we knew from the tests. Her toes were something I still had not received an adequate explanation on, I told Glenn.

We got to the hospital, parked, and went straight to the room. Mom was barely aware of the movement in the room as we entered. Glenn went to her, naturally smiling, and she noticed a countenance on her boy's face that had been absent for years. To see her involuntary, immediate happiness was a true blessing for me. I saw her the way I always had as a child at that moment. It was the final time.

I took Glenn home, where everyone else got the chance to see the "new" Glenn. No one else had seen the dilapidated state of his mouth and teeth before as a result of his self-imposed solitude. However, his teeth and smile were beautiful, and everyone was happy for him. The next day we were all at it again.

The doctor had not been back, and all of us felt like we were just coasting along with no break one way or another. I changed the blanket on Mom's bed, looking specifically at her toes. The two previously mentioned toes were deteriorating completely to black and purple. I was taken aback. Something was clearly not right.

I summoned the nurse, and she explained the doctor needed to discuss some things with me. I called the doctor and left a voice message that it was terribly urgent and to please give me a call.

Almost an hour later he called back. He said Mom was septic and bleeding on the inside due to the perforations in her bowels. The black and blue toes were a result of the lack of blood circulating properly.

At one point in his remarks the doctor said, "If your mother survives…"

"Wait. Did I hear you correctly, doctor? Did you just say 'if she survives'?"

The doctor hesitated a moment.

"We are doing everything we know to do. Stabilization is a priority. Your mother is very sick on her insides. I am very sorry."

Mom's system was delicate and weak. She was placed on a breathing ventilator. I spent some time with her cleaning her face, brushing her hair, and talking. I don't know if she heard me, but I mentioned Jesus a lot. I read somewhere once as the disciple Peter's wife was being crucified in front of him, he lovingly reminded her to remember The Lord. I told Mom to remember The Lord as I gently rubbed her.

I returned to the house and made calls requesting everyone be there. What I had just learned changed everything. I clearly understood what the doctor had said. Mom was dying.

Everyone accepted the news uniformly. Seeing Mom for days in the condition she was in with no noticeable improvement had conditioned us all for the time of acceptance. In the name of hope, two more days passed as we all waited for a miracle. Her condition only deteriorated.

Aunt Kathy and Uncle Gene needed to return to Kentucky. Everyone converged on the hospital together one last time. Uncle Gene, Aunt Kathy, Nadine, Melina, Myra, Michelle, Glenn, and Mom's friend. For a couple of hours each of us were with and around her. There were tiny glimpses of consciousness here and there, but they were miniscule. They provided a tiny second of hope for a different reality, but were quickly quelled.

Then came the time when everything had been said and everyone had their opportunity to say goodbye. Aunt Kathy left that hospital room knowing she would never see,

Martha, her sister, again in this life. There are no words for these moments. Only love, memories, prayers and tears.

We all left and returned to the house. There, everyone prepared to return to their lives. There was nothing more to do. Uncle Gene and Aunt Kathy headed north up the interstate. Myra and Michelle had flights to catch.

The following day Glenn, Nadine, Melina, and I returned again to the hospital. Nadine and Melina were close to her. I had few words of comfort even for Melina. Sometimes in life and death words possess no comfort. It is what it is. I did my best to model for her how we meet these grave and serious times in life. How we look ahead to our faith in Christ and His promises to us. I shielded her from nothing. Both of them spoke with Mom and took adequate time with her. Then they left her for the last time. Glenn and I called the nurse.

As we, her two children, watched, the ventilator was removed. The nurse quietly left the room. Glenn was on one side of her and me on the other. We both held one of her hands. Nothing was said for a time as her little chest rose and lowered from breathing.

I prayed and asked for her forgiveness, to please forgive me for not being a better child to her. That I loved her so much and was thankful to God for the mother he gave me. I prayed intensely that she would see Dad again very soon in the presence of Jesus Christ. Glenn was silent in his own pain and prayers.

A little over two hours after the machine had been removed, she made a curious movement I will never forget. Almost as if she was preparing herself for a journey, she licked her lips slightly and adjusted her shoulders.

Glenn and I looked at each other, acknowledging what we had just seen. We looked back at her and she was gone. The lips she had only moments before lightly licked were slightly open. I prayed and prayed for her to be in no more pain. It was May 7, 2014.

Chapter 29

Glenn and I did not speak as we drove home. I called Myra, Aunt Kathy, and Mom's friend to let them know what they already knew. That night I put out clothes for her and assembled her things. Two days later, Glenn, her friend, and I laid her to rest in the mausoleum near my father.

I immediately began planning a memorial for her in Lexington. Gordon and Karen Walls, longtime family friends, helped immeasurably with the details and arrangements, as did Myra and Aunt Kathy. Many people were affected by the news and reached out to us.

Mom had constructed walls in her later years and restricted access to herself from people she had been close with for years of her life. This was not "Martha," and people knew it.

I had countless conversations with countless people who were deeply saddened. I returned all phone calls and answered all letters. It was exhausting, but everyone deserved to hear something from us, from me, about Mom.

A number of people who had been involved with the takedown of Dad tried to get through. Perhaps they simply wanted to show their respect. Perhaps it was wrong of me to ignore their attempts, but I had nothing to say to them.

Ironically, at that exact time an organic fruit and vegetable distributorship in Sarasota was contacting me as a result of my "Andrew packet." They were in need of a Production Department head. The day before we were leaving for Kentucky, I interviewed with them and was offered the job. It was extremely close in scope and responsibilities to what I had done at Nadine's uncle's company in Germany. However, the volume and number of personnel was much larger. I couldn't believe it. It was a for real job with a real salary. I had done it.

When Mom passed away, I was still just delivering food, driving pool cars, and talking about making it. It was important to me, and I had prayed that she would see my success. God has amazed me time and again with answered prayers and beyond. This was not to be one of them. I wanted my mother to see me coming back and achieving a level of success as much as anything I had ever wanted. He denied me this.

We traveled to Lexington, and the memorial was held at Southland Christian Church. It was wonderful to see the people who attended, almost all of whom I had not seen in over 12 years, some for many more.

Both Dad and Mom held a special place in the hearts of many. People authentically cared for them. As Glenn and I stood, they waited their turn to share with us stories and loving memories of what seemed like many lives ago.

Ralph Hacker, a very well known and beloved broadcast executive and sports commentator, had been a valued friend of the Wilkinsons for years and was there in remembrance of Mom. He recalled the "Martha" character that had endeared itself to so many through genuineness, compassion, and humor. Ralph spoke perfectly of the ability she had to be herself in the midst of those who were high powered and influential just the same as folks on the farm or main street. Both Dad and Mom would have been profoundly grateful for his remarks, as Glenn and I were.

A person both Dad and Mom loved dearly, Judy Rose, filled the air with her wonderful and powerful voice. I am certain it pleased both The Lord and my parents.

Then, as I had done only months earlier for my grandmother, I stood from my seat and took the podium. As

I acknowledged those in attendance, I felt significant pressure. However, it wasn't from the audience. I stood before all of those people, and my past was no secret. As I gripped the sides of the podium, I felt shame. Here was a four-time convicted felon standing to honor Martha S. Wilkinson and her life.

I felt like every eye in the auditorium was fixed on me thinking, "Is the best they have to offer for Martha? Andrew? Could they not find someone else? Could Ralph not do this?"

I hesitated for a moment. As I stared out across the bodies in the chairs, I could only think of one person. My father. I could hear him in my head, "This is it, boy. Please do your mother and I proud. Forget everything else. Get this one moment right. For us."

As I thanked everyone for coming, my voice was shaking. I had no prepared remarks. I had prepared with intense thought and prayer. I spoke of the loving, loyal daughter, wife, and mother who had graced all of our lives. That it went without saying my father never could, or would, have reached the levels of business or political success he had without the steady presence of his wife and partner. If Wallace Wilkinson was the motor, or power, of the Wilkinson family that provided the thrust, Martha, was the stable, firm frame that housed all the moving parts. She was the one who held the family together. She never let any one of the three of us down.

She supplied absolute love, commitment, and dedication throughout her entire life for Wallace, Glenn, Andrew, and many others. Dad could be in Glasgow buying a bank or in Germany setting up a lumber company. It didn't matter. Mom created the environment for us to be a family. She was the ultimate partner for Dad and a prize of a mother for

Glenn and me. Her involvement was across the board — in business, politics, and her children's schooling.

She loved unconditionally, and she gave unselfishly to the point it was her trademark. The majority of souls in this life are those who give and take. Mom was of another form. She was a pure giver, never taking anything.

Still I can remember Mom tossing a ball with me in the yard. I recall noticing to myself, as a young boy, that she had no idea what she was doing with a glove and a ball. Even as a child it occurred to me that she was doing it just for me. Mom baked cakes for the Scouts, drove the carpools for practices, and rode horses or motorcycles with us. Roles, formal and informal, were the ones she played.

Glenn and I both attended Sayre School in downtown Lexington from kindergarten all the way through 12th grade. She served as trustee and then as the first chairwoman of the school board.

Overseeing all of our farm operations was also a loop on her jeans. Dad had a number of European business partners for a time. The Europeans all had a great affection for Mom.

The people of Kentucky also had a great affection for her. She was a magnificent First Lady and an indispensable secret weapon on the campaign trail.

I shared a story, I believe, that captured everything Martha Wilkinson was about. In the mid-nineties Dad had been talking with an investment banking firm in New York City. They were holding their annual retreat in Alaska, and we were invited to go. My father naturally came to Glenn and me to see if we were interested in going. The jet we had at the time was more than capable of flying to Alaska, and we would be taking it if we went. On board would have been the two pilots, Dad, Glenn, and me. Mom went to Dad and expressed her wishes to go along with us.

I remember it very well. My father said to her, "Of course, Mother, you are more than welcome to go with us. I didn't think you would be interested in that sort of trip, so I didn't ask you."

Her reply was, with tears in her eyes, "I do want to go. I want to go because you, Glenn, and Andrew will be on that plane. If anything happens, I want to be there."

What a woman, wife, and mother did God grace us with. That is how she lived her life. When something happened, she was there. And more happened than we ever could have imagined.

I ended my remarks by asking all those in attendance to pray with me. I thanked God for the overwhelming gift and blessing He had given us in the form of Martha Wilkinson. I knew she was with Jesus. I knew of nothing more I could add or say.

The books of Proverbs, Exodus, and Ephesians, among others, in the Bible, instruct us to honor our father and mother. I had not always given my parents the honor they deserved. I hoped that I had, yes, done my father and my mother proud the one last chance I had to do so.

Many of those present approached me after my remarks wanting to reassure or encourage me. Glenn never uttered a word to me about what I had said about our mother and her life. I saw and heard from those I never believed I would over Mom's passing. On the other hand, I was deeply surprised at others who chose to remain silent.

Chapter 30

Nadine, Melina, Glenn, and I returned to Sarasota. It was spring. I began my new job immediately. My new employer was a private company run by the man that founded it and his family. Approximately 15 years earlier, he had been operating a small, organic blueberry farm on his own land. He began transporting them to the east coast of the state where he saw a market.

During this time consumers in the United States began paying more attention to how things are that they and their families eat are grown. Other organic farmers needed someone to help them get their product distributed. What started out as a one truck and refrigerated trailer operation quickly grew. It really grew.

When I got there it was around 150 employees that worked out of a 90,000-square-foot office and refrigerated warehouse space. Around 20 trucks were dropping off and picking up every day. It was impressive, and I had real respect for what the founder had been able to do in a relatively short amount of time.

I settled in pretty quickly. I was familiar with the basics — production and processing, customer specifications, orders and schedules changing, employee issues, etc. Due to the explosive growth there had naturally been operational and organizational challenges that were rearing their collective ugly heads. I had three supervisors in the Production Department who were very good at what they did. They were also very good at doing things their own way. Bending them to my will, operationally speaking, and simultaneously building a trusting relationship with them was going to be a trick. They knew the ins and outs of the place extremely well, and I needed them.

The Production Department sorted, cleaned, and packaged or repackaged all sorts of organic fruits and vegetables. The inside of the production and warehousing space was cut into four equal squares. Each square was a different section of refrigerated warehousing with different temperature settings for the types of product it held. For instance, all of the leafy and flowering plants were in the cooler that required the coldest temperature while potatoes, onions, and beans were stored in another cooler with a different, higher temperature. The production room itself stayed at 42 to 45 degrees. There was no sitting down, and the days lasted as long as it took to fill the orders and get them on the trucks.

Production, warehousing, and transportation can be grueling work. The norm is 10 to 12 hour workdays, not eight. All of us were dressed like it was winter. We had several days that lasted well beyond 15 hours in there. Not everybody can do that type of work. One has to be somewhat mentally fit to do those jobs day after day for an extended period of time.

Most of the production room workers were from Cuba and South America. My three supervisors and their workers consistently performed and delivered with very heavy workloads. Daisy was close to retirement age and had been with the company since it had started. I often marveled at how long and hard she could work while at the same time maintaining a positive attitude. I would bring in a couple of boxes of Dunkin' Donuts with me on Saturdays at 6 a.m. as a simple gesture to show my appreciation.

I guess I was pretty tough as I first started with them, and it was bumpy for a time. People don't like change, and when change needs to take place, my philosophy is simple. I go in as an authority first. Reasonable, respectful, and professional, but as an authority. When I have established that I am not a pushover and will have to be dealt with, then comes the personal relationships. I love getting to know about people and their lives. I like to care about people.

My three supervisors, in time, became my three ladies in production. I learned as much from each of them as they did from me. Later we would laugh about how I used to drive them crazy (and still did sometimes). Marta, Leci, and Estella were excellent workers and fine people. I am thankful our paths in life crossed.

I had a partner in the production office, Sierra. I focused on the operational side of production and she handled the administrative and internal matters. It was a perfect fit. Although I see the need for it sometimes, I am not an office dweller. I like to get out and deal with people to see what really is going on. Sierra was an ace on the company's operating system and knew each customer's preferences and hang-ups inside and out. I am proud of the work we accomplished.

Always before in my life I could get people to do things simply because of who I was. That certainly did not apply anymore. I had to come in and make some serious changes in a department that consisted of about 35 to 45 full-time employees. Organizational, procedural, and structural changes are what I was brought there for.

People are far and away the most valuable asset of companies. They need to be treated well, fairly, and with respect. When we treat people well and work to earn their trust, they recognize this and will reciprocate positively every time. People must know that they are appreciated.

My hat is off to lower and middle management everywhere, the ones who appreciate their people and get things done. They are on the front lines. They're not allowed to break down. Breaking down is not an option. In every department (especially production and transportation), managers must work effectively and closely with others in pressurized environments and difficult circumstances. Decisions are made in the front. Execution happens in the back. A hallmark of any truly successful company is revealed in how it treats its people.

How grateful I was for the opportunity I had! I was probably over-grateful to them. My hire was a personal milestone of profound significance. I was no longer in Germany at Nadine's family's company where no one knew me or anything about me. I was back home where damaging information about me was readily available. My hire was proof I was back. I could get a job. From walking out of prison to that moment had been a long, arduous road. So my ultra, genuine gratitude might have come across as insincere at times; I don't know. I do know that it wasn't. My new job was a game changer for me.

Nadine, Melina, and Glenn were home most days. This was absolutely acceptable to me. Moves are stressful, let alone an international one. On top of that, one of all of us had just died. I was going to make sure Nadine and Melina had the proper space and time to be acclimated to their new home. In addition, I had prayers that Glenn being around them would have a productive effect. And it did.

I can never sit in judgment of my brother. I had once taken my own severe toll on my mother. I too had, at one time in my life, contributed to my mother's loss of stamina and foundation. Thank God, I had been restored and redeemed with Mom. She had accepted me back to her with love and joy. Glenn had continued to be very hard on her. Glenn knew it, and the chance had been lost to make things right. This tormented Glenn in his soul. This is one of the finest examples of what only Jesus Christ can do. He will take these crushing, fleshly pains and deep sufferings from us. He will replace them, when we go to Him, with forgiveness, peace, understanding, and strength. But we have to go to Him.

"I am the way, and the truth, and the life; no one comes to the Father but through Me," is what Jesus told the man in the Gospel of John. This is not popular to say in the world today. In fact, the world hates it. It always has. I love it. The world takes this as a weapon and uses it to divide people. I don't speak of other's condemnation or judgment. I do, however, speak joyfully about the certainty of my salvation. What use is a God we cannot be sure of?

I spoke to Glenn on many occasions about his faith, what he believed, and how the healing he yearned for and needed was a well springing from only one Source.

On the day I was released from prison, I remember very well the specific thoughts and prayer I had about one thing in the future. I hoped to return one day to help the men and women on the inside of the compounds. Clearly, there are residents guilty of horrendous and heinous crimes who must endure severe punishment in our nation's prisons. There is a joke about "jailhouse religion" not being quite sincere enough. When the gates fly open, people often forget all about that Bible they were always clutching. However, it is also gloriously true that Light shines brightest in the darkest places. A prison is a dark place, and there are broken people there. At the point when a person breaks, they are prepared to accept the reality of God. I was broken too.

I had nowhere left to run to or turn to in the back of that transport van. Absolutely everything was gone or destroyed. Inside and out. God had my attention. My cold heart was prepared for Him in my brokenness. A significant portion of the prison population wants to, and can, change their lives. Punishment and rehabilitation need to be one big, collective strategy and goal. Now they operate as two different things. There are millions of lives to be reached and helped with prayer and a real focus on helping convicted felons. Everyone wins when they become again, or perhaps the first time ever, a contributing member of society.

I joke, to myself only, that I had put out an APB (All Points Bulletin) to all sorts of law enforcement agencies and community groups. I wanted to be involved somewhere with somebody. There is absolutely nothing wrong with serving food or other types of activities as a volunteer. I have done it and will again, but I really wanted to get involved in lives that had hope to change. All authentic change comes from hope first. Hope is the conduit from despair to action. Death ends hope. I know what hopeless feels like.

Finally, I received a response from a veteran of the law enforcement and corrections community in Florida. We met in Ybor City, the historic Latin Quarter of Tampa Bay, for coffee and a light lunch late one morning. It was so cool. My persistence had paid off. She introduced me to the administration at the Hardee Correctional Institution in Bowling Green, Florida.

Hardee is approximately 70 miles northeast of Sarasota. The prison boasts of a faith program that has been, by any measure, successful. There is evidence that the introduction of voluntary, regular faith programs in prison camps decreases violence and recidivism, bolsters morale, and improves relations between captors and captives. Besides, I know it to be true. I'm around it all the time.

God Behind Bars is the Department of Corrections' nationally recognized prison ministry. They offer an opportunity for live worship, addiction recovery, resources for re-entry into society, and ongoing support in the time after release. Two years before, when God Behind Bars came to Hardee, it was a rough place with violence occurring regularly, mostly prisoner on prisoner. Today, the difference is seen and acknowledged.

Raeanne Hance is the Executive Director of God Behind Bars in Florida, and a person through whom God answered my prayer. An extra facilitator was needed for the morning class on Thursdays. Would I be interested? She got me going with the training and the background check to work within the state's prison. I jokingly explained there might be some red flags coming back when they run me in the system! I tell Raeanne all the time that God answered a prayer for me through her. We have become close friends, and I will always be grateful to her for being the one to let me give back.

I have travelled to Hardee once a week for two years as of the time of this book's publication. The day I go there is my favorite day of the week. It is a closed security prison, which means there are men who will die there. There is a program and material I facilitate, but I also bring my own messages and lessons. I serve as a link to the outside world and fill them in on current events. We discuss God, faith, forgiveness, repentance, love, suffering, race, manhood, and all sorts of other things. I don't tiptoe around. I say what I have to say with love and respect. They tested me a little to see what I was about in the beginning, but they have let me in. A rapport has developed that lends itself to listening and learning. Nothing is forcing anyone to be there. Therefore, there is, outside of some yahoos that we weed out, sincere motivation to change.

I bring something with me to that prison. Nadine and I have an inside joke.

I said to her once, "Sweetheart, I actually like being at the prison. Does that sound weird?"

Seeing the opportunity for one of her cute little jokes she said, "Uh, yeah" as she widened her eyes.

I like being there because a difference can be made. One person can introduce a difference. I call it the three C's.

They are caring, committing, and connecting. That I care enough to listen and want to know them. That I am committed enough to drive 140 miles round trip one day a week to sit among them. That I can connect enough to help them feel love and respect. Many of them have never had that. Christ has a very special way of breaking down barriers and opening hearts. I have seen it so many times. The men will begin to interact and trust. The fruit will begin to grow in the lives of these men. It truly is awesome to be a part of.

One of our assignments was to write about the past and examine our life. What and/or who made us what we had become? Did we own up to it? Did we know the damage and pain we had brought to the lives of others? Over 100 were turned in. Most were around a page long.

That night I brought them into the bedroom, and let Nadine read some while I read. It was profound. Most of them described a childhood and life complete with experiencing many of the darkest sufferings in this world. Abuse, neglect, assault, molestation, addiction, abandonment, among many others, are words used to describe the lives I read about. Between my own time in prison and that moment reading with Nadine, I knew we have a responsibility to help as many of them as we can.

I am a believer in personal responsibility, accepting consequences, and the punishment/rehabilitation model if it is used effectively, but I have seen many people who never had a chance from the start. With God and the proper approach, causes are not lost. Lives will change. It is a given.

I have befriended a man, Leo Schofield, at Hardee. Leo was convicted in 1989 of murdering his wife, Michelle. She was brutally stabbed to death. He has maintained his innocence since the beginning. There is no physical evidence linking him to the murder, with holes up and down the prosecution's case. There are those in the legal profession, investigative journalists, and law enforcement officials who have studied the evidence and believe Leo is innocent. He is not innocent due to an utter lack of evidence; he is actually proven innocent by the evidence.

This is not a case of shadow of doubt, per se. I have researched the case myself. I also have spent hours with this man who has been in prison for nearly 30 years. We have gone to The Lord in prayer together. He has faithfully done the work of Jesus Christ while behind bars.

On the compound he is known as their humble, spiritual leader and is respected for illustrating how a Christian man lives. When we met, I believed there was a strong chance Leo didn't do it. That's not the case anymore. I am fully convinced Leo is a man convicted of a crime he did not commit.

I believe in our system of jurisprudence, but it is not perfect. The ball is dropped sometimes. When that happens, it is our job to pay attention and pick it back up.

As of the time of writing this book, an explosive new revelation has come forth in Leo's case resulting in a judge ordering the state prosecution to prove within 60 days why Leo should remain in prison. Of course, this is huge. It looks good and there is cautious joy.

During one of our opportunities to pray recently, I asked Leo how and what he was feeling. I'll never forget the look in his eyes as he explained to me how many times his and his family's hopes have flown on wings only to be crushed into the ground. I beheld a man truly weary.

"Andrew, will you pray for me?" Leo asked.

"Of course, you know I will, Leo," I said.

"Please pray only that I can accept God's will for my life. Whatever His will is for me, that I can go on. That I can continue. I don't know how much more I can take."

I was listening to a man who has not taken a free breath of air in 28 years. I know what pain is. I have felt free fall, confusion, and sadness on any scale of measure. But the forgiveness and absence of bitterness in Leo's life are proof of God. Our flesh is not capable of such things. Leo receives this power from The Holy Spirit.

I know this power. I felt it in the back of that prisoner transport van — broken, beat up, and chained like a beast, with nowhere left to hide. As I rose up from the metal grating scraping on my skin and lifted my chin into the air, it was like I was being blown up with air. It was the air of life. The Holy Spirit had come in. I have my Bible, yes absolutely, but I also know what happened. I also know I could not have "created" that moment for myself. I had nothing left in my spirit, heart, character, and imagination. I was totally bankrupt. No one will ever be able to tell me what happened didn't happen. I was there and I thank God for it.

John the Baptist said, "He must increase, but I must decrease." So, on a practical level I was in a good spot for God to get a hold of my attention. The more cushy and "hassle free" our lives are, the more difficult it is for us to recognize God and our need for Him. It is our sin nature. He has placed knowledge of Him and our need for Him into our hearts. But our spirits become dulled and numbed by sin and separation from God. Our hearts are then blanketed with false sense after false sense of pride and independence.

Money and worldly success are not evil. Making them the primary focus of our lives is. There is an image we think of when we hear the word evil. Pictures come to mind of brutal mass murderers, blood and gore, even Satan himself. Evil is, plain and simple, anything not of God. Absolutely everything that stands in our way of getting to God is evil.

The thing is, this is precisely the same power Jesus used to live a sterling and stainless life. It is the power that held Him up so He could be sinless and worthy. It is the power that enabled Him to pray for those who were brutally executing Him. This power, which God gave His Son, is available to us on a grand scale. There is no difference in it, and it is given with grace and mercy to us.

I see how it easy to miss this power in our lives. I have missed it before. This power must be received with a heart of prayer, repentance, and thankfulness. It won't come any other way. Repentance has become this "harsh" word today. Repentance simply means we know how we have and do fall way short of God's glory, we are sorry for our sins against Him, and we want in His name not to be controlled by sin. All we have to do is come clean. He is there with open arms, waiting. There is no condemnation in Christ Jesus.

Nadine and I teach Melina that if all else fails, she must tell the truth. If she is honest, no matter how bad the situation, then we can work with her and go forward. But if we can't believe her and trust her to tell us the truth, then all sorts of damage is done to our relationship with her.

This dynamic runs directly into our relationship with our Father. If we are truthful with Him, we save ourselves from damage to our relationship. Anyway, He knows exactly where we have been, what we have done, and what we are thinking about. It's not like we are keeping secrets.

Chapter 31

Daily life continued for us — Nadine, Melina, Glenn, and I. The four of us did seem to find a "family" thread running through each of us — me, the girls, and crazy uncle "Glenny." Glenn had a real relationship with both Nadine and Melina. He and Nadine spent a lot of time talking about everything under the sun. He helped her when she needed it with something she was trying to get done or figure out. I never had a negative thought in terms of how he would act with Melina or if I could trust him completely. Before too long, Glenn had a little buddy who hung out and went places with him.

The band, Rascal Flatts, had a tour stop in Tampa that Nadine and I picked up some tickets for. It was Nadine's first country music concert, and we made a weekend trip out of it. Melina and Glenn held the fort down in Sarasota. They played putt-putt, made pancakes, and watched a couple of Melina's movies together. We returned from Tampa to find both Glenn and Melina doing very well.

All of this was very good. He was again enrolled in some online classes, and his marks were consistently excellent. Glenn's problem was never brain capacity. I didn't dig too much into the details of his schooling. Not yet. Other things needed to develop first. And I never had a problem with that. But at some point I was going to inquire of Glenn to where all of this schooling was realistically leading.

Glenn had been very alone for a long time. His marriage was never a real one in terms of deep, meaningful things. It never got there. I noticed that Glenn lamented over his marriage dissolving, but never really the person.

Functioning lives were happening all around him, which had not been seen in quite some time with Mom. Things were contagious, with morning showers and shaves, salads and water, and an e-cigarette replaced real ones. Glenn lost about 20 pounds and looked good.

Unbeknownst to us, he had created a profile on a couple of online dating sites. For a split second I was taken aback when he shared this with me. But after a moment of letting the thought settle, I realized this is how our world functions. It is not how I met someone, but that doesn't mean it can't work for someone else.

We had some fun together creating his profiles "staging" photos of him and Melina. Each of them showing a handsome, sweet, family guy out in the yard with his niece. It wasn't long before he was getting and giving hits. Some initial back and forth online chats soon gave way to phone calls with real conversations. One of these conversations was with Nitzel Rocio Guerra. Nitzel was from and lived in Panama. Her work in international sales brought her to the United States frequently, specifically Florida. Her friends and family called her Ro. Ro was warm, pretty, and professional. Her previous marriage had produced a daughter who was in high school in Panama City. Ro came to Sarasota several times and everything about her suggested she was a fine person, perhaps a little lonely but doing something about it.

Everyone liked Ro, but more specifically, how Glenn was with Ro. They had been talking longer than they let on. It either came naturally or they had already settled into a comfort zone that suited them. Laughter was heard coming from Glenn's room once more. Ro did very well with Melina. It was not awkward if the two of them had a pair of minutes to spend together. Glenn, Ro, and Melina, just the three of them, played miniature golf, went to the store, and even went shopping. Melina received a new nickname from the two of them, "Squishy."

Glenn and I, the two surviving heirs of our mother's estate, needed to have numerous meetings with attorneys and discussions between us. One afternoon, we sat together and squared away the ownership of a few personal items not designated in Mom's will.

He went into older brother mode on me, "Little brother, it's just the two of us now. Dad and Mom are gone. Let's make them proud. Let's push ahead, two brothers in the world."

His voice reminded me of an earlier time in our lives. The same as for many, many memories, we were at the farm. It was autumn, and a number of us were riding horses and motorcycles in a group. We had ridden down the side of a big cornfield and come to a corner gate. Glenn, on his trusty steed, dismounted. While the rest of us watched, he looked out across the landscape in his Stetson. Spitting some tobacco, he crouched down grabbing some earth in his hands.

With dirt sifting through his fingers, squinty-eyed just like Clint Eastwood, he said, "Well, boys, It's gonna be a long winter."

All of us sat quietly for a moment before we started laughing so hard we almost fell off of our horses! It was hilarious. It was classic, vintage Glenn.

In a matter of months, Glenn had managed to make a big wide turn. It wasn't a 180, but it registered on the radar. He was in movement. Glenn had come alive again. I had destroyed my life and subsequently had taken all the necessary steps of putting it back together. So, I recognized the legitimacy of what my big brother was doing. There was a long road ahead. However, some of the early steps were behind him. We all noticed and remarked about the positive changes that had taken place.

It had been six months since Mom passed away. A number of medications had been prescribed to Glenn for various reasons. There were pills for high blood pressure, high cholesterol, hypertension, sleeping disorders, and so on. For a man in his early forties, Glenn was on a significant amount of meds. But there was more.

Glenn was diagnosed with Hepatitis C. It had moved beyond the beginning stages. There was evidence of liver damage and issues with his gallbladder. The prognosis was a jolt to us, but all in all things were addressable, treatable, or curable.

By this time we knew Ro was close to her parents and daughter, had close friends, and was successful at her job. She could have had prospects elsewhere if she chose, but the attachment formed between Glenn and Ro was undeniable. We all saw the connection. I had no idea what the future did or did not hold for them. That there wasn't a special attachment isn't true.

Glenn shot Ro straight about his life, our life, and the medical situation. As long as he was serious about getting better and staying healthy, Ro was still on board. That's when I understood how serious things were between the two of them. Collectively, all of the matters in Glenn's life had the potential to repel women. It didn't not go unnoticed by me how Ro was willing to invest herself in my brother.

Fall eased into winter. Glenn was eating healthy, drinking water, not smoking, and keeping normal hours of being awake and sleeping. He was trimmed down and, with his beautiful teeth, appeared like a different person than previous years. Evidence of the health issues, however, could be detected. Sometimes his eyes looked a little yellow and red, itching fits drove him crazy, and he felt pain in his stomach and chest. He was in and out of doctors' offices for several weeks while test were administered, results were studied, and a treatment plan going forward was being put together.

Meanwhile, Glenn and Ro dropped a bomb. They had become engaged, and they had a plan. After Glenn got thorough the health issues, he was going to move to Panama City. There, he and Ro would be married and start a life together. Apparently, Ro, between her family and well-paying job, had eyed the private real estate market for some time. She was interested in buying small properties, and fixing them up to sell or rent. The same as is done here in the United States. That part sounded less crazy than the getting married part.

If Glenn could be healthy and stay on the ball, this might be the start that he needed. He had taken six years of Spanish between high school and college. A couple of times when we were in Mexico dove hunting I had heard his Spanish in action. He could shore it up to a great operational level in Panama in no time.

Who were we to stand in the way at that point? Nadine and I congratulated Glenn and Ro. We truly did give them our best wishes. It was the middle of November, and I had an idea. We should make a photograph of Glenn, Ro, and Melina for a Christmas card. Glenn could send his first Christmas card in a very long time, and Ro could use it to send to her family and friends in Panama.

We had some decorations in the front sitting room of the house. Dad and Mom's official state portraits still hung on the wall where Mom had them. Glenn became irritated when I wouldn't let him take the picture in blue jeans. He returned in chinos and a polo shirt. Still not the best for a Christmas card, but what the heck? I wasn't going to argue with him about a Christmas card.

Glenn was seated in a chair with Melina in his lap. Ro was seated to their left in another chair. The images of Dad and

Mom were behind them on the wall. I had not started giving my direction yet for the shots I wanted to capture while playing photographer for the night. All of us were relaxed and laughing about something. Seeing Glenn naturally happy with Melina in his lap and Ro on his left did my heart so much good. I took a picture of the moment — the smiles, the body language, the ease of the mood.

It was the last picture taken of my brother. Six days later, Glenn was gone.

Chapter 32

Ro left Sarasota for a business trip. With her work finished, she returned to Panama City for a few days. It was a Wednesday, and Glenn had been to a couple of doctor's appointments in the morning. I was off of work, and we all were home. It was a beautiful southwest Florida winter day. Nadine had a couple of errands to run, but wouldn't be gone long.

Glenn, Melina, and I were in the kitchen while I did some prep work for dinner. He talked about Ro, Panama, and getting out of Sarasota. Glenn had spent some of the most lonely and disillusioned years of his life in Sarasota. Indeed, he had done much of the damage himself, but nonetheless, it was a very dark place for him. I wasn't anyone to speak against new beginnings elsewhere.

Nadine came home, and we all ate dinner. Often we sat at the table, but sometimes I would just make the food and tell everyone to dig in when they were hungry. Everyone had to clean their own dishes.

Glenn and Melina went to their respective bedrooms, Nadine was in the bathroom working on her nails, and I worked on my laptop for a few minutes.

Glenn had his room set up like "Bud Fox" in "Wall Street." There were numerous computer displays. Certainly a home entertainment mecca for a five-year-old. Glenn would put on Melina's favorite TV programs and she was in heaven. Often they would watch movies or shows together. Glenn knew by heart many of the song lyrics in the movie "Frozen."

We constantly had to pull Melina out of Uncle Glenny's playroom when it was time for bed. But this night was different. Glenn went into her room and stayed with her until it was bedtime almost an hour later.

I was in the kitchen making some dessert, and Nadine was with me. The door to Melina's room was open, and we could hear some of what they were talking about.

At one point Melina asked Glenn what he wanted from Santa for Christmas to which he answered, "I already have the best present in the whole world. I have the best niece ever."

They continued their conversation as Nadine and I looked at each other, without speaking, acknowledging the tenderness of the moment.

A few minutes later, Glenn quietly emerged from Melina's room. As he gently pulled the door shut, I was in the hallway as well. When he saw me, I nodded my head and squeezed his shoulder.

Melina was asleep, Nadine was in bed, Glenn retired to his room for his nightly video call with Ro, and I reclined in the big leather chair in front of the television in the living room.

As I checked out my loyal go-to channels, History, Travel, Discovery, and the like, I heard the chatter of Glenn and Ro's conversation. Just as I had, by this time, 50 other times. With his door closed I could still hear him clearly, but only identify that it was Ro's voice on the other end of the conversation.

It wasn't long before I slipped into a nice pre-mattress slumber. I don't know how long it lasted until Glenn's voice stirred me. He and Ro were still going strong. I rose from the recliner and looked at my watch. It was after 11:30 p.m. I grabbed my phone and walked into the bedroom where Nadine lay asleep already. I went to my side of the bed. That is when the phone rang.

It was Ro calling. I thought immediately there might be a line or connection problem and their call was dropped. Nadine and I dealt with it many times in our courtship. With ringing phone in hand, I kind of skipped through the kitchen and living room to Glenn's bedroom door.

"Hey buddy, I have Ro on the..."

The door to the room had glass panes with a curtain on the other side that wasn't completely drawn. I looked through and saw Glenn laying flat on his back on the bed, his toes pointing in the air. His hands and fingers were restricted like electrical pulses were shooting through his body. I heard Ro's voice screaming through the computer audio speakers for Glenn to get up.

"G-L-E-N-N!" I busted through the door with my shoulder and lunged toward him.

"Oh God! Please no! Please God!"

As I reached him in panic I looked to my right and was horrified to see Ro, her trembling hands over her mouth. No two eyes have ever shown me true human terror like hers did in that second.

I stood over Glenn and grabbed his shoulders while I still saw life in his eyes. I don't know if he ever knew I was there. Everything seemed like it was divided up in to its own space, but we were all connected.

"Glenn! Oh God...oh God. Please don't...Glenn, don't...I can't, I can't! God, please! Please!" I desperately cried.

I had taken a CPR course in Germany and frantically began compressions on his sternum. Glenn, both eyes still open, was staring straight ahead. Where was the phone? I frantically searched for the phone with one hand, across the bed, under the pillows, while I meaninglessly continued compressions with one hand.

"Ro! Where is the phone? I can't find, oh God, where is the phone? Nadine! Oh God, Nadine! Come here, please! Nadine, quick!"

I was in a state of controlled panic. My breathing was interchanged with whimpering as my fingers wrapped around the phone under Glenn's shoulder. As my hands shook so much it was difficult, I dialed 911 for my brother.

I put the phone between my shoulder and jawbone. I started my compressions again. I looked at Glenn's face again. One eye had closed and the other, half open, stared blankly over my shoulder. I knew his heart had stopped.

"911. What is your emergency?"

"My brother. He's dying. His heart has stopped! I'm doing CPR. Please come now!"

"Sir, what happened?"

"I think it's a heart attack. His fingers were clenched!"

Nadine must have been in as much terror as Ro first, and then me, as she ran into that horrible room. The 911 operator had instructed me to get Glenn's body off of the bed and onto the floor. Nadine took the phone as I scooped Glenn under his arms and shoulder blades and tried to pull him onto the floor as gently as I could. I controlled his torso, but as the back of his feet hit the floor with a thud, I understood the situation. God love Nadine, she had just come into this horrid scene, and now she was talking to a 911 operator, trying to coach a frantic me, looking at Glenn on the floor, and seeing Ro, who had just watched everything from her bedroom in Panama City. The scene was brutal. There are no other words for it.

As Nadine talked to me through the 911 operator, I continued CPR. But I knew it was over. Whatever had gone so terribly wrong wasn't going to change because I was on top of him pushing down on his chest. I knew only God could provide a miracle and this was going to require that. The ambulance and police arrived within minutes of each other. They came through a double French door leading outside from the room.

I didn't want to let Glenn go. I knew this was the last real contact I was ever going to have with him. As they pushed me away from him, I started to my feet with burning anger. It was the kind of rage I felt when I decided to hit the man that had thrown my things out on the jail floor. Even more so. I wanted to destroy. I wanted to hit something and tear the hell out of it. Whatever it was, I wanted to hurt it. I wanted to hurt me. I looked wildly around the room for something I could grab. Then, I looked at Nadine. Water was running down from her red eyes and she was still holding the phone in the air by her face. My rage left me. It is very easy, automatic almost, for us to question God in times like this. For us to wonder where He was.

As I took Nadine in my arms and hugged her tightly, I knew where God was. He was right there in that room with us. The Lord was there and His arms were outstretched to us. He felt every ounce of the maniacal pain we did. He knew that pain and much worse. At the hand of man, and the righteous wrath of God over the sin of mankind was poured onto Him.

As the paramedics hovered over Glenn, Nadine and I took hands and we prayed to God in the name of Christ. I don't know if it was a prayer or more of a calling out. We accepted His will, but prayed that Glenn could be saved. We prayed for Glenn's soul. We are His sheep and He is our shepherd. He knows every single one of us. And we know His voice.

The insanity, dark confusion, and sinful anger left. We could function then. We felt a level of strength and understanding. Nadine went to Ro on the computer display.

I stood in a haze watching the professionals with the lifeless body of my brother. Several minutes had passed at this point. They had used a defibrillator. I'll never forget the sound and the image of Glenn jumping from it. I would watch that, and then turn to see Nadine crying and trying to help Ro. Then I would turn back to Glenn.

If a man doesn't understand there is a God at this moment, then he won't believe. We are not in control like we love to try and tell ourselves.

Ro, who had only 20 minutes earlier been talking with Glenn, now watched as they prepared to carry him away. Glenn's time of death was called and his body was taken to the ambulance outside.

As I went through the house to get my jacket, it dawned on me. Melina never woke up. Less than 50 feet away, everything might as well have been right outside her door. An ambulance, a police car, a fire truck, the lights flashing, the sirens wailing, the screaming, oh God, the screaming. Melina was not sick or getting sick. God showed His mercy to Melina that night. He had compassion for her and spared her the awful scene that Nadine, Ro, and I had to endure.

I left the girls not really talking, but basically being traumatized together. I think at that point some of Ro's family and her daughter were with her. I gave my account of events and answered all the questions law enforcement had.

During some of the most difficult times in my life I have experienced "fuzzy" mode. Everything just seems to be fuzzy and not clear. I don't remember much about what was said or done. I don't remember following the ambulance down to the hospital. I recall sitting in a waiting room and a doctor informing me the cause of Glenn's death was a massive heart attack. Unless Glenn had been in a hospital, he most likely still would not have survived it.

The doctor also informed me the instances of a heart attack for this age group are small. However, the vast majority of these infrequent heart attacks result in death.

My brother, Wallace Glenn Wilkinson Jr., was 44 years old. I entered the large room where he lay on the gurney. There was a chair. I walked to him and looked over him. I was grateful someone had closed his eyes.

My heart was heavier than it ever had been. I felt like I had been physically attacked. Although there was tragedy and pain surrounding Dad's and Mom's deaths, there was somewhat of a natural progression of things in motion. As children, we expect to say goodbye to our parents one day.

No one is ever prepared to watch their brother or sister die like that. Let alone Ro, who couldn't be distracted by at least trying to help Glenn. No, she had to sit there helpless thousands of miles away, and watch. The threads of our lives — Nadine, me, and Ro — will forever run through the needle of November 20, 2014.

My heart was so heavy; the words came out of me like they were being pushed. "What happened, buddy? Oh God, Glenn. What happened?" My voice was hoarse and weak.

For several minutes I sat collapsed, motionless in the chair with my forehead and hands on the gurney. My mind was turning the pages of my life's photo album. Many pages turned with images and memories of Glenn and us together. Memories of the four of us together before the nightmare began.

Finally, I rose to my feet and took the necklace that Ro had given him off of his neck. I kissed his forehead. Then I told the only brother and sibling I ever had goodbye.

Dad, Mom, Glenn, and I had gone through so much together. I couldn't believe I was the only one left. Walking to the door, it was as if I was walking through a portal of two worlds. I was leaving one world and entering another. I was no longer, and never would be again, a son and a brother. Now, I was a husband and a father.

Two hours had passed since I left the house. I returned to Nadine sitting alone in the room in which we had only hours earlier witnessed death. The room was a complete wreck. The space on the floor where Glenn had been was an empty hole. It seemed completely unreal. Ro's family had taken control of what they could in Panama City. It seemed like a hurricane had blown through. Now was the assessment of the damage.

Melina continued to sleep in the calm and quiet that belied the previous bedlam. The silence was so awful. Both of us were in shock and disoriented. There was nothing else we could do. We sat on the bed together and wept.

Perhaps Nadine was able to sleep for an hour or so; I never slept. The sun rose a couple of hours later. As soon as it was full in the sky, I called Myra. Once again, she was immediately on her way to Florida — for the second time in seven months. This time bringing her girls, Katherine and Lizzie, with her. Then I phoned Aunt Kathy and Uncle Gene. By this time, the number of bad telephone calls made within our family over the years was getting, well, bad. Of course, they were upset and shocked. Carola, already in the United States for her work in the thoroughbred industry, and Ro each headed to Sarasota.

Melina awoke in the morning her same sweet self as she always does. All I know to say is that Nadine and I simply couldn't bring ourselves to sit Melina down and tell her. At that point, I don't think either one of us were capable of handling it with the responsibility to Melina's feelings we had as parents. Simply put, we knew learning Uncle Glenny was gone was going to give Melina a lot of pain. That physical death is a reality of life is one of the most important lessons that we learn. Melina learned it with Glenn, and she loved him very much. It hurt her and Nadine both. Both of them loved Glenn, and he them.

Nadine had lost a grandmother she was close to in Germany a couple of years earlier, but until then her experience with death was minimal. That was not so anymore. Everything about that night slapped us hard in the face several times.

During the very difficult task of being in the room and sorting through Glenn's things, I found a Bible. On the inside cover he had written a date from two years earlier. Under it he wrote, "I accepted Jesus Christ as my personal Lord and Savior." I pray so much it is so.

Over the course of two days everyone showed up. All in all it was eight of us, and being together gave us all a lot of strength. Melina is close to Katherine and Lizzie, so that part of it was perfect. The three of them pod around together. Katherine, the wonderful, responsible older one, leads the two little stinkers, Melina and Lizzie, around. Later, we learned that Katherine slipped and told Melina about Glenn.

Nadine and I went to her and did the best we knew how in discussing such things. Trying to explain to a beautiful young child about God, life, and death in a profoundly traumatizing moment is very difficult to do. Christ always needs to be at the center of any explanations or reasons given about anything. Totally every experience we have here, Christ endured magnified before He accomplished everything on the cross and afterward. Jesus also knew the intense sadness we feel when death is involved. Jesus loved Lazarus, whom he raised from the dead. As The Lord watched Mary and the other Jews weeping, He wept. Everything about life that is deep and heavy I always connect to the suffering, love, forgiveness, and glory of Jesus Christ.

As we all came together and discussed Glenn's life, something came into focus. Although Glenn had made wonderful strides in his health recently, he had also abused his body for many years. Health was never really a priority of his. The strains of the last 10 years had become unbearable to his system. It just shut down quickly and severely. Along with the trauma of losing him, the trauma of the experience itself was something we were all dealing with.

Within a day, news spread to Kentucky about Glenn. There was an article in the Lexington newspaper. As I read about Glenn's life, it didn't say husband or father. It didn't say numerous things I wish so much life had not denied my older brother. But I know that Glenn denied himself. The Bible tells us exactly what God wants us to know, but there are some secrets of God that remain His. Maybe we will learn some of these things when we are in eternity with Him.

Glenn visiting Melina the night he died was an intensely spiritual event. Nadine and I have discussed it as rational adults who were there. We believe Glenn was somehow led to go to Melina. By The Holy Spirit or his own spirit, we do not know. We saw how he went to her like never before. On some level, he was saying goodbye.

Love and support poured out from the years of our lives past. Many people who had not heard from or seen Glenn in years, but knew the real him, reached out to me. God used many of them to hold me up.

Of course, Myra was there. Myra has been there for me many times in our lives, I'm afraid much more than I have for her. I hope she knows she will always be my sister.

David Dean was a very close friend of Glenn's in high school and college. My parents always really liked Dave. Dave was always one of those guys who had style and was loaded with charisma. Like so many of our friends, Glenn and Dave were buddies first, and then Dave and I became friends.

Both Myra and Dave planned and coordinated Glenn's memorial at Sayre School in Lexington. Sayre is where Glenn and I attended kindergarten through 12th grade. Over the years, the Sayre community was another on the long list of things we had walked away from.

I have known Gordon and Karen Walls for over 30 years. We had lived across the street from Karen's parents, who were close friends of Dad and Mom's all throughout my childhood. Gordon, with his own measure of charisma, was the only person I can ever remember my dad letting call him "Wally." Gordon and Karen played instrumental roles in both Mom's and Glenn's memorials. Gordon is a very sound Christian. Last summer, while having dinner at his house, his spiritual maturity showed itself clearly over my sometimes-overzealous immaturity.

Having said and written thank you, I still wonder if Myra, Dave, Gordon, and Karen really know how indebted I am to them. Their love, support, and efforts are what made both memorials happen.

God always provides for us in our deepest hour of need. Glenn did not have a will, and the decision of what to do for him really was not a decision at all. Glenn was cremated and his ashes are with Nadine, Melina, and me.

One day it is my prayer to have Dad, Mom, and Glenn all together in a place that is proper for them. I am prayerfully and with trust awaiting this day.

Many people I had not seen in years were at Glenn's memorial. It did my heart such good to feel hugs and warmth that I recognized. Michelle Lambert is a dear friend that life had separated from me for 20 years. Michelle also had experienced dealing with pain as the public watched. We never really talked about it, but I believe mutual respect and understanding were always a cornerstone of our friendship.

I walked into the area of the memorial and one of the first things I saw was Michelle walking to me with her purposeful, confident stride the same as always. So often we don't appreciate and know the depth of the ties and bonds we make when we are younger. Or maybe we do, but we just lose them. Either way, when we hugged I knew I was home.

For the third time in 14 months, I stood before others to speak of a life that directly influenced the human being I became. My heart was ripe for abandonment and pain. The truth is, if I had not had Nadine and Melina in this time I could have buckled. This was a time I could have obliterated things. I could have started obliterating limits that had come into my life through God and some hard, hard lessons. That is my nature.

But as I stood again looking at the faces that looked on me, I remembered that portal I walked through. That life, that Andrew is gone. I have to let him go. The blessings in my life don't need that Andrew.

As I began, I spoke of the fortune God had bestowed on me in that I had a father, a mother, and a brother who all loved me very much. Glenn had been in our younger years a little rougher on me than he should have been. But somewhere along the way a transformation had taken place, the result of which was a fiercely loyal and dedicated brother. My older brother was my own private "break in case of emergency" tool. If I ever was in need, danger, trouble, or whatever, Glenn was the person I needed to call first. And he had received a lot of calls from me.

Yes, there was room to go down a deeply sad, tragic road. I chose not to. For whatever reason, Glenn got knocked off track and he never could get back on. He was a human being. But I knew that human being and the array of good and wonderful things about him. The people there that day did as well.

I was happy and grateful I could bring with me news of positivity and life tasted once more by my brother. He did not die in a place of the sort he had been in earlier. Glenn had felt again. Ro had brought color into his landscape. Nadine and Melina had introduced conversations, fun, little private jokes, and stories. There had been love and laughter. I thank God Melina and Nadine knew him as well as they did.

As I left there that day, I did it with an attitude of thanksgiving. If Glenn had not experienced some of the things in his life that he did, his death would have been something altogether different. God gives and He takes away. He does it in His way, and I have come to understand that in my life.

I returned for the first time to Greenbrier and saw that the extra large lot Dad had developed years ago was now divided up with several homes standing. The girls and I traveled the almost 30 miles on I-64 through horse country to the Governor's Mansion in Frankfort like I had done so many times.

From Frankfort, we drove another 30 miles south on US-127 to the place we used to call Wilkinson Farms. Oh, how I knew that drive. I could hear us shouting, riding, and having times I wish so much I could just go back to one time.

273

The pull was enormous, and I had to drive to the main brick house, take a left over and up to the barn, drive past the white barn and through the gate at the silo, and then head left to and past the office. There, down in a thicket of trees was Mom's cabin. Although still standing, it is a much different cabin than the one of my past. Gone are the cut grass, blooming flowers, and swept, lit walkways. The corncrib party barn where Freddy the farm cat stayed was falling down. Large tree limbs, resting now, had broken through the roof, porch, and windows.

Without Dad, Mom, and Glenn, and to see Mom's cabin alone with time passed by like that was one of the saddest moments in my life.

Chapter 33

The pressure, strain, and difficulty of 2014 had been immense. Beginning with our separation for four months while I worked as hard as I could to make preparations for my family, then my mother's rapid decline and death, and then Glenn's death and the night itself. We were just barely functioning. It had left us a little bit crazy. We were pretty much in shock as a result of the whole year, not one specific event.

It is precisely these times when followers in Jesus Christ can take heart. In the world we will have pain, suffering, and chaos, but we can have peace through Our Savior. He has overcome it. And where He is, we are going. It's not easy. In fact, it's impossible to comprehend these things without The Holy Spirit. But we have it, I have it, and I understand. This is Our Hope. What else do we have? I have heard or seen nothing as good.

The three of us headed to a cabin in the mountains, woods, and waterfalls of western North Carolina. The company I worked for was extremely gracious when I requested some time away with my girls. All of us were exhausted, and the need to get away was front and center.

For 12 days over the course of Christmas, we snuggled and played games by the fire. We drank hot chocolate, and cooked bacon and eggs for breakfast. I sat on the wooden front porch and sipped my coffee while the cold mountain air arose my senses. Lake Toxaway was the local community, and we explored the area. We hit the trails with horses and hiking boots. We ate at a great old diner in Brevard before we finished some Christmas shopping at O.P. Taylor's toy store in the old downtown. It was really a good time, Nadine and I dancing around with all of our plans so Melina wouldn't figure things out.

I have always heard the language of that part of the country, and I'm not referring to the dialect but the language of the mountains. Like all the majestic things and forms created through The Lord, the mountains also reveal God's invisible character to us. Nadine was introduced to that part of my country, one of the most beautiful. And hopefully, Melina will recall it well.

Those 12 days in the mountains made it possible for us to start the rest of our lives together. From there, we again returned to Florida to start fresh. We left my mother's house and signed a lease for a home we all found comfortable.

As much as the time in North Carolina was a blessing, the wounds were all still very raw for the three of us. For months it was common for me to find Nadine alone in the house somewhere crying in silence. Melina was experiencing great sadness for the first time in her life. It hurt me to see her crying, understanding but not understanding. I was learning to live without any surviving member of my family. I handled Glenn's last affairs and was determined to focus on moving forward in life with my family.

Walking through the house all of a sudden could become a 50-foot walk of sadness. I would see a photograph of the four of us, or the three of them. Reminders dot the landscape of my life — a Wilkinson Blvd. road sign, a Martha's cabin sign, a lifetime of photos, memorabilia, and belongings of what truly was another lifetime ago. I painstakingly sorted through every storage room, garage, box, closet, file, and drawer. I made the decision once and for all what to keep and what to rid ourselves of.

There are three large trunks packed with the most revealing things about the lives and characters of the Wilkinson family — Wallace, Martha, Glenn, and Andrew. One day in the future I will take my daughter to sit by these trunks. We will explore for her who her family is, and I will honor the memories and lives of the people I can only speak of to her.

The challenge for me most often is when I think of one I will think of another, and then another, and then the four of us. I am the only one who survived what happened to us 16 years ago. Everyone else died as a direct result of the collapse. The bankruptcy was the beginning of the end for Dad, Mom, and Glenn. I was with each of them as they drew their last breath.

There is no dispute that the Wilkinson story is sad. As long as I am in the flesh, the pain will always be there. But what a blessing to be with them as their time here was over. What a gift from God.

We were basically alone in Sarasota at this point. We were praying for God to provide some direction for a church home. Nadine was visiting different congregations with Melina as I was working on Sundays, giving my job priority over my faith. Sunday was a busy day in production. We were getting out orders for the beginning of the week that usually changed at the last minute. Along with this, many times we were waiting to "flip" incoming trucks with fresh produce. Sometimes that practice made the Production Department warehouse and loading docks a literal madhouse.

In my absence, some of the advances we had realized disappeared. I didn't take it personally. I was the one who really cared about the new direction; it was my direction. I had established authority, but not trust yet. There was still some unconscious and conscious resistance to some of the new things I had introduced. So when I wasn't there, there was some slippage.

Still very much in mourning for my mother and my brother, I was back in the coolers and the office. A couple of weeks into my return, I went to talk to our box maker. We had a position with the sole responsibility to prepare cardboard boxes for production needs. I am a stickler for a clean, organized work area. When I'm in charge, clean up and organization are performed during work activities — not after. I had spoken before to the box maker about keeping his workstation in order. That day, his workstation was not in acceptable shape, so I approached him in my scope of authority and questioned him.

This man was illiterate and I, along with the founder's sister, had researched several reading and writing programs for him. We had given him good information accrued from several different resources and watched to see what he did with it. Over time, we understood he was not interested in learning to read and write.

He became upset when I sternly asked why he was not doing his job the way I had asked him to. Ultimately, he cussed at me using the f-word twice and raising his voice. It was quick and severe how I verbally responded to him. While others watched, I gave him a tongue lashing with my finger in his chest as the pain from everything else in my life came out of my windpipes.

I had lost my cool in a big way, and I knew it. At least 15 other people watched Andrew the Christian chop this guy down. The employee's actions were intolerable. However, my response was a total failure — first as a Christian, and then as a professional.

The man went home for the day, and I went straight to the front office and told them what happened. I even knocked on the owner's office door, went in, and explained myself to him. I knew I was better than the way I had acted, and I was apologetic. As much as I felt guilt for the company, I had just damaged The Kingdom of God. I clearly illustrated my hypocrisy.

We all are hypocrites on some level. Hypocrisy is not political, cultural, racial, or anything else designated to one group of people. Hypocrisy is part of the human dilemma. It is part of our sinful nature and the only one never to have possessed it is Jesus Christ. In each of us, our tolerance levels for what offends increase when other things about something or someone fall in line with our belief system.

I can stick to my guns with the best of them, but when it is time to fess up and apologize, I will. I believe it is a hallmark of strong character to admit wrongdoing and ask forgiveness. I willingly approached the box maker and offered my apology. He apologized in turn, and we established a good working relationship again.

I was on fumes, frazzled, and going through many emotional and spiritual issues. We had no close friends or family nearby. The Lord put it heavy on my heart that I could not continue alone. Going it alone is one of my calling cards. If I am in that mode, then something is or will be wrong.

I decided to immediately do two things. First, I scheduled an appointment with an appropriate psychologist for me and my Christian faith. Second, I went from doctor's office to doctor's office to have tests performed to gauge my health.

Although under some extenuating circumstances, three out of four members of my family were gone. All of them were young or relatively young. I needed to learn the state of my health, and prepare some things for Nadine and Melina in the event Our Savior called me home. I was seriously grateful to learn I was in decent shape. There are some "not so young anymore" issues at play, but for the most part my health is intact.

Melina, our sweet, wonderful daughter, was of concern to me. Bless her heart. Over the course of our lives, Melina has shown us as long as she is with Nadine and I, she can be a happy, vibrant child. She brings so much into the lives of her mother and me.

In Germany, we moved three times, and then the whole "American" experiment started. We moved four times in less than two years. We have dragged Melina all around. Never has she uttered a word of complaint. As a baby and toddler, Melina would grab gently with her hands and fingers. If she was next to you on the sofa, it wouldn't be long until you felt her little fingers softly touch or pinch you. In fact, our nickname for her is "Pinch." We knew this could also be a time for Pinch to act out. It was a strange time; all of us had the potential to act out, really.

But we didn't. Praise The Lord. The three of us stayed close and drew strength from each other. God has blessed each of us through the other two. Melina came to me, visibly upset, on a particular occasion.

As parents we learn the grade scale for the severity level of tears. It runs from "silly" all the way through "legit." The tears streaming from Melina's eyes were legit and showed disturbed sadness. She had heard talk somewhere of marriages ending, divorces, and custody battles. What if she ever had to choose from me or Mami? She wouldn't do it, she told me. There was no way anybody could get her to choose. Oh, the pure innocence of childhood. She talked to me as if, when she would refuse to choose, things would all be settled and nobody would have to choose because "we all would be living together perfectly happily forever."

I hope Melina can fully understand one day that if I can, I will always choose, even seek, pain for myself before I let her experience that same pain. If I can, I will always take it for her. Although I understand many people in divorces have said something similar, I truly believe that it would have to be something super serious for Nadine and I to be even remotely pulled apart. We have bled for what we have. I know it is held as something worth fighting for with both of us. Because we already have. There is a trust between us that had to be achieved. And we did. In terms of marriage, that is just enormous.

Chapter 34

For me, one of the biggest factors to staying focused and healthy, other than prayer and active fellowship, is being involved in the lives of others. There is a lot of pain and suffering out there. The world in which we dwell is fallen. I don't think, at this point, that statement is relegated to being only a Christian opinion. All one has to do is open their eyes, ears, and senses. The fallenness can be overwhelming. War, murder, violence, disease, addiction, human trafficking, and we scream in rage-filled protest over the right to do some of the most unspiritual things imaginable.

There is love, beauty, and meaningful, good things too, for sure. But these are not the defining elements of our current world. They are from God and they burst through, jumping up and down, screaming, trying to get our attention. All of these things and universes more were created through Christ and show us the way back to Him through the muck and mire of this world.

I say again, there is good in man. After all, God made a conscious decision to form us in His image. This innate goodness shines forth in natural ways. However, the deceit in the Garden of Eden of Adam and Eve by Satan was the biggest heist in all of human history, and souls are what he stole. He introduced sin to soil the perfection in our relations with God.

People love to hear about salvation, but they do not care to hear about sin. They are part of the same cross and cannot be separated. Instead of being irritated in our pride when we must endure hearing about sin, we should be talking about the greatness of our God. How we were separated from Him, but He has provided a way back to Him because of His love for us.

I have told the following story to people several times. One day during my lunch hour, I was at a gas station near my job. I noticed a guy in front of me with a pair of work gloves hanging from the glove clip on his belt. It caught my eye because I had misplaced my gloves in the coolers at work several times. I asked him where he found the glove clip and he told me his employer provided it for him, that he didn't know where to find them. He left. I paid inside, and also left. As I was getting back into my truck, the guy walked up with the glove clip in his hand and offered it to me.

"Here," he said. "Take these. I can get another pair at work."

"For real, man?"

"Yeah, take them. I'll get another pair. I hope they help."

I looked at him, "Thank you, my brother. They will. I appreciate that." I spoke with gratitude and respect.

He recognized my tones. Then he nodded back, communicating the same tones in return without words.

He was black.

All over the United States, every single day, there are genuine, respectful interactions between races in the grocery store, post office, or wherever; there are people living with one another in harmony.

In prison, I had and have had some of the most honest, productive discussions about life and race in my life. There was no political correctness. Oh no, you can't show up on a prison compound talking about political correctness. Political correctness is seen as a luxury for people who have the time and comfort to focus on those things. You don't see political correctness at the barbershop, corner mart, and car wash like you do in the schools, boardrooms, clubs, and gyms.

It was really no big deal for that guy to give up his clip for me. He was going to get a replacement from his boss. The point is that man, completely from self-will, decided to do something nice for me. These things happen everywhere all the time. But it's not salacious, violent, or oppressive enough to hold our attention.

There is racism, and horrible things have been and are done in the name of it. Racism is born from fear, and fear is part of our fallen nature. The solution to the global, ageless struggle of racism, which exists everywhere, is God. God alone can remove racism from the hearts of men. Because we all stand absolutely equal in front of Him.

I naturally engage in small acts of respect and kindness. I enjoy being helpful to people or even, perhaps, making their day better. I hold doors, I help carry things, I wave to the trash guy, I give a thumbs up to the guy holding the stop sign. These are all very small things but they, in my opinion, carry a wallop in terms of the good done.

I've always had respect for authority, even though I was taunting it half the time. For years, I have approached police, firefighters, and soldiers offering thanks from me and my family. It's like my own personal way of saying to people that we may be divided into groups by society, but we are all in this together. I like to convey this in my actions, deeds, and words.

Many verifiable good deeds of law enforcement go largely unnoticed by the public and media. Again, it doesn't draw as much attention when a police officer, out of the compassion in their heart, helps a battered wife run away from a crack addicted, abusive husband, as it does for something else. Such as when that police officer feels terrified for their life and discharges their weapon in self-defense or in error from the ungodly pressure at that split moment in time.

Back in 2006, inmates in Florida's state prisons were required to have a clean-shaven face at all times. We were given a daily razor that we used and turned back in. Shaving every day is a problem for some black people because of the way their neck hair grows around their throat. Not a lot, but some. The skin can be easily irritated by a razor being pulled over it. Naturally, a lot of the black inmate population asked for and received medical passes allowing them not to shave every day. Many of the people who asked for the medical exemption from shaving really had no problem with skin irritation due to shaving. They were just lazy and didn't want to shave.

It got kind of ridiculous how many black guys had the pass not to shave. We all knew that most of them didn't have a problem with shaving. The prison staff realized this too, but none of them wanted to deal with being called a racist if they didn't issue a pass to someone. A significant portion of the black population in the prison used the guards not wanting to face a racism accusation as leverage for what they personally desired. In this case, it was the desire not to shave.

All groups of people do this, and it is no surprise the black guys at Franklin Correctional did the same thing. They saw something they could use as an advantage for what they wanted to accomplish, and they used it. Therefore, their collective exploitation of the shaving rule was generally accepted. Everyone knew it and accepted it. We even discussed it. It's just how it was because the guards let it happen.

Nowadays, a journalist or some other person not associated with prison in the least would call me a racist over simply sharing that experience. They'd have absolutely no clue what happened or why it happened, no understanding of the environment it took place in, and call me a racist for simply talking about it. This is what political correctness does. The reality of the situation at the ground level is not what is expressed. This type of thing definitely exists today and hurts race relations. The truth is bent to fit a narrative, and people believe it as it is presented because they don't know any better. They weren't there either. A story about how a man of color in prison is being forced to bloody up his neck with a razor sells much better than the same guy giving a glove clip to a white guy.

This is particularly grievous for me because the other half of my family is in Germany. As little as good race relations are illustrated here, they are hardly ever shown across the Atlantic Ocean. What Europeans have to digest about race in the United States, outside of the entertainment industry, is pretty much always the worst scenario. I would say the vast majority of Europeans believe that the United States is a place of severe racism, even though millions and millions of us twice-elected the first African-American president in our country's history.

There are all sorts of biases across the world. In every single country people have negative feelings about other groups of people. But somehow along the way, racism became purely a white against black American thing.

As a Christian, I know God does not see any color other than red — the red of Jesus's blood that makes me perfect and blameless to look at. I have prayed with many men of all different races. I have hugged them, and they have hugged me. I have written letters of encouragement, and met family members who have waited a very long time for anything good. I have cried and laughed with them. We have shared the hardest regrets in our lives and the biggest dreams, hopes, and fears. I have made sure they had a nice outfit to wear when they walk back into life, no longer a prisoner of man's system. I am not only volunteering. In the Similitudes of the Gospel of Matthew, Jesus says we are to let our light shine before men in a way that lets them see our good works and that glorifies God. Of course, Christ is our light. I am one of the ways, I pray, the light of Jesus Christ overcomes the darkness.

When I help others, the focus is taken off of me. I spent over 30 years selfishly paying attention to the man in the mirror. We all see where that got me. The truth is I can never blame what happened to my father for the shape I ultimately ended up in. The foundations of my own collapse were there beforehand. I could have walked down the exact same path of self-destruction in a life where there was no bankruptcy and still bunches of money. I was arrogant on the outside and afraid on the inside.

Josh Hopkins is an old, good friend of mine. Hop, as we call him sometimes, is a successful actor and director in Los Angeles. Growing up he was handsome, athletic, funny, and personable. This guy was made for California, and girls got downright silly over him. The guys loved hanging out with him. Hop and I were part of a group of Kentuckians who went to Auburn University in Alabama.

A couple of years into his studies, Josh dropped out in pursuit of his dream of becoming an actor. He went after it with a humble, maniacal work ethic and desire to learn the craft. I think it is safe to say that his parents, Larry and Carolyn, while believing in him did not want him to leave school. Hop stayed true to his vision and kept on trucking.

Years later, Josh is living and working in California and has made it on any scale of measure in the industry. Back in school there were always kids jealous of him. I am sure there are some today still jealous of his success and celebrity. I too was jealous of Hop, but for a different

Andrew Wilkinson

reason. I saw him stand firm for what he wanted and believed in for his life. He went to his folks and talked about it and took action. I never had the guts to do that.

In my teen years I knew following my father's footsteps and taking over the companies he started might not be what I wanted for the focus of my life. For Glenn, it was clear that is what he wanted. That was his choice, and that was okay for him. I felt different from that early on. Looking at things just for a bottom line is not something I am good at. Activities on a more human level attracted me much more. I wanted to do something on my own, to be tested. Deep down I believed I had what it took to strike out on my own; I just had no clue how to do so. Teaching is always something I believed I could do.

I have a cousin, David, who my parents loved very much and has his own incredible story of perseverance, sacrifice, and hard work. David, also living in Los Angeles, is a world-class pianist and classical opera teacher. His career has taken him all over the world, and now he professionally resides at Pepperdine University in Malibu, California — literally on the West Coast.

Like Josh, David knew what he wanted, went for it, worked hard, and made the sacrifices. He was a prodigy on the piano out of Casey County, Kentucky. It is a community of good people in the heart of the Bluegrass, but classical music is not something the area is known for. David was sharp, quiet, and not average at all. There was always a special quality to him. David, no doubt, endured a lot at the hands and mouths of other children growing up. Children are capable of dispensing hellfire pain. But David did the work and was in New York, Europe, and now Malibu. He too staked his claim in life, went for it, and got it.

I believed I was being forced into a life I knew wasn't what I wanted. Of course, I was not forced at all. In the beginning, it is true; Dad might not have understood where I was coming from. He came from a place of real, down and out poverty. He hated it and worked all of his life not to remain in it. That I somehow was refusing everything he was willing to hand over to Glenn and me could very well have troubled him. However, as intimidating as Dad could be, he also was fair and reasonable.

If I had come to him with a plan and a well-thought out explanation of what I wanted, it would have been a really good start with him. Then, after some time, he and Mom would have seen I was serious and they would have supported my endeavors. I know it. There were simply a lot of things. My father had hundreds of employees, and had very ambitious plans to further grow his businesses. He needed help doing these things. So for me to give even the slightest indication that I wasn't going to be involved would have been a pretty big deal in my family. I shrank from the pressure.

I allowed all of this to create unhappiness in my younger life. This is why I absolutely could have gone down the road I travelled regardless of other circumstances. Instead of facing things, I jetted off to New York or California and spent in a weekend what some made in a year. It was fear. Fear stopped me in my tracks, and I lived in it for a big segment of my life. The fear of letting my father down shut me down completely. It was a fear of him looking at me and not being proud of me. A fear of everyone watching and what they would have been thinking. And that is my fault, not Dad's. The choices I made in my life influenced by my fear did far worse damage than what my father, who loved me, ever did or would have done.

Today, when I see myself in the mirror, I know who is looking back at me. It's a guy whose brokenness should have sent him to his grave a thousand times. I see the grace, mercy, compassion, and love of Jesus Christ staring me back in my face. I am not that as much as I wish I was. I see a man who has, at this point, experienced quite a bit.

At times it does seem like I have lived many different lives. An irresponsible young man of privilege and influence, a shocked and staggered man in the financial demise and death of his father, a selfish self-transformed victim bent on his own destruction, a prisoner and a free man simultaneously, an ex-con learning how to be a productive citizen and apply his faith to real life, a man learning how to be a man, husband, and a father in a foreign country, and a man who lost the final remnants of a life that once was when his mother and brother died upon his homecoming.

Oh, but there is so much more. I have a beautiful woman of God who loves me, and together we have a wonderful child. Nadine is the prayer warrior of our family and whose natural, God-given goodness of heart keeps me in check. We follow the Biblical structure for our home. I am the head of our household. This means I am the leader servant for my family just the same as Christ was to His disciples. This is a huge responsibility and an honor from God that I have Nadine and Melina to be responsible to and for. Nadine accepts this role for me and because she does she gains tremendous sway and authority over me. Both of us are built up by the other.

People can and will interpret this the way they want to. Some will even have a problem with it, and that is their problem. Up to our limitations without God, what Nadine and I have is a potent mix of man-woman power. The structure we have is a formidable way to deal with life, and God gave it to us. It is my job to be thankful and hold her up for what God has blessed me with. I am not better or more important than any other member of my family. However, because there is no struggle between us for control, our love can flourish.

This is called old-fashioned today, I believe. Some call it much worse. We are nothing of the sort. There are elements of an old-fashioned lifestyle that carry great value. However, it is not something that accurately describes us.

A little over a year from the beginning stages of writing this work, I went to Nadine and asked what she thought if I took it on. I believed I was ready. By this point, I had been in front of other groups of people on various occasions and some of them had approached me afterward. In conversation, I was often asked if I had given thought to writing about the past years of my life. Nadine and I both knew it was a full-time endeavor, which meant quitting my job.

Nadine, my partner, supporter, and helper, agreed that we could do it if I was really ready to sit down and walk through my whole life in detail. Her encouragement meant more to me than a ship full of gold. She went out of the house to work in retail while I stayed home and worked. That also meant I was the point man for driving to school, cooking and preparing meals, housework, laundry, and the myriad of other incidentals that come with living life in a family.

I resigned my position at my employer and thanked them for the wonderful opportunity they had given me. I certainly wished them well in the future. But, much like Germany, it was time for me to move on. I was still on my way somewhere.

The home is a much overlooked and vastly important part of the family. Actually, the amount of truly good, meaningful things born in the home is infinitely more than that which is born outside of it. All of the other members in a family go out into their day with a send-off from the one in the home primarily responsible for these things. There is the lunch made with a little note, the outfit that was ironed and the patch put on it, the massage given, the buttons sewed on, the deep scratch cleaned, the play lines practiced, and much, much more.

With us, everybody does what is required at the time and we don't get bogged down in labels and roles. We do whatever we have to do to get through whatever time we need to get through. I take pride in preparing a meal for my family and fixing it the way I know they like. I also take pride in Nadine and Melina knowing if something ever happened, if something threatened them, that I would do everything I know how to protect them from harm. I would lay down my life for them.

I know Melina's favorite color and the special little configurations she can do with her toes. I know Nadine's thought process even while she talks in her sleep in German or English (it depends on her mood). I have fun having a discussion with her while she sleeps and telling her about it in the morning.

As parents, our policy is not to hide Melina from things or the world. There is a limit to what a seven year old can understand and process. However, there is just too much out there to attempt to always shield and cover. We discuss things as they come at us, and we prayerfully figure out a way to do so. God is at the center of most of our conversations. Or I should say, His connection to the particular moment or topic at hand.

One of my biggest pet peeves is bunching the dirty silverware up in the first couple of bins of the dishwasher, instead of spacing the knives, forks, spoons, and whatever else out toward the back of the washer. Another one is clumped up toothpaste in the cap of the toothpaste. Oh yeah, leaving hair all over the bathroom floor after using the hair dryer is one too. The point is we have sort of a mantra in our house that goes, "It is not more work; it's just not being lazy." Meaning that the little things we do all throughout the day in the name of being thorough, don't add up to much work. But when these little things are neglected, there is exponentially more work at a later time. To teach Melina things like this is to directly affect the way the rest of her life is conducted. I take it very seriously, and I pray one day Melina will sit with me and be thankful for the manner in which Nadine and I raised her. In her life, she is the one who has to ultimately choose her decisions and beliefs.

Chapter 35

I believe absolutely there is a God. I am a person on this earth who has lived enough of this life to make a decently credible decision for myself. God is real. Billions of other souls have and still will come to the same conclusion. I choose to follow Jesus Christ. I have specific reasons why I do so. They are spiritual, experiential, and logical. I have experienced the power of The Holy Spirit in my life, and no one can ever tell me I haven't. We don't have all the answers, but the ones we need are all around us in everything that He made and the Bible.

I think about things like no one has ever been able to credibly speak of a sin Jesus committed. And how the world, the accuser and father of lies, and his legions have tried. I see how in a room full of people all sorts of religions can be discussed in relative calm, but when the name Jesus is spoken, people become angry and irritated. We have noticed paranormal television shows where the name of Jesus Christ is routinely the ultimate tool to overcome dark forces and demons. I think of the 40 God-inspired writers who penned 66 books over the course of 1,500 years and their unbelievable ability to stay on The Point of all time.

The game "telephone" is played when the participants sit in a circle and start with one player and a word. The starter will whisper the word in the ear of the person next to him and so on and so forth until the last player hears the word. One word, much of the time, is changed in the course of 20 or 25 people whispering it to another. For me, the clarity and accuracy of what the Bible provides over 1,500 years, 40 authors, and 66 books about The Lord means one thing. It was from one source of divinely inspired knowledge, which was God. I see the transformed lives of people in the

Bible, of history, and of today. I see clearly how, when left to his devices, man does not establish limits and thresholds are crossed that should not be. I have seen the light and love of Christ burst through in the darkest of lives. I have felt the love of Christ during a group hug in prison with a room full of men in tighty whities.

The emotional spectrum we have is directly from our Creator. Everything we feel, He also feels. The difference is, He feels in perfect holiness and we don't. There is one characteristic or attribute of God that, to me, flat out proves His existence. That is love. Love didn't just occur. It didn't come into being from an explosion billions of years ago. Evolution hasn't performed its magic over numerous millennia resulting in love from an extremely base form of the emotion. Love is how we can get back to God.

The fiery and dedicated leader of the disciples, Peter, tells us that our salvation through the love of God is a theme that the angels are very interested in. God's love for man is a matter that fascinates the angels! And His redeeming, forgiving love manifested itself through Jesus Christ and His atoning death on the cross. Wow, that is love! That is a love I want to know and receive and learn to give. And I can; we all can.

It's true — all of the jets, helicopters, and boats are gone. The tickets, passes, comps, and closet full of handmade clothes are gone. The garage full of something new and shiny every six months no longer exists. The need for people to recognize me when I walk into a room has been put down.

But today, I have Andrew Wilkinson and an understanding of who he is. And that is worth far more than anything man has created, does create, or will ever create. What I don't understand, I realize that I don't and might never. When I see my life, it is accurate to say I see sadness, pain, and tragedy. But I really am nothing special. It comes to us all one way or another. There is a word for it. Life. And not only is it sometimes not pretty, it can downright knock us out cold on the dirty, hard, and wet ground.

Someone once said that having money and losing it is much worse than having never had money at all. That same someone obviously missed the invaluable lessons there were to learn about God, self, and life.

Please understand; I am not touting my program or way of doing things. But I could never say before that when I had "everything," I really had nothing. Now, I don't have a lot in terms of what the world calls wealth, but I have enduringly more than I have ever had in my life. I don't hate money, for crying out loud, but I know its proper place in my value system. My life will not be defined solely by the pursuit of it. I will work hard and do the best I can to provide for my family. Nadine has interests of her own. There is a lot of good life left to live.

Today's given meaning by society and the press of being a Christian is equal to standing on the roof of a church and yelling, "I'm perfect and so are all Christians!"

That is twisted. The contrary is actually true. Being a Christian means I acknowledge that I am inherently a sinner. Although there are good qualities about me because I am made in God's image, my sin nature separates me from God. God, through His Son, Jesus Christ, has shown me mercy and grace by forgiving me and not holding my sins against me. Christ lived a sinless life, was crucified on the cross, endured the wrath of God resulting from sin, rose again to physical life in three days confirming His victory over death, and now He sits at the right hand of the Father as The All Worthy One. He will come again. Because of all this, and my belief in it, I have a Savior and salvation for my soul. This is what it means to me to be a Christian.

I am far from perfect. In fact, left to my own devices I could be a train wreck again. I pray to God, through and in the name of Jesus Christ, and He is very active in the affairs of my life. I see it happening all the time. Other Christians do too. We are not mad people. We have taken off the masks (or should) and have gotten real about things. God shows up and does stuff. Plain and simple. He loves, He gives, He teaches, He waits, He secures, He hears, and so much more. And, yes, when we need to understand or accept something, He will discipline us. There are not enough theses and dissertations that can be written to truly describe what Christ did and accomplished on the cross for us.

When I see someone with wealth or who appears to have wealth, I don't sit in silent envy. I wonder, do they know a lot of the things I do? Do they know, if everything was stripped away, who they are? Where would they turn? What would they do?

I sure did not know. In my case, money and the trappings of wealth served as distractions. Distractions that I allowed to keep me from knowing who I was. Distractions that I allowed to deceive me about my need for God and a Savior. I have known many persons of significant wealth who, quite frankly, were very unhappy. Money is a needed, very convenient thing. The physical world revolves around it. But it does not determine in the least who we are and what our time here means.

I remember my family and the way we were every day. Reminders are too numerous to count. They are all around me. So many things about who I am are connected to that life. There were four of us who experienced those very hard years together. Now, three of us have gone and one remains.

Yes, I can feel the loneliness and sadness from time to time; I still dwell in the flesh. But I don't stay there. I don't stay there because I don't have to. I have a God-given understanding that allows me to dwell in His light, not my darkness. Thank The Lord I don't have to be that beat up, chained up, pitiful mess I was in the back of that prisoner transport. I am a victor! I have victory over death because He defeated it on and after the cross. I have life because, through Christ, I have been forgiven and restored, not to a perfect life, but indeed a life.

All my days I will think of and miss Dad, Mom, and Glenn. Hearing Dad yell he was ready and then seeing him exit the double doors of his bedroom, cap in hand and sock feet. Displaying that sly grin I loved. Singing "Rose Colored Glasses" on the front porch of the cabin with Mom as it was sunset in central Kentucky. Knowing that Glenn and I, brothers, always came together in life when we needed to. Every single time.

I also have trespassed against people in my life. I have many regrets and acknowledge the number of mistakes I made. To those of you I hurt at one point in my life or another, I am sorry and I ask your forgiveness. Today, I have the eyes to see the pain and damage resulting from my selfish, immature, and insecure decisions, attitudes, and actions. As The Lord who so graciously forgives us has, I ask you to please forgive me. I know I must also forgive.

My mind and my spirit both have been bent like a massive steel beam under tremendous pressure and strain. Complete with sound effects like the creaking and moaning of a single piece of railroad track being tied into a bow. Jesus Christ and His life give me the understanding I need to deal with the life I've had.

And to those of you reading now, it gives the understanding and power you need for your storms. The beauty isn't life itself, but rather the navigation through the storms of life with The Supreme Compass, knowing all the while we come out golden on the other side. That is where the beauty is. That is where the glory is. And that is where we will be with Him.

Prison allowed me to get out of the bubble that was modern society. I spent much time looking back into that bubble from the outside while I was on the "inside." Sometimes I literally would daydream that I was an alien coming to this planet. I tried to process what it would be like to see, for the first time, things that we obsess over and the drastic measures we employ to achieve the desired effects.

In my opinion, we do not teach personal responsibility anywhere near the level it should be taught. There is a quick fix, remedy, and solution to and for everything in our culture. How is it that people will act responsibly when they live in a culture of not having to deal with the consequences of their actions, even to the point of taking an unborn baby's life.

It seems to me there is a "free for all" going on spiritually. We invite and accept many things about God that please us, sound good, and don't arouse our fears. We discard the elements of God's love, grace, mercy, and forgiveness that inconvenience us. There are responsibilities we acquire when we accept God's offer of free salvation through Jesus Christ. We cannot accept Grace and continue to live and focus on things not of God. The very good news is that He waits for us. He is patient, and His love never diminishes or changes.

At some point life becomes life to all of us. No one advances through life without pain. Family and loved ones leave us, others betray or forsake us, and bad things just happen. It is a part of the human dilemma that we are forced to endure. But the amount of pain and suffering is directly linked to our perspective of life and God. When we are absorbed by ourselves, it is overwhelming and can crush us. When we have the proper perspective, we can get through anything no matter how tragic or devastating.

I did not always understand this. But I do now. I do now because Jesus Christ taught me. We all have journeys, roads travelled that shape us into the people we become. Some are unbelievable, some are fantastic, some are downright brutal, and some are uneventful. However, they are all the same in that they are unique to us. God bombards us with wisdom and truth. It surrounds us. In terms of His existence there are no secrets.

The question is, are we so caught up in lies and myths of here and now that we never see what He is trying to show us? We all have a story of how we open our eyes and truly live, or buy into an existence that defines us by what people think and how much stuff we get or have. Every single one of us has this story. This has been mine.

Society is incredibly loud. If only we, all the people screaming and pointing fingers at others around this country and world, could for one day pray with intent. If we could do that, the results we would see from our collective prayer would boggle our minds. What would come in the form of answered prayers, undoubtedly and by any measure, would greatly exceed the benefit of man's efforts fighting, struggling, and toiling.

There is a severe lack of respect, decency, and civility among us all as Americans, which is disturbing. Assistance should be given, programs are beneficial, and the government can do good things, but wise is the man who searches beyond the government for answers and solutions.

I enjoy writing and speaking immensely, but there is another vision in my life. I know there are many men, women, and juveniles currently incarcerated somewhere who can still get it right. As I have said, they are not lost causes. They need and deserve real help.

To me, there is immense honor associated with someone who has been on his back in life and again stands firm on two feet. When all the elements are firing — a true desire to change, hope and motivation, God's presence in their lives, and belief in their efforts from others — lives do change. When they do, to me, it is one of the purest reasons why we are here. For the rest of my life, I intend to be personally or professionally involved with the ongoing assistance and rehabilitation of men and women who have been incarcerated.

For years I was missing in action from my extended family; for over 10 years I was out of the picture and missed important occasions, accomplishments, and coming together in times of need. I have spoken to family members and expressed my desire to have Nadine, Melina, and me connected to everybody. I look forward with great anticipation to planning trips to see David in California, Duey and Karla in South Carolina, Debbie in Richmond, Kentucky, and Aunt Paulette in Lexington. My family has forgiven me and taken me back without ever a hint of guilt or shame. Support and love is what I have received from them. God, through Christ, has restored me to heights I previously only hoped for.

I accept with a full heart the man of today over the money of yesterday. It is the absolute truth that if given the choice, I would, in a second, choose my life and who I am today over what was. There wouldn't even be a momentary pause for effect. I am healthy, feel strong, and yearn to earn the love of my wife and daughter, even though I don't have to. My life has been quite a puzzle so far. As a result, I have gathered insights, experiences, and commentaries. I am fallible and have to always remind myself that both Nadine and Melina need to experience things on their own rather than from my instructions, good intentions, and sometimes dogged advice giving.

There still are times when I feel as if when I'm not suffering, I am not worthy. I know this is nothing from God. This is my flesh and the adversary manipulating and twisting the way they both do so very well. Through Christ and with Nadine, Melina, and others in our lives, I still am learning to chill out, relax, and enjoy.

God has answered our prayers in search for a church home. We believe we have found a place of worship with proper doctrine and fellowship. My beautiful wife, Nadine, found it and brought our family to it. Sometimes I can hardly believe how blessed of a man I am when I hold her. No, she is not perfect, but she is absolutely a blessing God bestowed on me. We both have friends and have connected with others in the church. Our hearts have been opened again to the fellowship, and we are grateful. There is an active, genuine outreach and missions department at the church and this pleases both Nadine and I, but especially her. To see Nadine witness to others about how The Lord has completely changed her life is heartwarming and joyful. I will, Lord willing, participate in my second mission trip. We will leave for Guatemala a little more than halfway through the summer of 2017. I am very much anticipating this experience.

When someone asks if they can pray for me, I always reply yes. I ask them to pray that I continue to grow in Jesus Christ and that I always carry an attitude of love and gratitude to Him for what He has already done for me. After that, any blessings The Lord bestows on me and in my life are a bonus.

I see something about my life. God has shown me immense favor. Blessings from heaven have always flowed down onto me. I am not a man to be pitied. The opposite is true. I am a man who has understanding in a world that is fallen and quite frankly, going crazy. I am not an authority on anything other than how the impact of God, through Jesus Christ, has changed and saved my life.

My hand is in Nadine's, my hand is in Melina's, and we will walk together into the horizon knowing love, beauty, and good are there. We will laugh and take joy in the presence of laughter and joy.

The storms are there too. But it's not the storm's power that is unbelievably overwhelming. It's the love and power of God in our lives that is.

Acknowledgements

To my wife, Nadine, and our daughter, Melina. Other than my faith, they are the two grandest blessings in my life. Without their love, patience, and belief in me this work would not have been possible.

To my extended family in Lexington, Kentucky for wholly accepting me again after more than a decade of enduring pain at my hands. I love you all.

To Stephanie Mojica, my writing mentor at The Carnegie Center in Lexington, Kentucky, for her patience and professional skill in dealing with me, a first-time writer. After our first meeting I was confident in the dexterity of her understanding of me and my vision.

To Moments in Time photography studio in Sarasota, Florida, for creating the shots used on the cover. Fred and his team showed great aptitude.

To Frank's Designs in Sarasota, Florida, for a quick understanding of what my vision was. Frank and Anna were a pleasure to work with, offered sound advice, and provided me with a cover I am proud of.

73266316R00172

Made in the USA
Middletown, DE
12 May 2018